Stephanie Ke

FUN PLACES
to Go with
Children in

Southern California
6th EDITION

CHRONICLE BOOKS
SAN FRANCISCO

For Nora and Eddie.
With special appreciation to Terry Gillen.

Copyright © 1997 by Stephanie Kegan.
Cover photograph copyright © 1997 Roger Paperno.
Maps copyright © 1997 Eureka Cartography.

Printed in the United States of America.

Library of Congress Cataloging-in-Publication Data:
Kegan, Stephanie.
    Fun places to go with children in southern California / Stephanie
Kegan. — 6th ed.
        p.   cm.
    Rev. ed. of: Places to go with children in southern California. © 1992.
    Includes indexes.
    ISBN 0-8118-1516-1 (pbk.)
    1. California, Southern—Guidebooks.   2. Family recreation—
California, Southern—Guidebooks.   I. Kegan, Stephanie. Places to go
with children in southern California.   II. Title.
F867.K29   1997
917.94'90453—dc21   96-48550
                                                                CIP

Cover design: Martine Trélaün
Book design: Karen Smidth
Composition: Words & Deeds
Cover photograph: Children's Zoo at the San Diego Zoo

Distributed in Canada by Raincoast Books
8680 Cambie Street
Vancouver, B.C. V6P 6M9

10 9 8 7 6 5 4 3 2 1

Chronicle Books
85 Second Street
San Francisco, CA 94105

Web Site: www.chronbooks.com

Contents

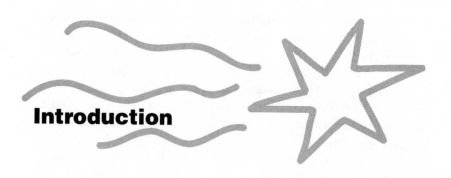

Introduction

TWENTY YEARS AGO, when I set out to write a guidebook to Southern California for people with children, the idea was a fairly novel one. At the time, no books on the subject existed on the shelves of Southern California bookstores. Would anyone in a region regarded as a playland for adults even be interested in a book that focused on places to go with *children?*

As it turned out, parents were—and so were teachers, scout leaders, grandparents, tourists, and lots of others. The book you are holding is the sixth edition of *Fun Places to Go with Children in Southern California.*

In the past twenty years, as I have gone from being a childless young writer to a parent who, with every new edition, had to contend with a different-aged child, I have had the humbling experience of having to live with my own advice. The straightforward criteria I applied in the first edition to selecting appropriate places to go with children have become more complex with each succeeding edition.

Twenty years ago, I tried to look at each place through the eyes of a child: Just how tall do you have to be to see over the gate in front of the exhibit? Are the docents or proprietors friendly to children? Can you make noise? Can anything be touched? Are there places nearby to run and be active? And so on.

Those considerations now share space with many others. How, for example, do you persuade a thirteen-year-old that there are places worth visiting in Southern California that contain neither a gravity-defying thrill ride or a heart-stopping water slide? Where can you take a baby or a toddler and still have a good time? How does a family with children of different ages find someplace they all can enjoy? Is it safe for families to go to this or that part of town? Does every activity for children have to be a hands-on one? And what about school field trips?

In *Fun Places to Go with Children in Southern California,* I have tried to compile a guide to this vast, diverse, and magnificent region that can be used by families with children of any age, as well as by teachers and anyone who enjoys a family atmosphere. The book is geared to residents of and visitors to the eleven counties that comprise Southern California. Since families have different needs, I have tried to include enough information in each listing so that parents and kids can select places that are just right for them. To make the task easier, a suggested age range for each destination is included. But remember, it is just a suggestion. Older kids can still have a good time doing activities geared primarily toward their younger siblings.

Since 1977, when the first edition of this guide was published, the opportunities for families to have fun together in Southern California have mushroomed. Twenty years ago, for example, there were no children's museums in Southern California, and few opportunities for hands-on learning in ordinary museums. Today, in addition to all the wonderful children's museums, nearly every major museum has areas and programs designed with children's needs in mind. Opportunities abound to get close to nature, to experience history in a way that makes it come alive, to explore science, and to just have a plain old good time. And, despite the odds, some terrific attractions have managed to stay pretty much unchanged in twenty years. The people at the Bob Baker Marionette Theater in Los Angeles are still putting on marvelous performances for kids; the little trains are still chugging in Griffith Park and at the Santa Barbara Zoo; and you can still visit the Morro Bay Aquarium for fifty cents and tour the restored historic village at Laws near Bishop for free.

Unfortunately, some things *are* harder for families these days. Although the emphasis of this books remains on low-cost family fun, there are simply not as many places to recommend that are free anymore. If you get irritated having to pay for a formerly free attraction, remember—in this era of cutbacks—an entrance fee may be the only way some doors can be kept open.

To address one other important concern: While panhandling transients have made venturing to urban centers feel less safe, do not be deterred from visiting attractions in downtown areas. If I felt unsafe visiting somewhere with a child, it did not go into this book. (If your children are unused to seeing panhandlers, you might think about how you are going to answer their questions as to why someone is asking for money, why you are not giving it, etc.)

The places described in this book have been arranged, as much as possible, by location and proximity to one another to make planning for outings easier and to give parents a backup in case something doesn't work out. Keep in mind that—although the proliferation of children's museums and hands-on activities is wonderfully exciting for all of us— not every attraction we take children to needs to be a hands-on one. There is a great deal to be said in our pentium-paced world for the experience of just looking, of quietly listening. Over the years of writing these books, I have seen children dazzled by paintings on a museum wall, captivated by elderly docents who manage to make history come alive in old adobes, and mesmerized by koi swimming in the pond of a botanical garden.

Since this is a book of places to go with children, places that appeal only to children but drive adults crazy are not included. The emphasis is on places to see, rather than places to stay or activities to do such as skiing, miniature golfing, ice skating, etc. However, if in the course of researching the book, my family and I stayed at a comfortable child-friendly hotel, had a good meal with kids, or tried out a fun activity, I have passed that information on here.

Finally, having been humbled by my experiences as a family-guide-book writer and parent, I will not offer any helpful hints for traveling in the car with kids. A few pointers I can offer:

- Always call ahead. This is the most important advice I can give. I have gone to a place that I just knew would be open, only to find it closed that day for lack of volunteer staff. I have also driven up and down the street looking for a place that I knew was there, only to learn that it had been replaced by something else the week before. And I am supposed to have learned something in twenty years.
- The prices and hours are accurate at the time of writing, but as we all know, prices are always going up and establishments often change their hours.
- Local chambers of commerce and tourist offices are great sources for free maps, brochures describing local activities, and hotel and restaurant guides. If you are a member of the Automobile Club of Southern California, you will find their tour books, maps, and services, as well as discounts on hotels and attractions, invaluable.
- Although this advice may seem terribly obvious, be sure to have a good map handy and to study it before starting out. And remember to take this book along in the car.
- A box kept in the trunk of your car packed with a few items can prepare you for just about anything. Include a blanket, a package of paper plates, paper towels, and a few utensils to give you the option of an impromptu picnic. A simple first aid kit stored in the box can save an outing. Ditto a change of old clothes and shoes for the kids.
- Dress in layers. In Southern California it is frequently cool in the morning, hot in the afternoon, and quite cool in the evening.

Most important of all:
Have fun!

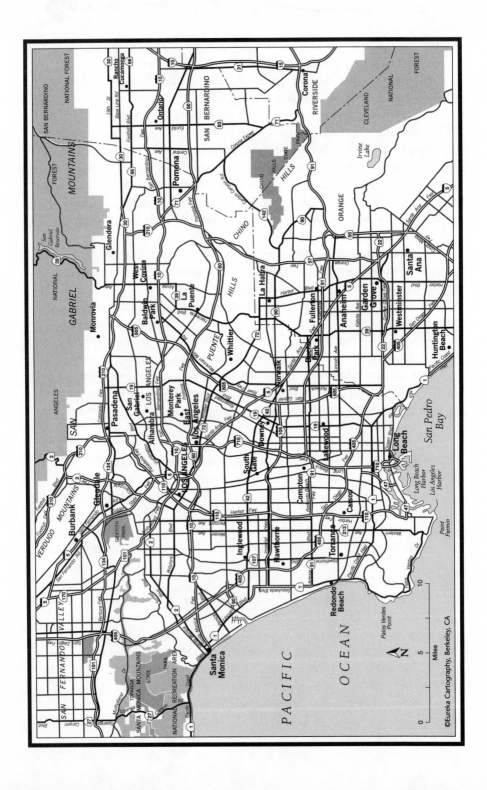

©Eureka Cartography, Berkeley, CA

Los Angeles County

YES, LOS ANGELES HAS earthquakes and its share of problems. But Los Angeles County also offers scenic beauty, great weather, a rich history, a wealth of cultural resources—some just for kids—and the vitality of a culturally diverse population. Stretching from the ocean across a huge metropolis, north into snowcapped mountains, and beyond into the desert, Los Angeles County is a place where kids can experience just about every kind of outdoor activity imaginable, from surfboarding to tobogganing. Children can see places in this county that served as ranches for cowboys, hideouts for bandits, sets for movie stars, and gooey traps for prehistoric beasts.

Perhaps one of the most exciting things about Los Angeles is its ethnic diversity. Within a few downtown blocks, kids can get a taste of Japan in Little Tokyo, China on North Spring Street, and Mexico on Olvera Street. All in all, there may be a greater variety of things to do in Los Angeles County and better weather to enjoy them than anywhere else in the country. What's more—despite budget cuts and the spiraling cost of just about everything—there are still plenty of places here for families to have fun without spending a bundle.

Los Angeles, however, is not a very manageable area. No one place provides a representative sample of what the area has to offer. It is difficult—although not as hard as it once was—to get around without a car. Metrolink offers commuter rail service from Orange, Riverside, San Bernardino, and Ventura counties into Los Angeles. Bus lines run throughout the county, and subway and light rail lines run to places in Los Angeles. For bus, Metrolink train, and Metro Rail Line information, phone 800-266-6883. The Los Angeles Convention and Visitors Bureau (phone: 213-689-8822), located downtown at 685 South Figueroa Street in the Hilton Tower and in Hollywood at 6541 Hollywood Boulevard, are excellent resources for tourists.

Downtown Los Angeles

● El Pueblo de Los Angeles Historic Monument

Between Main Street, Sunset Boulevard, Macy Street, Alameda Street, and Arcadia Street. (213) 628-1274. Open daily. Free. Visitors Center located in the Sepulveda House, 622 North Main Street (front entrance) and W-12 Olvera Street (rear entrance). Monday–Saturday, 10 A.M.–3 P.M. **Ages 6 and up.**

In 1781, forty-four bedraggled men, women, and children arrived from northern Mexico after a difficult seven-month journey to found the pueblo of Los Angeles. The settlers—eleven families of predominately black, Indian, and mixed heritages—built earth huts around a central plaza, changing forever the lives of the native Indians living nearby. The city grew up around the plaza, and today the area and its original buildings are preserved as El Pueblo de Los Angeles Historic Monument. It's a lively, fun place—as well as a historic one—that includes the city's first firehouse and its oldest street, recreated as a Mexican marketplace.

A good place to begin your tour is at the Visitors Center, located in the 1887 Sepulveda House. (You can enter from either Main or Olvera streets; the Victorian facade faces Main Street.) Constructed in the East-lake Victorian style, the Sepulveda House was a commercial building with an upstairs rooming house. The Visitors Center, housed in a restored Victorian shop (it once sold fireplace mantels), shows a free eighteen-minute film on the history of the pueblo on request. As you leave Sepulveda House toward Olvera Street, you can peer behind glass to see a recreated boardinghouse kitchen of the 1890s and the restored bedroom of Señora Sepulveda, the building's original owner. Work is under way to restore the upstairs rooms in the house.

You can also take a free guided walking tour of El Pueblo Tuesday through Saturday from 10 A.M. to 1 P.M., on the hour. The tours begin at the Docent Center, 130 Paseo de la Plaza, located next to the firehouse on the south side of the Plaza. The tour docents are well informed, friendly, and accustomed to children. (Kids should probably be in upper elementary school or older to get something out of the tour. Families with younger children can pick up a brochure at the Sepulveda House for a self-guided tour.) The guided tours last about forty minutes and include the Pico House, the city's first three-story hotel, which you cannot see on your own. The Pico House and some of the Plaza's other buildings are in a slow process of being restored, and there is something to be said for seeing them before they are completely restored.

● Olvera Street

North of the Plaza between North Main and Alameda streets. (213) 628-1274. Daily, from about 10 A.M. to around 8 P.M. Some shops close later in the summer. **Ages 6 and up.**

One of the oldest streets in Los Angeles, Olvera Street was transformed from a rundown dirt road into a brick-paved Mexican marketplace lined with shops and *puestos* (stalls) in 1930. Bustling, full of tourists, and very commercial, Olvera Street still manages to convey a colorful sense of the past. Children can see candles being dipped, a glassblower shaping glass, and other artisans at work. At the north end of the street is a water trough carved by mission Indians in 1820.

Marvelous piñatas and Mexican handicrafts ranging from inexpensive to expensive are sold in the marketplace. There are a number of places to eat, including La Luz del Dia (southwest corner of Olvera Street), where, if you climb the stairs leading to the restrooms, you can get a good view of the women making tortillas by hand. Musicians usually stroll around Olvera Street, too.

The Plaza, south of Olvera Street, is a good place to stop and rest. Once the center of pueblo life, the Plaza now hosts a number of celebrations including the Blessing of the Animals, Mardi Gras, and Cinco de Mayo. The iron-grilled kiosk in the middle of the Plaza serves as a center for concerts.

● Avila Adobe

10 Olvera Street, El Pueblo de Los Angeles Historic Monument. (213) 680-2525. Daily, 10 A.M.–5 P.M. Free. **Ages 6 and up.**

The Avila Adobe is the oldest existing residence in the city of Los Angeles. Built in 1818 by Francisco Avila, one-time mayor of the pueblo, the seven-room adobe was the pueblo's most elegant dwelling. Saved from demolition in the 1920s by some civic-minded citizens, the adobe was completely restored—using original building materials—after being damaged in the 1971 earthquake.

The adobe has been furnished in the style of a typical well-to-do California family of the early 1840s. You'll see the father's office, where he kept his ledgers and the cowhides used for barter, the indoor kitchen (most cooking was done outdoors) with its wooden bathtub, and the parents' bedroom. Kids, of course, will be most interested in the children's bedroom with its cowhide bed, wooden cradle, chamber pot, clothes, and dolls. Outside is a packed-earth patio with an outdoor kitchen and an old wagon.

● Old Plaza Firehouse

134 Paseo de la Plaza (southeast corner of the Plaza). (213) 680-2525. Tuesday–Saturday, 10 A.M.–3 P.M. Free. **Ages 4 and up.**

Built in 1884, this two-story red brick building was Los Angeles's first official fire station. It has been authentically restored to the era of the 1880s and is now a museum of early fire-fighting memorabilia. One of the first fire engines used in the city is on display, along with an original pumper and a chemical wagon. There are a large number of photographs, a collection of fire hats, and some old fire alarms, which the firefighter on duty will ring for you.

● One-Day Train Rides

Union Passenger Station, 800 North Alameda Street. For reservations and information, phone (213) 624-0171. **Ages 5 and up.**

Is there a kid (big or small) who doesn't love trains? The grand Union Station, with its marble floors, big leather chairs, and flower-filled patios, is a fitting starting point for a train adventure. You can travel either to San Diego or Santa Barbara and back easily in a day.

The Amtrak to Santa Barbara leaves Los Angeles every day at 9:10 A.M. (arriving in Santa Barbara at 11:36 A.M.) and 11:35 A.M. (arriving at 2:15 P.M.). Trains leave Santa Barbara at 2:15 P.M. (arriving in Los Angeles at 4:55 P.M.) and 6:50 P.M. (arriving at 9:25 P.M.). After the train passes through the San Fernando Valley, it goes through two tunnels under the Santa Susana Pass to the Simi Valley. The train stops at Oxnard and then travels right along the Pacific. There is a full dining car for the treat of a moving lunch. Round-trip excursion fare is $29 for adults; children ages 2 to 15 are half fare.

Heading south, trains leave every day for San Diego, about every two hours starting at 6:35 A.M. The trip takes about two hours and forty-five minutes. The last train from San Diego leaves for Los Angeles at 7 P.M. With younger children you might want to ride only as far as San Juan Capistrano, where you can have lunch at the Capistrano Depot and walk to the mission. Round-trip excursion fare from Los Angeles to San Diego is $33 for adults—to San Juan Capistrano, it is $21. Children ages 2 to 15 are half fare.

Amtrak and San Diego Mini Tours also offer package tours to the San Diego Zoo and Sea World. For more information on the tours, call Amtrak and wait on the line for an Amtrak operator.

Reservations are required for the Santa Barbara train and are a good idea for the train to San Diego.

● Gateway to Transportation/The Gateway Transit Center

800 North Alameda Street, behind Union Station at the corner of Vignes and Cesar Chavez streets. For bus, Metrolink train, and Metro Rail Line information, phone (800) 266-6883. **Ages 5 and up.**

If Union Station represents the glory days of rail travel past, the Gateway Transit Center—behind and connected to Union Station—is the future. Designed to be the major transportation hub for Los Angeles in the twenty-first century, the $300 million transit center integrates bus and rail services to Los Angeles from neighboring counties.

So few children in Southern California have experience with public transportation that riding to or using it in downtown Los Angeles can be an adventure in itself. Metrolink offers commuter rail service from Orange, Riverside, San Bernardino, and Ventura counties and Santa Clarita, Burbank, and Glendale into the station. The Red Line Metro Rail runs underground from the station through downtown to the intersection of Wilshire Boulevard and Western Avenue. The light rail trains of the Metro Blue Line connect with the Red Line at the Seventh Street Metro Center and run south to downtown Long Beach. The light rail trains of the Green Line run between Norwalk and Redondo Beach, connecting with the Blue Line at the Imperial/Wilmington station. In downtown, you can get just about anywhere you want to go on a mini Dash bus. The service operates Monday through Saturday with a fare of 25¢.

You can plan a trip entirely using public transportation—for example, the Children's Museum is a four-block walk or Dash ride from Union Station—or you can incorporate a subway trip into your activities downtown.

Your family should also enjoy seeing the new Gateway Center itself. More than a mere transportation hub, the center is also a massive work of public art. Los Angeles artists, selected in an open competition, have designed everything from mosaic fountains to elaborate bus bench pavilions. On the lobby floor of the glass-domed center are bronze likenesses of trout, turtles, and other water life that once made a home in the Los Angeles River. Winding along one side of the lobby is a serpentine-shaped tile bench topped by a flowing river sculpture complete with stone fish imbedded in its base. The sculpture is fed by a mountain-like waterfall studded with artifacts excavated from the original Chinatown site underneath Union Station. On the opposite side of the lobby is a large aquarium. Be sure and look outside at the bus bench pavilions topped with curving, creature-like metal skeletons.

● Chinatown

Bounded by Sunset Boulevard, North Hill and North Spring streets, and the Pasadena Freeway. The main gate is located at 900 North Broadway near College Street. Open daily. Free. **Ages 5 and up.**

Chinatown is the historic center of Los Angeles's large Chinese-American community. The present Chinatown dates from the 1930s, when the original Chinese settlement, located southeast of Olvera Street, had to relocate to make way for Union Station.

North Broadway is the main street of Chinatown. Located here are Chinese restaurants and groceries, fresh fish and live poultry markets, as well as new shopping plazas. Central Chinatown in the 900 block of North Broadway is the section geared to tourists. As you enter the plaza through the pagoda gates, point out the carved animals and fish along the rooflines to your children—the animals provide the buildings with good luck. The shops along Gin Ling Way, although catering to tourists, are fun for browsing—you'll find lots of kites and inexpensive toys. At night, lantern-covered lights brighten the plaza.

The area along North Spring Street serves the community rather than tourists. The herb shop at 701 North Spring Street is particularly interesting.

Although in recent years the cities of Monterey Park and San Gabriel have eclipsed Chinatown as places to go for gourmet Chinese food, Chinatown still contains many good, moderately priced Chinese restaurants. Since Chinese families take their children out to eat with them, nearly every restaurant here is accustomed to children. For something different, you might try a dim sum lunch at the **Empress Pavilion** (988 North Hill; 213-617-9898) or **Ocean Seafood** (747 North Broadway; 213-687-3088). **The Phoenix Bakery** at 969 North Broadway is a great place to pick up dessert.

● Philippe The Original

1001 North Alameda Street at the intersection of North Main, Alameda, and Ord streets. Located one block north of Union Passenger Station on the fringe of Chinatown. (213) 628-3781. Open daily, except Thanksgiving and Christmas, 6 A.M.–10 P.M. **All ages.**

There are so few places you can take your children in Los Angeles that look the same as they did forty or fifty years ago that Philippe's sandwich shop would be worth the trip just for the experience. However, the food's good, too. One of the oldest restaurants in Southern California, Philippe's is known for its french dip sandwiches. You line up at the counter, tell the server your order, then carry it to a wooden booth or a

long wooden table with stools. There's sawdust on the floor, press clip-
pings on the walls, a glass-cased candy and cigar counter, an old-fashioned
scale, and lots of tradition.

● San Antonio Winery and Restaurant

*737 Lamar Street off the 1700–1800 block of North Main Street. (213)
223-1401. Monday–Tuesday, 10:30 A.M.–6 P.M.; Wednesday–Sunday,
10:30 A.M.–7 P.M. Free.* **Ages 6 and up.**

Commercial wine making in California started on the site of what
is now Union Station in downtown Los Angeles. Louis Vignes planted a
vineyard there and established a wine-making business in the 1830s. The
San Antonio Winery, founded in 1917 and still run by the original family, is the last winery in Los Angeles still in operation. On a self-conducted
tour you'll see the original winery buildings, built from boxcar sidings,
and some of the wine-making equipment, including the enormous aging
vats. In addition to wine tasting for adults, there is an Italian-accented
delicatessen and sandwich shop on the premises. You can eat at a table
among the casks of aging wine.

● Los Angeles Children's Museum

*310 North Main Street in the north end of the Los Angeles Mall at street
level. (213) 687-8800. School year: Saturday, Sunday, and some holidays,
10 A.M.–5 P.M. Summer: Monday–Friday, 11:30 A.M.–5 P.M.; Saturday
and Sunday, 10 A.M.–5 P.M. The museum is open weekday mornings year-
round for groups of ten or more children with advanced prepaid reservations.
For group reservations, phone (213) 687-8825. Admission: $5 per person;
under 2 years, free.* **Ages 2–11.**

The Los Angeles Children's Museum aptly describes itself as a
place "where kids can touch the world." Children are encouraged to
touch, handle, feel, wear, ride, probe, construct, design, and otherwise
discover the museum's many exhibits. In the "City Streets" exhibit, for
example, children can crawl through a drainage pipe, see what is beneath
the sidewalks, walk on a catwalk, don the uniform of a firefighter, take
the wheel of a city bus, and sit astride a police motorcycle. In the "Cave
of the Dinosaurs" exhibit, they enter a cave to discover dinosaur footprints, bones, and holograms. In the "H_2O: The Story of Water" exhibit,
children can float a boat through locks and dams, pedal a bicycle to
create a vortex, and generally play with water while happily getting
somewhat wet.

At Club Eco, the museum's environmental clubhouse, children find
out firsthand the value of recycling. In the Recycle Art Studio, they use

egg cartons, paper tubes, Styrofoam bits—you name it—to make, well, whatever. One of the most popular and enduring exhibits is the "Sticky City," where giant foam shapes with Velcro tapes offer all sorts of wild construction possibilities. The Children's Museum has a spectacular Lego construction area, a recording and a video studio for kids, a computerized pianocorder, a children's theater, and much more.

In addition to its permanent exhibits, the museum offers a year-round program of workshops and special events. Included are live performances by singers, storytellers, dance groups, and other entertainers and opportunities to interact with artists. A museum shop sells children's books, educational games, and toys.

● Little Tokyo

Bounded by First and Third streets from Main to Alameda streets. **Ages 5 and up.**

Little Tokyo is the heart of Los Angeles's large Japanese American community. It is an active district with scores of businesses and restaurants. If you come here in the morning, you may see the shopkeepers starting their day by washing their windows just as their counterparts in Japan do. As in Japan, the moderately priced restaurants here have plastic displays of their food dishes in their windows.

Little Tokyo contains both newer shopping malls and original commercial buildings. With stone paths, the **Japanese Village Plaza Mall** (between First and Second streets, near Central Avenue) is easily recognized by the traditional fireman's lookout towering over the First Street entrance. In addition to shops and Japanese restaurants, the mall contains a number of Japanese-accented fast-food places where kids can try a bowl of *ramen gyoza* or an *imagawayaki* (sort of a dessert pancake).

Weller Court (between Los Angeles and San Pedro streets at the corner of Onizuka Street) is a three-level outdoor mall of shops and restaurants overlooking a central court. It is located on a broad pedestrian walkway, named in honor of *Challenger* astronaut Ellison S. Onizuka and containing a monument to him.

Yaohan Plaza, located at Third and Alameda streets (the entrance is on Alameda; there is underground parking), is the newest shopping center in Little Tokyo. On the ground floor of the three-story center is a Japanese supermarket with a dazzling variety of Japanese foods. Just browsing through the aisles can be an educational experience. There is also a large bookstore here that includes Japanese children's books, and a variety of other shops, restaurants and snack bars.

At the corner of First and Los Angeles streets is the impressive New Otani Hotel. Take the elevator to the fifth level and stroll in a lovely, genuine Japanese rooftop garden with waterfalls. While adults will be soothed by the garden's serenity, children will be fascinated by the odd perspective that comes from being high above the city streets while seeming to be at ground level.

The Japanese American Cultural and Community Center at 244 South San Pedro Street (phone: 213-628-2725) has displays and information on cultural events, such as Children's Day, held in May in Little Tokyo, and summer workshops for children.

● Japanese American National Museum

369 East First Street at the corner of Central Avenue, Little Tokyo. (213) 625-0414. Tuesday, Wednesday, Friday, Saturday, and Sunday, 10 A.M.– 5 P.M.; Thursday, 10 A.M.–8 P.M. Adults, $4; seniors, students, and children, $3; under 5, free. Free every Thursday from 5 to 8 P.M. and all day on the third Thursday of every month. **Ages 8 and up.**

The Japanese American National Museum is the first museum in the country devoted to the experience of Americans of Japanese descent. Housed in a restored former Buddhist temple, the museum's changing exhibits use videos, photographs, artwork, personal histories, clothing, letters, and artifacts to convey aspects of Japanese-American history, such as the World War II experience of Japanese Americans. Hands-on activities for children are usually a part of the exhibits.

The museum also offers special workshops and activities for children and events geared toward families. Ask for a schedule of museum events to be sent to you.

● The Temporary Contemporary

152 North Central Avenue. (213) 626-6222. Tuesday and Wednesday, 11 A.M.–5 P.M.; Thursday, 11 A.M.–8 P.M.; Friday–Sunday, 11 A.M.–5 P.M. Adults, $6; students and seniors, $4; under 12, free. Admission fee includes a same-day visit to the Museum of Contemporary Art at California Plaza. Free to all every Thursday, 5 to 8 P.M. **Ages 10 and up.**

In 1983, the Temporary Contemporary opened in Little Tokyo as an exhibit space for the Museum of Contemporary Art while the new museum building on Grand Avenue was being constructed. The temporary museum, located in a pair of converted warehouses, proved so popular that it became a permanent auxiliary of the Museum of Contemporary Art.

Older children will enjoy the interesting warehouse space and many of the changing exhibits. Younger children may find some of the artwork frightening. The museum is easily accessed by wheelchairs and strollers. It makes a nice outing for parents with babies.

● *Los Angeles Times* Tours

145 South Spring Street, between First and Second streets. Free parking at 213 South Spring Street. (213) 237-5757. Monday–Friday (except holidays), at 11:15 A.M. Minimum age is 10. Free. **Ages 10 and up.**

No reservations are needed for this forty-five minute tour of the *Los Angeles Times,* which takes you through the editorial area, wire room, composing room (where the news stories are assembled into page form), and distribution area. A separate tour of the *Times* printing plant is available by reservation. Group tours are also by reservation.

● Grand Central Market

Broadway and Hill streets between Third and Fourth streets. (213) 624-2378. Monday–Saturday, 9 A.M.–6 P.M.; Sunday, 10 A.M.–5:30 P.M. **Ages 5 and up.**

The block-deep Grand Central Market is a far cry from the local supermarkets or shopping malls that most kids know. More than fifty independently operated stalls sell everything from rare spices to octopus to pigs' heads. It's exciting to see all the produce piled high and the eggs spread out, seemingly by the acre, instead of in Styrofoam containers. Plastic wrap is practically unheard of; butchers put your meat in waxed paper, and vendors place your produce in paper bags. Kids can watch tortillas moving along the conveyor belts of a *tortillería,* and parents— if they want—can get their blood pressure checked at a health food stand. There are a number of places in the market to have a counter lunch.

The majority of the market's customers are Spanish speaking and most stalls have bilingual signs and staff. The market has recently undergone a major renovation, but its heart is still in the same place.

● Angels Flight

Upper station is behind the Watercourt in California Plaza, between Olive Street and Grand Avenue and Third and Fourth streets. The lower station is next to the Fourth and Hill Street entrance to the Metro Red Line. (213) 626-1901. Daily, 6 A.M.–10 P.M. A one-way trip is 25¢. **Ages 5 and up.**

For sixty-eight years from 1901 through 1969, the twin cars of the Angels Flight funicular shuttled passengers up and down a steep incline of 315 feet from Bunker Hill (once a desirable residential neighborhood) to the heart of downtown Los Angeles. By the time Angels Flight was dismantled in 1969, Bunker Hill was a blighted area set for urban renewal as a commercial center. Responding to the outcry against dismantling Angels Flight, the city promised the little railroad would be saved and put back in place one day. Twenty-seven years later, the city made good on its promise and the beloved railway is back in operation after an extensive restoration.

Now located a half block south of its original site, Angels Flight has been rebuilt using the original wooden cars—with a new steel undercarriage—and original station house and archway. The short, steep ride on the funicular is not only historic, but great fun. (The best seat is at the far end of the car.) You pay at the station house at the top.

Angels Flight is just a short distance from the Grand Central Market, the Museum of Contemporary Art, the Wells Fargo Museum, and the Los Angeles Public Library. It is just steps away from the Fourth and Hill Street entrance of the Metro Red Line subway station at Pershing Square. For a real rail adventure, you can take a Metrolink Commuter Train into Union Station and the Red Line from Union Station to Angels Flight. (For Metrolink, Red Line information, phone (800) 252-7433.)

Your children will want to see the Watercourt, the dancing, upward-squirting fountains, in California Plaza behind the station house at the top of Angels Flight. Every summer, California Plaza presents free noontime and evening concerts in an outdoor performance space. Phone (213) 687-2159 for the schedule.

● Museum of Contemporary Art

250 South Grand Avenue. (213) 626-6222. Tuesday and Wednesday, 11 A.M.–5 P.M.; Thursday, 11 A.M.–8 P.M.; Friday–Sunday, 11 A.M.– 6 P.M. Adults, $6; students and seniors, $4; under 12, free. Admission fee also covers a same-day visit to the Temporary Contemporary. Free to all every Thursday, 5–8 P.M. **Ages 7 and up.**

The artwork at the Museum of Contemporary Art begins with the museum building, a stunning red sandstone structure with pyramid-shaped skylights designed by the Japanese architect Arata Isozaki. Inside the bright galleries are displays from the museum's permanent collection—international paintings, sculpture, photography, and environmental works from the 1940s on—and changing exhibits. A free guide introducing families to contemporary art and MOCA's permanent collection is available from the information center.

The museum sponsors special workshops for families with children aged seven to thirteen that combine gallery tours with art projects focused around a selected exhibition. The workshops are free, but require reservations. For information and reservations, telephone the museum's education department at (213) 621-1751. Patinette, the museum's cafe, offers indoor and outdoor seating and exceptionally good food.

Although almost everyone will appreciate seeing the outside of the museum building, the courtyard fountains, and the interesting outdoor sculpture, a visit inside is best made with children who are at least seven years of age. The museum acoustics are such that one small child can make a great deal of noise. More important, young children may find some of the artwork frightening.

● Los Angeles Philharmonic Symphonies for Youth/ Open House at the Bowl

Los Angeles Philharmonic Association, Education Department, The Music Center, 135 North Grand Avenue, No. 405, Los Angeles, CA 90012. (213) 972-0703. June–August: (213) 850-2000. **Ages 3 and up.**

Each year the Los Angeles Philharmonic performs concerts especially for children ages six through twelve. The forty-minute concerts have special children's themes and are geared for their attention spans. Each piece of music is introduced with informative remarks by the conductor, and there are appearances by outstanding guest artists. Storytellers, narrators, puppets, and young soloists are also featured parts of the programs, which are designed to instill an appreciation of music in children. The concerts are held in the elegant Dorothy Chandler Pavilion at 10:15 A.M. on five Saturdays during the school year, with a variety of children's activities taking place an hour before the concerts. Seats are $6 to $8.

Special half-hour concerts for younger children are offered in a program called Open House at the Music Center. The concerts for children ages three to six are held from 11:30 A.M. to noon on three Saturdays during the school year.

The Philharmonic Association also offers children an outstanding summer arts festival at the Hollywood Bowl. Called Open House at the Bowl, the festival offers six weeks of performances and workshops for children on weekday mornings. The lively programs include performances by dance, instrumental, theatrical, and puppet ensembles. A different program is featured each week. Performances are held Monday through Friday at 10:00 and 11:15 A.M. on the Open House Stage, located in the Box Office Circle area.

Workshops for children ages three to twelve follow the performances at 11:00 A.M. and 12:15 P.M. The workshops, which are divided into age groups, relate to the performances and might include making puppets or instruments, learning magic, or participating in music or drama. The festival also exposes children to the Los Angeles Philharmonic Orchestra, which rehearses at the Bowl most weekday mornings.

Open House at the Hollywood Bowl is very popular and space in the workshops is limited, so make your reservations early. For more information, phone (213) 850-2000.

● Wells Fargo History Museum

333 South Grand Avenue on the northwest corner of the Wells Fargo Bank Center; entrance is on the corner of Third and Hope streets, up the stairway. (213) 253-7166. Monday–Friday, 9 A.M.–5 P.M. Free. **Ages 6 and up.**

Stagecoaches are the highlight of this shiny public-relations museum devoted to Wells Fargo history. Children can see (but not touch) a restored nineteenth-century Concord stagecoach. A partially built coach, along with original coachmaker's tools, gives children an idea of how stagecoaches were built. There is also a stagecoach cabin that children can climb into; inside they will hear a tape that describes an 1859 stage journey from St. Louis to San Francisco.

In a replica of an 1850s Wells Fargo office, complete with gold scales and a safe, kids can sit at the desk and try their hand at sending a telegraph message. (The display includes a code book.) Other displays that would interest children include Winchester rifles, gold nuggets, nineteenth-century reward posters, Pony Express saddles, steamer trunks packed with clothes, and a nineteenth-century letterpress used to duplicate documents before the age of photocopiers. A fifteen-minute video on the history of Wells Fargo plays in a small theater.

● Los Angeles Bonaventure Hotel

404 South Figueroa Street. (213) 624-1000. **Ages 6–12.**

Although the Bonaventure Hotel no longer seems quite as futuristic as it once did, the hotel is still fun for a look around. With five skyscraping mirrored cylinders and glass elevators gliding outside, the hotel is hard to miss. You can enter the hotel lobby, located in the square base of the building, from either Flower or South Figueroa streets. The rather space-age lobby, circled by reflecting pools, is several stories high, with overhead balconies. Don't miss taking a ride on the glass-walled elevators; it's quite a thrill for kids to see the view outside as they zoom up thirty-five floors on the exterior of the building.

There are several inexpensive places to eat or snack in the hotel's shopping gallery, or you might want to head over to the rather elegant McDonald's in the Court at Wells Fargo Center. To get to the Court, take the skywalk from the fifth floor of the Bonaventure that leads east over Flower Street. On the other side of the skywalk, you'll find the new Stuart

M. Ketchum downtown YMCA. (Take a peek inside to watch the swimmers through the glass in the lobby.) Then continue along Fourth Street to the Court at Wells Fargo Center (350 South Hope Street) with its lovely skylit atrium and indoor garden. The McDonald's inside the Court, decorated in mauve and gray, has a terrace that offers a great view of downtown.

● The Los Angeles Central Library

630 West Fifth Street, between Flower Street and Grand Avenue. General Information: (213) 228-7000. Children's Literature: (213) 228-7250. Monday, 10 A.M.–5:30 P.M.; Tuesday and Wednesday, noon–8 P.M.; Thursday–Saturday, 10 A.M.–5:30 P.M.; Sunday, 1–5 P.M. Free. Validated parking with an L.A. public library card is available in the 524 South Flower Street garage beneath the Maguire Gardens. **Ages 3 and up.**

Not only has the Los Angeles Central Library been restored to its original glory, but it is now bigger and more beautiful than ever before. An outpouring of public support—and money—led to a ten-year rehabilitation and expansion of the library after it was badly damaged by arson in 1986. The new library, now the third-largest central library in the nation, consists of the restored original 1926 pyramid-peaked, Egyptian-style building, a large new wing, and gardens.

The original building contains one of the loveliest children's libraries you are likely to ever see. You reach the children's library through an elegant, mural-covered rotunda with a bronze chandelier of the universe hanging from the ceiling. Located in the former history library, the children's library has restored historic murals lining the walls, a custom animal-patterned carpet, leather chairs, and lamps that are replicas of the 1920s originals. In addition to plenty of comfortable space for reading, there are areas for videotape viewing, a multimedia center, and a separate young children's library with scaled-down old-fashioned furniture.

The centerpiece of the children's library is the KLOS Story Theater, with tiered seating, large video screens, and a velvet-curtained puppet theater. Puppet shows, video matinees, story times, and other special events are held regularly in the theater. Phone the children's library for the schedule.

Teenagers have their own distinct library space, Teen'scape, located on the second floor near the popular library. Teen'scape also offers a homework center and special activities for teens, such as drama and computer workshops and stargazing. For information on Teen'Scape, phone (213) 228-7290.

The Mark Taper Auditorium, a handsome 235-seat space in the new wing of the library, is the site of additional activities for families with both young and older children, including concerts, plays, and readings by actors and authors.

Walk-in tours of the library are available daily (telephone for the times), and you can certainly see it on your own. Don't miss taking a ride in the elevator lined with old catalog cards and seeing the fanciful chandeliers in the atrium of the new Tom Bradley Wing. The library also includes a small museum-type store and a fast-food cafe.

Directly across the street from the Fifth Street entrance of the library are the **Bunker Hill Steps,** a monumental stairway some have compared to Rome's Spanish Steps, leading up Bunker Hill. The steps are lined with restaurants and food carts, grassy terraces, fountains, and a stream. (You don't have to climb all the stairs; you can take the escalator.)

● Pacific Stock Exchange

233 South Beaudry. (213) 977-4700. Weekdays, 8:30 A.M.–1 P.M. Free. **Ages 10 and up.**

The trading floor of the Pacific Stock Exchange is second in size only to New York's. You can get a firsthand look at the action from a viewing gallery on the twelfth floor. Tours can also be arranged for high school students.

● The Flower Market

700 Wall Street. **Ages 6 and up.**

The 700 block of Wall Street is lined with wholesale flower markets that open in the middle of the night to sell flowers and plants to the city's floral trade. The public is welcome after 9 A.M. each weekday and on Saturday. By 11 A.M., the stock is pretty much depleted. Even if you don't buy any flowers, the flower district is a lot of fun to see.

East Los Angeles

● Lincoln Park/Plaza de la Raza

3501 Valley Boulevard. Park entrance is a block east of the intersection of Valley Boulevard and Mission Road. Plaza de la Raza: (213) 223-2475. Free. **All ages.**

This park is the home of the Plaza de la Raza (Place of the People), a community-supported Mexican American cultural center. Cultural instruction with a Latin emphasis is given in classes that include dance, music, arts and crafts, piano, guitar, drama, and other subjects. There is a small fee for the classes, which are open to all. Plaza de la Raza also sponsors presentations of Mexican American music, dance, drama, and other cultural events.

Scattered among the parks' forty-six acres are picnic tables, barbecues, a gymnasium, ball fields, and a swimming pool. The park has a lake with ducks to feed, and where youngsters can fish. There is also a children's playground with an Aztec motif.

● El Mercado

3425 East First Street. (213) 268-3451. Monday–Friday, 10 A.M.– 8 P.M.; Saturday and Sunday, 9 A.M.–8 P.M. **Ages 5 and up.**

You can give your children a taste of Mexico without going farther than East First Street on a visit to El Mercado, a bustling three-floor indoor Mexican market. On the main floor is a large supermarket surrounded on the outside by stalls selling everything from piñatas to fresh shrimp. Most interesting of all is the *tortillería* where you can watch the conveyor belts carrying fresh, hot tortillas. Upstairs is a series of restaurants and snack bars where you can sit at a table and watch the action on the mezzanine below while you eat. Mariachi bands are usually strolling around, too. In the parking lot behind the market is a mural of actor Edward James Olmos.

South Central Los Angeles

● California Museum of Science and Industry

700 State Drive, Exposition Park. Located off the Harbor Freeway (110) at Exposition Boulevard. (213) 744-7400. Daily, 10 A.M.–5 P.M. Free. **Ages 5 and up.**

The second-largest science museum in the country, after the Smithsonian Institute in Washington, D.C., the California Museum of Science and Industry is a fascinating museum for kids. Children can not only touch the exhibits in this museum, they can activate them, manipulate them, go inside them, and even converse with them.

In the Earthquake exhibit, children can feel a realistic simulation of a large-magnitude earthquake (warn them what is coming); in the Bicycle Company exhibit, they can design their own bicycles on a computer and then become managers of a bicycle factory; in the Creative Computer exhibit, they can create their own computer art. Mathematical principles are demonstrated in displays complete with ringing bells and flashing lights. A temporary structure, Science South, houses a favorite exhibit: live chicks hatching in an incubator. (Chicken farmers bring the eggs to the museum every other day and take the newly hatched chicks back to the farm).

Some of the most exciting exhibits are housed in the seven-story **Aerospace Building.** Included among the displays are the actual Gemini 11 space capsule, the Apollo 12 lunar descent engine, the Interstat III communications satellite, a T-38 Air Force trainer, and a replica of the Space Shuttle. On the ground floor, children can design their own airplanes, tap into a weather satellite, or call up a satellite image of another part of the world. Outside is the Air and Space Garden, which includes a United Airlines DC-8.

In the **Hall of Health,** the focus is on choices people can make to enhance their own health. At the Health for Life exhibit visitors insert personalized "credit" cards to check their breathing, pulse, heart rate, balance, stress level, and other vital signs. Another exhibit provides clear and understandable information on AIDS.

In addition to its permanent displays, the Museum of Science and Industry features touring exhibits from museums around the world. These offer something new several times a year. The museum also offers a superb program of Saturday and summer science workshops for children ages five through thirteen. Each workshop is geared to a specific age level. For example, young children can learn how animals adapt to their environments or about ocean surprises, while older children can build their own rockets, design their own planes, or take a trip aboard a marine research boat. For a schedule of classes and an application, phone the Science Workshops Hotline, (213) 744-7440.

The museum is currently undergoing a major program of renovation. The museum complex and the educational programs will continue during the construction.

● IMAX Theater

State Drive and Figueroa Street, Exposition Park. (Next to the Aerospace Hall.) Open daily. For program information and admission prices, phone (213) 744-2019. **Ages 6 and up.**

A part of the Museum of Science and Industry, the octagonal IMAX Theater offers viewers a five-story motion-picture screen, surround sound, and a sense of being inside the action. The films take you into outer space, under the ocean, to far-off continents, and into the eye of killer storms.

● California Afro-American Museum

600 State Drive (at Figueroa Street), Exposition Park, across from the IMAX Theater. (213) 744-7432. Tuesday–Sunday, 10 A.M.–5 P.M. Free. **Ages 6 and up.**

The contributions of African Americans to art, science, education, politics, religion, and sports are honored in this museum of art in Exposition Park. Galleries, containing changing exhibits by African American artists, lead from a central atrium sculpture court. The museum's permanent collection includes indigenous African art, colonial and nineteenth-century paintings and drawings, twentieth-century sculpture and paintings, and contemporary works in a variety of media. Among the art that children should enjoy seeing are African masks, headdresses and ceremonial costumes, and contemporary sculpture created from discarded objects. A number of the pieces should provoke conversation between adults and kids. For example, *The Door*, by David Hammons, shows the outline of an African American pressed against an actual office door labeled Admissions Office.

Special exhibits for children are sometimes offered, as are free workshops for families. During the Christmas season African American artists and craftspersons demonstrate their work in the Sculpture Court.

● Natural History Museum of Los Angeles County

900 Exposition Boulevard, on the west side of the Rose Garden in Exposition Park, one block east of Vermont Avenue. (213) 744-3466. Tuesday–Sunday, 10 A.M.–5 P.M. Adults, $6; seniors and students ages 12–17, $3.50; ages 5–12, $2; under 5, free. Free first Tuesday of every month. **Ages 3 and up.**

Above all else kids want one thing from a museum of natural history: dinosaurs. At the Natural History Museum of Los Angeles County, children need only to walk as far as the foyer to see a pair of eighteen-foot-tall dinosaurs locked in battle. The dinosaurs, a tyrannosaurus rex and a triceratops, are made from a combination of real bones and casts.

Other dinosaur exhibits include a cast of the complete skeleton of a mamenchisaurus, the largest-necked dinosaur ever discovered, the skull of a tyrannosaurus rex, and models of an allosaurs and carnotaurus. After seeing the dinosaurs, your kids will probably want to head to the museum's **Discovery Center,** a hands-on, exploratory center designed for all ages. Located on the main level, near the original rotunda area, the Discovery Center gives kids the opportunity to handle all sorts of artifacts and scientific specimens. They can touch the skeleton of a camarasaurus dinosaur, take fossil rubbings from a realistic-looking rock wall, study water drops under a microscope, use a magnifying glass on small specimens, and check out discovery boxes filled with special activities and things to examine.

Children will also want to visit the museum's **Insect Zoo.** The zoo features more than thirty live exhibits of insects and their relatives, including Madagascan hissing cockroaches, giant African tiger beetles, velvet ants, black widows, hairy scorpions, and tarantulas. Kids operate a Bioscanner camera-video system to get a really upclose look.

The third-largest museum of its kind in the country, the Natural History Museum is too big to see all of it in a single visit. Among other highlights for children are the habitat halls showing North American, African, and exotic mammals in their natural environments; the hall of birds, featuring electronically animated bird habitats; the megamouth shark display; and the walk-through gem vault in the Gem and Mineral Hall. Kids will also enjoy the multimedia Chaparral exhibit, which surrounds them in the sights, sounds, and even the smells of a chaparral ecology.

The museum also has exhibits on American and California history and Native American and pre-Columbian cultures. In addition to the permanent collection, the museum presents traveling and changing exhibits that feature interactive displays and special activities for children.

The Natural History Museum also offers school tours, summer nature workshops for children ages three to thirteen, and monthly special family events in the Discovery Center. For more information on classes, school tours, and the Discovery Center, phone (213) 744-3414.

● Exposition Park Rose Garden

900 Exposition Boulevard. Daily, 7 A.M.–5 P.M. Free. **All ages.**

Adjacent to the Natural History Museum is one of the largest rose gardens in the nation. The sunken garden contains more than sixteen thousand rosebushes. Lawn-covered paths lead through the garden, making it a lovely place for a stroll. There are covered gazebo-like areas for sitting, and if your visit is on a weekend you may catch sight of a rose garden wedding.

● Los Angeles Memorial Coliseum Tours

3911 South Figueroa Street, Exposition Park. (213) 748-6136. Tours: Tuesday, Thursday, and Saturday on non-event days at 10:30 A.M., noon, and 1:30 P.M. Adults, $4; seniors, $3; students, $2; under 12, $1. **Ages 8 and up.**

Built in 1923, the Los Angeles Coliseum is the home of the University of Southern California Trojans football team. The Coliseum was a major site of the 1984 Olympics, as well the 1932 games. A one-hour tour of the historic stadium takes you through the teams' locker room and training facilities, the press box, Coliseum Club, and onto the field. Reservations are required.

Watts Towers/Watts Towers Art Center
1765 East 107th Street, Watts. (213) 847-4646. Art Center hours: Tuesday–Saturday, 9 A.M.–4 P.M.; Sunday, noon–4 P.M. Free. **Ages 6 and up.**

Sabatino Rodia, an Italian tile setter, devoted thirty-three years of his life to the construction of these soaring towers. Single-handedly, he wired steel reinforcing rods together into a lacy structure, stuccoed them with cement, pebbles, cup handles, old dishes, and other cast-off items. The neighbors made fun of him, calling his towers junk, but Rodia worked on anyway—often suspended by a window washer's belt. By the time he died in 1965, his towers were recognized as remarkable works of art. Tours of the towers grounds have been suspended temporarily while the towers undergo structural repairs. You can see the towers from outside the fence, though. The Watts Towers Art Center (up the block at 1727 East 107th Street) displays the work of local artists and has special exhibitions.

● Dominguez Adobe/Rancho San Pedro
18127 South Alameda Street, Compton. (213) 631-5981. Tuesday and Wednesday, 1–3 P.M.; second and third Sunday of every month, 1–3 P.M. Free. **Ages 8 and up.**

Juan José Dominguez was a soldier with Father Serra's original expedition from Mexico to found the California missions. He was rewarded for his long service with a seventy-five-thousand-acre Spanish land grant that covered the area south of the Pueblo de Los Angeles to the water. The land grant passed to Juan José's nephew Manuel, who built a ranch house on it in 1826. The land is now covered by more than a half-dozen different cities, but you can still see the ranch house, which has been restored as a museum.

North Central Los Angeles

● Heritage Square
3800 Homer Street, three miles north of downtown Los Angeles. Exit the Pasadena Freeway (110) on Avenue 43, go east to Homer Street (just on the other side of the freeway), then south to the end of the street. (818) 449-0193. Saturday, Sunday, and Monday holidays, 11:30 A.M.–4:30 P.M. Guided tours at noon, 1, 2, and 3 P.M. Ticket gate closes at 3 P.M. Adults, $5; seniors and ages 13–17, $4; ages 7–12, $2; under 7, free. On Fridays, there are no tours,

but the grounds are open 10 A.M.–3 P.M. and admission is free. **Ages 10 and up.**

Heritage Square is a haven for some of the city's endangered Victorian buildings. Eight significant structures, which would have otherwise been demolished, have been brought together in this ten-acre park. The buildings, including an 1897 church and the Palms Railroad Station, have been arranged in a village setting of lawns, shade trees, and period lampposts. The restoration work, supported by public contribution and carried out by largely volunteer craftsmen, is going slowly. So far the 1887 Hale House, originally at Avenue 45 and Figueroa, has been completely restored and furnished with period furniture. On a guided tour, you can see the interior of the Hale House, as well as some of the buildings that are in the process of restoration, including a octagon-shaped farmhouse. (The unrestored buildings are as interesting as the restored ones.)

Children probably need to be at least ten years of age to enjoy the tours. Fridays, when there are no tours, might be a fun time to come with younger children. You are welcome to bring a lunch and picnic on the green. The museum's information line gives information on upcoming special events, such as Christmas season festivities. School tours can be arranged by calling the museum office at (213) 796-2898.

● Southwest Museum

234 Museum Drive, Highland Park. From central Los Angeles, take the Pasadena Freeway north to Avenue 43, go left on Avenue 43 to Figueroa, right on Figueroa, left on Avenue 45, right on Marmion Way, and left on Museum Drive. (213) 221-2164. Tuesday–Sunday, 11 A.M.–5 P.M. Adults, $5; seniors and students, $3; ages 7–18, $2; under 7, free. **Ages 8 and up.**

Perched on a hill overlooking Highland Park, the Southwest Museum looks like a monastery. The museum is devoted to the history and culture of Native Americans, particularly those of California and the Southwest. The best way to enter the museum is through the long tunnel on Museum Drive which is lined with dioramas depicting Southwestern Indian life. (Children have to be about four feet tall to see the dioramas without being lifted. Preschool children might find the somewhat dark tunnel frightening, and children should probably be at least eight years old to enjoy the museum in general.) At the end of the tunnel is an elevator that takes you up 108 feet to the museum.

Inside the museum, some of the high points for children are a large totem pole, Native American headdresses and clothing, a replica of a Chumash Indian rock art site, some fascinating masks, a collection of Hopi kachina dolls, and a full-size Southern Cheyenne tepee.

The museum also sponsors workshops for children and adults, festivals, films, and family programs.

● Lummis Home

200 East Avenue 43, Highland Park. From the Pasadena Freeway (110) take the Avenue 43 exit. (213) 222-0546. Friday–Sunday, noon–4 P.M. Free. **Ages 8 and up.**

Near the Southwest Museum is the home of its founder, Charles Lummis. A noted writer, editor, archaeologist, historian, and Western enthusiast, Lummis built his home by hand using local stones, hand-hewn timber, and telegraph poles from the Santa Fe Railroad. A curator from the Historical Society of Southern California will be pleased to give a personal tour of this remarkable home, pointing out Lummis's early California memorabilia and his photos of Southwestern Indians. Children should be at least eight or nine years old to appreciate the home. Outside is a lovely garden of native California plants.

Los Feliz and Hollywood

● Griffith Park

Main entrances on Los Feliz Boulevard at Vermont Avenue, Western Avenue, and Riverside Drive. Griffith Park lies just west of the Golden State Freeway (I-5) roughly between Los Feliz Boulevard on the south and the Ventura Freeway (134) on the north. Freeway off-ramps leading to the park from I-5 are Los Feliz Boulevard, Griffith Park (direct entry), and Zoo Drive. Approaching the park on the 134 Freeway eastbound, take either the Forest Lawn Drive or Victory Boulevard off-ramp. From the 134 Freeway westbound, take Zoo Drive or Forest Lawn Drive. After leaving the freeways, follow signs into the park. (213) 665-5188. Daily, 6 A.M.–10 P.M. Bridle and hiking trails and mountain roads close at sunset. Free. **All ages.**

Children in Los Angeles have the largest city park in the United States for a playground. Covering more than four thousand acres, Griffith Park offers picnic areas, children's playgrounds, hiking and bridle trails, a famous zoo, a fascinating museum of the American West, a miniature railroad, an outdoor and indoor museum of transportation, pony and stagecoach rides, an observatory and planetarium, an old-fashioned merry-go-round, and plenty of other kids to play with. A free map of the park, including hiking trails, is available at the Ranger Headquarters and Visitors Center, 4730 Crystal Springs Drive.

● Griffith Observatory and Planetarium

2800 East Observatory Road, located at the north end of Vermont Avenue, on the south side of the park. (213) 664-1191. Hall of Science is open daily in summer from 12:30–10 P.M. Winter hours: Tuesday–Friday, 2–10 P.M.;

Saturday and Sunday, 12:30–10 P.M. Free. Planetarium shows summer and holidays: Monday–Friday, 1:30, 3, and 7:30 P.M.; Saturday and Sunday, 1:30, 3, 4:30, and 7:30 P.M. Winter: Tuesday–Friday, 3 and 7:30 P.M.; Saturday and Sunday, 1:30, 3, 4:30, and 7:30 P.M. Ages 13–64, $4; seniors, $3; ages 5–12, $2. **Ages 5 and up.**

The Griffith Observatory houses one of the largest public telescopes in California. It is open for free viewing every clear evening, except Monday, from 7 to 9:45 P.M. In the summer, it is open daily from dark until 9:45 P.M. For a recorded message on the current planet positions and sky events, phone (213) 663-8171.

The **Hall of Science,** in the observatory, has exhibits in astronomy and the physical sciences. Highlights include a pendulum showing the rotation of the earth; a six-foot, three-inch-diameter globe of the earth; a seismograph, which reacts to the vibrations of feet stomped on the floor; and a submarine periscope.

A huge projector fills the seventy-five-foot dome of the adjacent **Planetarium** with realistic views of the skies as they appear at any time from any point on earth. The hour-long presentations change regularly. Shows are selected for their dramatic appeal as well as their astronomical interest. Children under five are not admitted to the planetarium shows—as they might find them frightening—except for the special children's presentations at 1:30 P.M. on Saturday and Sunday (daily during the summer).

Older children and teenagers will enjoy the **Laserium** show at the observatory. It's a laser-light concert with high-fidelity rock or other music and impressive special effects. Shows are held evenings, Tuesday–Sunday. Children under five are not admitted. For Laserium information, phone (818) 901-9405.

There are plans for a $25 million expansion of the observatory. The work, which will take years to complete, will be done in stages. The first stage is construction of a subterranean addition twelve feet beneath the observatory's front lawn. The observatory will remain open during the expansion.

● Travel Town

On Zoo Drive near Griffith Park Drive, Griffith Park. (213) 662-5874. Monday–Friday, 10 A.M.–4 P.M.; Saturday and Sunday, 10 A.M.–5 P.M. Closes one hour later during the summer. Free. **All ages.**

The largest collection of steam locomotives west of the Mississippi River is located in this relaxed outdoor museum. In addition to locomotives, there are boxcars, cabooses, dining cars, and even yellow streetcars from the old days in Los Angeles. Children can climb aboard most of the trains, including the locomotive cabs, and let their imaginations run wild.

Travel Town is undergoing a major restoration. Volunteer groups are working to restore the railroad cars, and a new acquisition, an operating diesel switch locomotive, is helping to move cars. Some of the restored passenger cars are open at set times. On Saturdays, you may see volunteers at work laying new track.

An indoor area of the museum houses an exhibit of fire-fighting equipment to tell the story of the Los Angeles Fire Department from 1869 to 1940. A refreshment stand has indoor and outdoor seating. There are plenty of benches and shaded picnic tables, and you can picnic on the lawn. A miniature train leaving from Travel Town's restored Southern Pacific depot circles the perimeter of the outdoor museum. (Children ride for $1.25; adults, $1.50). You can also arrange to have your child's birthday party in the Travel Town Birthday Car, which is decorated just for kids. The car comes equipped with air-conditioning and a refrigerator/freezer.

On Sundays from 11 A.M. to 3 P.M., the **Los Angeles Live Steamers Club** members operate their own miniature steam engines on a layout of track east of Travel Town. The tiny trains are authentic in every detail and children are welcome to ride them for free.

● Los Angeles Zoo

5333 Zoo Drive in Griffith Park near the intersection of the Ventura and Golden State freeways. (213) 666-4090. Open every day except Christmas, 10 A.M.–5 P.M. Ticket sales end at 4 P.M. Adults, $8.25; seniors, $5.25; ages 2–12, $3.25, under 2, free. Free parking. **All ages.**

After weathering some tough times, the Los Angeles Zoo appears to be on the rebound with a new director, improved exhibits, and increased funding. A major new exhibit, a naturalistic forest habitat for chimpanzees, should be completed by mid 1997.

More than 1,200 animals from all over the world live on the zoo's eighty acres of landscaped, hilly terrain. The animals are grouped by area of origin—Africa, Eurasia, North America, South America, and Australia—residing in moat-enclosed environments. The Los Angeles Zoo also participates in a number of cooperative breeding programs for endangered species. Some of animals in these programs that you can see include Arabian oryx, mountain tapirs, golden lion tamarins, and a gerenuk herd. The zoo also contains a koala bear exhibit, an aquatics section, an aviary, a reptile house, and a children's zoo called "Adventure Island." Animal shows are scheduled daily. There are snack bars, picnic areas, and play-grounds inside the zoo. Strollers and wheelchairs are available to rent.

The Los Angeles Zoo also has a number of programs for children geared to their age level. These include hands-on activities and a chance to learn about zoo animals for younger children and, for older kids, career days and zoo sleep-overs. During the summer, weeklong zoo camps are offered for preschoolers through eighth graders. Other programs include zoo overnights and camping trips for families. For information about family, children's, school, and youth group programs, phone the zoo's education office, (213) 663-4819.

● Gene Autry Western Heritage Museum

4700 Zoo Drive in Griffith Park at the junction of the Golden State (I-5) and Ventura (134) freeways, across from the zoo parking lot. (213) 667-2000. Tuesday–Sunday, 10 A.M.–5 P.M. Adults, $7.50; students and seniors, $5; ages 2–12, $3. Free parking. **Ages 3 and up.**

The Gene Autry Western Heritage Museum is an exciting, major museum devoted to the history and culture of the American West. Seven permanent galleries designed by Walt Disney Imagineering, along with special exhibits, depict the history of the West from the early explorations of the Spanish conquistadors to the present day. Exhibits range from tra-ditional displays to elaborate and creative multimedia presentations.

The focus of much of the museum is on the real, everyday lives and occupations of the people who helped settle the West. For example, the tools and personal belongings carried on a journey west are featured in an exhibit with sounds and voices from the past. As counterpoint to this "real" West, the museum also depicts the West of romance created in films, television, novels, advertising, and art. Adults may get a kick out of seeing cowboy toys and lunch boxes just like the ones they had as kids. A "screen test" offers kids a chance to get on a bucking saddle and see themselves on television in a Western movie.

The docents are friendly toward children, and many of the exhibits offer children an opportunity to participate. The *Los Angeles Times* **Children's Discovery Gallery,** on the lower level on the building, is a walk-in, hands-on exhibit area for children. Classes, workshops, and spe-cial events for children take place regularly at the museum. Events for the whole family include Western serenades in the outdoor court, radio plays in the **Wells Fargo Radio Theater,** and concerts and film programs in a 250-seat theater. The Golden Spur Cafe, open daily, serves breakfast, lunch, and snacks. All museum areas are wheelchair and stroller accessible.

● Merry-Go-Round

Located just off Griffith Park Drive near the main concession stand in Griffith Park. Winter hours: weekends and holidays, 11 A.M.–5 P.M. Summer hours: daily, 11 A.M.–6 P.M. **All ages.**

Crafted in 1926, this lovely, old (but well-preserved), four-abreast carousel offers rides for children and adults for $1.

● Pony, Stagecoach, and Miniature Train Rides

Crystal Springs Drive near Los Feliz Boulevard, Griffith Park. Pony/ Stagecoach: (213) 664-3266. Tuesday–Sunday, 10 A.M.–4:30 P.M. Train: (213) 664-6788. Monday–Friday, 10 A.M.–4:30 P.M.; Saturday and Sunday, 10 A.M.–5:30 P.M. **Ages 1–10.**

Children as young as a year old can ride the ponies here. A track of slowly walking ponies lets kids take their first rides with mom or dad walking next to them. A separate oval course has a medium track for children three years and older and a fast track for children seven and older weighing up to one hundred pounds. Stagecoach rides are also offered. Stagecoach and pony rides are $1.50.

Nearby is the Griffith Park & Southern Railroad, a miniature train that provides rides for children and adults. The fare for persons fourteen years and older is $1.75; for younger children, $1.25.

● Happily Ever After

2640 Griffith Park Boulevard (near Hyperion Avenue), Los Angeles. (213) 668-1996. Tuesday–Saturday, 10 A.M.–5:30 P.M.; Sunday, noon–5 P.M. **All ages.**

This children's bookstore is located in a cozy yellow house. Babies and toddlers have their own book area, which includes an inviting basket of toys in the center of the floor. Another room contains a blue couch and fine selection of books for preschool children through young adults. Picture books are arranged by subject—such as school concerns, siblings, and sleep problems—as well as conventionally by author. Books for parents are shelved in a separate room that includes a large chair. The store also sells some educational toys, wooden stamps, and book-related cassettes and videotapes.

A story hour for toddlers is held on the first and third Wednesday of each month from 10:30 to 11 A.M. With their parents, children hear stories, learn hand games, and sing songs. (No preregistration is necessary, although you should call before coming.) Happily Ever After will also special order books for you and provide free gift wrapping.

● Barnsdall Art Park

4800 Hollywood Boulevard. From the Hollywood Freeway (101), take either the Hollywood Boulevard or Vermont Avenue exit. The park entrance is on Hollywood Boulevard, one block west of Vermont. (213) 485-8665. Open daily. Free. **Ages 3 and up.**

Located on a hilltop surrounded by olive trees above the bustle of East Hollywood, Barnsdall Art Park has become a major cultural center in the city of Los Angeles. The park land once belonged to oil heiress Aline Barnsdall, who commissioned architect Frank Lloyd Wright to design her home, called Hollyhock House, on the crown of a hill. Today, the 13.5-acre park includes a municipal art gallery; an arts and crafts center; a junior arts center; and the Hollyhock House, which is open for tours to the public. The Metro Rail construction on Hollywood Boulevard has obscured the entrance to the park—and dampened its pleasantness—but the art facilities of the park are carrying on through the mess.

● Los Angeles Municipal Art Gallery

Barnsdall Park. (213) 485-4581. Wednesday–Sunday, 12:30–5 P.M. Adults, $1.50, ages 13 and under, free. **Ages 5 and up.**

The Los Angeles Municipal Art Gallery displays the works of contemporary Southern California artists in regularly changing exhibits. The gallery is a good place for kids to get acquainted with the artwork of others. Exhibits frequently deal with some aspect of the creative process—for example, how artists perceive ordinary objects such as a telephone. Folk art, conceptual art, and works in which children and others can participate are included in the exhibits. Most displays include statements by the artists, which help explain what their work is all about. The docents at the gallery are understanding with children and enjoy answering their questions.

Tours of the gallery are available for groups of children from kindergarten on up. The tour educators use a variety of techniques from role-playing to guided art projects to involve the children with what they are seeing. Tours need to be scheduled at least two months in advance.

● Junior Arts Center

Barnsdall Park. (213) 485-4474. Gallery hours: Wednesday–Sunday, 12:30–5 P.M. **Ages 3–17.**

The Junior Arts Center offers an excellent program of arts workshops for children and young people ages three through seventeen. The classes—which include painting, drawing, clay, photography, movement,

theater, film and video workshops, as well as other arts and crafts workshops—are taught by experienced artists and craftspersons. Workshop
sessions are generally divided into seven- to eight-week fall, winter,
spring, and summer quarters and a shorter December arts program.
Classes meet once a week and contain about twelve students.

The gallery in the art center has changing shows designed for children. Included among the special programs are family workshops,
children's film festivals, storytelling, and other events. A visual arts
program for children with disabilities is offered, and accommodations for
disabled children in other programs are readily available.

● Hollyhock House

*Barnsdall Park. (213) 662-7272. Tours: Tuesday–Sunday, 12, 1, 2,
and 3 P.M. Adults, $2; seniors, $1; ages 12 and under, free with an adult.
Tickets are sold at the Municipal Art Gallery, next to the house.* **Ages 10
and up.**

Aline Barnsdall's home was the first residence in Los Angeles designed by Frank Lloyd Wright, and it is the only Wright house open to
the public on a regular basis. Wright decorated the main house with styl-
ized designs of Barnsdall's favorite flower, the hollyhock. This remarkable
house was restored in 1974 and refurbished with many of the original
fixtures and furniture. In 1990, Wright's custom-designed living room
furniture was replicated and installed in the location of the original pieces.
The tour is best appreciated by older children and teenagers.

● El Capitan Theater

*6838 Hollywood Boulevard at Highland Avenue, Hollywood. (213) 467-
7674. Phone for show times and prices.* **All ages.**

The El Capitan opened in 1926 as a venue for music revues. In the
1940s, the theater was converted to a movie house, and its beautiful interior was covered. Fortunately for us, the El Capitan was saved by the
Walt Disney Company and Pacific Theaters, who restored the showplace
to its former glory. The El Capitan shows Disney movies exclusively on
its single screen. The ornate interior, including balcony boxes, stenciled
ceiling coves, and velvet curtains, has been either restored or recreated.
You can even sit in the balcony. On Thanksgiving weekend, the holiday
show opens with the latest Disney release, preceded by a live stage show.
Order your tickets early because the shows sell out quickly. After or before
a visit to the El Capitan, your family may want to cross the street to check
out the footprints in front of the **Mann's Chinese Theater.**

● John Anson Ford Amphitheater

2580 Cahuenga Boulevard East, in the Cahuenga Pass. From the south, exit the 101 Freeway at Cahuenga Boulevard and proceed north, following the Ford signs. From the north, exit the 101 Freeway at Barham Boulevard, and, following the Ford signs, head south on Cahuenga. A sign for the Ford will direct you to turn left, crossing over the freeway and into the Ford. Information Line: (213) 974-1396. Box Office: (213) 466-1767. Ticket prices: $7– $25. Family event discount cards and discounted series tickets are available. Telephone to request a season schedule. **All ages.**

Owned and operated by the county of Los Angeles, the John Anson Ford Amphitheater is a 1,200-seat outdoor performance site in a park setting. Summer evenings bring music, dance, and other performances under the stars. Picnic areas on the grounds open two hours before the performances, and there is also an outdoor cafe where you can purchase sandwiches, salads, desserts, and drinks.

The Ford also offers one-hour programs for children and their parents during the summer on selected Saturdays at 10 A.M. and selected Sundays at 4:30 P.M. The programs include dance, music, and puppet performances, and even Shakespeare for children. Some offer pre-show crafts and activities. The **Ford Family Fun Calendar**, available from the Ford, gives an age-appropriate suggestion for each family performance.

● The Hollywood Studio Museum

2100 North Highland Avenue, Hollywood (on the opposite side of the street and slightly south of the Hollywood Bowl). (213) 874-2276. Saturday, 10 A.M.–4 P.M.; Sunday, noon–4 P.M. Adults, $4; seniors and students, $3; ages 6–12, $2. **Ages 8 and up.**

In 1913, Cecil B. DeMille established Hollywood's first major film studio in a barn on the corner of Selma and Vine streets. Today the re-stored (and relocated) barn serves as a museum dedicated to the silent film era in Hollywood. A recreation of DeMille's first office in the barn has his boots under the desk. (The boots were quite necessary because he shared the barn with a horse.)

A twenty-minute video presentation on the museum and the history of Hollywood is shown in a small screening room. (If your children are young, ask to skip the film. It will not interest them.) Exhibits that will interest children include early motion-picture cameras, projectors, and stud lights; costumes, including Roman shields; models of the Spanish galleons used in early pirate movies; and the chariot from *Ben Hur.*

Telephone the museum before heading out as they sometimes have shortened hours due to a shortage of volunteer staff. You might want to combine this museum with a visit to the nearby Hollywood Bowl Museum.

● Hollywood Bowl Museum

2301 North Highland Avenue, Hollywood. On the Hollywood Bowl grounds, next to the Patio restaurant. (213) 850-2058. Mid-September through late June: Tuesday–Saturday, 10 A.M.–4:30 P.M. Late June through mid-September: Monday–Saturday, 10 A.M.–8:30 P.M. Also open Sunday evenings on concert days. Free. **Ages 8 and up.**

The recently rebuilt Hollywood Bowl Museum features exhibits on the history of the famous outdoor amphitheater. On the first floor of the sleek two-story building, you can watch videos and hear audiotapes of historic past performances at the Bowl. Upstairs are photographs and other memorabilia.

Mid-Wilshire

● Bob Baker Marionette Theater

1345 West First Street. (213) 250-9995. Reservations are required and can be made by calling the box office any day between 9 A.M. and 4 P.M. Performances: Tuesday–Friday, 10:30 A.M.; Saturday and Sunday, 2 P.M.; extra performances may be scheduled. $10 per person. Admission includes refreshments. **Ages 2–9.**

One of the oldest continuing theaters in Los Angeles is a puppet/marionette theater for kids. Children sit on the floor close to the stage and watch the Bob Baker marionettes perform in wonderful fast-paced productions. Kids meet the puppeteers after the show and then are served ice cream, cookies, and punch. (There's coffee for the grown-ups.) The whole experience takes about two hours and even very young children can appreciate it. The Bob Baker people are not only serious about the art of puppetry, but they also genuinely enjoy kids. Their holiday productions are a particular delight. Group and birthday party arrangements can also be made.

● Craft and Folk Art Museum

5800 Wilshire Boulevard. (213) 937-5544. Tuesday–Sunday, 11 A.M.–5 P.M. Adults, $4; students of any age with ID, $2.50; under 12, free. **Ages 8 and up.**

The Craft and Folk Art Museum displays crafts, folk art, and design from around the world. While some of the changing exhibits may not interest children, there is usually a hands-on workshop at the museum that will. For example, a recent exhibit on weavings included an opportunity for children to try their hand at weaving.

● The Carole & Barry Kaye Museum of Miniatures

5900 Wilshire Boulevard, across from the Los Angeles County Museum of Art. (213) 937-6464. Tuesday–Saturday, 10 A.M.–5 P.M.; Sunday, 11 A.M.–5 P.M. Adults, $7.50; seniors, $6.50; students, $5; ages 3–12, $3. **Ages 7 and up.**

An office building across from the Los Angeles County Museum of Art houses a rather amazing museum of elaborate miniatures—or dollhouses, as your children will call them. Built in a scale of one-twelfth or less, the miniatures are all authentic to the last detail. You'll see a remarkable miniature Fontainbleau with inlaid marble and detailed furniture, English manor homes, Southern mansions, gargoyle-trimmed medieval abbeys, and snow-dusted villages. The miniatures represent buildings from ancient Roman times to the present. One display features the first ladies of the United States in miniature. There is also an interesting gallery of eighteen-inch historical figures created by the artist George Stuart. Be forewarned: The museum exits into a large doll and dollhouse shop.

● La Brea Tar Pits/George C. Page Museum of La Brea Discoveries

5801 Wilshire Boulevard, Hancock Park. (213) 936-2230. Tuesday–Sunday, 10 A.M.–5 P.M. Adults, $6; seniors and students, $3.50; ages 5–10, $2; under 5, free. Free the first Tuesday of the month. Joint admission for the museum and the Los Angeles County Museum of Art: Adults, $4.50; seniors and students, $2.25; ages 5–12, $1. All-day parking is available for $5.50 with museum validation. **Ages 3 and up.**

For thousands of years, prehistoric animals were trapped in these pits when they mistook the shiny black pools for water and got stuck in the ooze. (The ooze was not actually tar, but asphalt created when crude oil surfaced through cracks in the ground and evaporated.) This asphalt ooze, however, was a superb preservative. Since 1905, when archaeologists began exploring the tar pits, more than four million fossils of plants, reptiles, insects, birds, and mammals have been recovered. Today, life-size fiberglass reproductions of some of the ancient animals—most notably, the imperial mammoths with their twelve-and-a-half-foot-long tusks—

recreate a bit of the scene at the tar pits thirty to forty thousand years ago.

The skeletons of the creatures uncovered at the tar pits are on display in the beautiful George C. Page Museum on the park grounds. In a nicely laid out exhibition space, you'll see the reconstructed skeletons of saber-toothed cats, giant ground sloths, dire wolves, mastodons, a twelve-foot-high imperial mammoth, antique bison, and extinct varieties of camels and birds. (Kids may be disappointed to learn that dinosaurs disappeared sixty-five million years before the La Brea tar pits were even formed.) An open-view paleontological laboratory gives children the opportunity to watch technicians as they clean, repair, and sort the many fossils still being prepared for research.

Many of the museum exhibits have been designed with children in mind. In the "Asphalt Is Sticky" exhibit, kids can actually experiment with the La Brea ooze. In other exhibits, they can touch the massive, asphalt-soaked bone of a giant ground sloth, watch an animated model of a juvenile mammoth, and see a hologram that forms a prehistoric woman from her bones. For two months every summer, families can watch paleontologists at work in Pit 91.

● Los Angeles County Museum of Art

5905 Wilshire Boulevard. (213) 857-6000. Tuesday–Thursday, 10 A.M.– 5 P.M.; Friday, 10 A.M.–9 P.M.; Saturday and Sunday, 11 A.M.–6 P.M. Adults, $6; students and seniors, $4; ages 6–17, $1; under 6, free. Free on the second Wednesday of every month. Museum: **Ages 6 and up.** *Classes:* **Ages 3½–12.**

The collections in the Los Angeles County Museum of Art range from ancient treasures to the very latest in modern art. The museum, the largest in the western United States, is composed of four main buildings: the Ahmanson Gallery on the west, the Hammer building on the north, the Bing Center on the east, and the 1986 Robert O. Anderson building in the front. There is also a pavilion for Japanese art and a sculpture garden. The buildings are united by a court and a stunning new museum entrance.

Children will probably find the ancient artifacts displayed in the Ahmanson Gallery the most interesting. Many of these pieces are at their eye level. The pre-Columbian Gallery is located on the plaza level; the Egyptian, ancient West Asian, ancient Persian, and Greek and Roman galleries are on the second level. Children probably will also enjoy seeing the costumes displayed on the third level and the impressionist art hanging on the second level of the Hammer Building. Baby carriages and strollers are permitted in all galleries except for crowded special exhibitions.

The **Bing Theater** in the Bing Center offers excellent film series, including many family films. Call the museum for the schedule. The Bing Center also holds a pleasant cafe. You can eat inside or out.

The museum offers art classes year-round for children and adults. Children ages three and a half through five participate with the parents in a variety of gallery experiences that include storytelling, games, and art activities. Classes for first through third graders feature storytelling, sketching from artworks in the galleries, and other art activities. Fourth through sixth graders study works of art in the galleries and do a variety of art activities. Classes generally meet once a week for five weeks. For more information, phone the art class registrar at (213) 857-6139.

Special school tours are also available for the fourth through twelfth grades. On selected Sundays throughout the year, museum tours are given for children aged five to twelve and their families. For more information on school or family tours, call the docent office at (213) 857-6108.

● The Petersen Automotive Museum

6060 Wilshire Boulevard at Fairfax Avenue. The parking garage entrance is on Fairfax Avenue. (213) 930-2277. Tuesday–Sunday, 10 A.M.–6 P.M. Open Monday holidays. Adults, $7; seniors and students, $5; ages 5–12, $3; under 5, free. Parking in a covered structure is $4 all day. **Ages 6 and up.**

Perhaps no one should be surprised that Los Angeles has an outstanding museum dedicated to automobiles and their place in the city's history. Located in the landmark former Ohrbach's Department Store building, the Petersen Automotive Museum displays more than two hundred rare and classic cars, trucks, and motorcycles. The first-floor permanent exhibits trace the history of the automobile. The cars are displayed in colorful surrounding exhibits such at a 1920s-era gas station or a uniquely Los Angeles street, and you walk through the exhibits to see the cars. Interactive computers allow kids to participate in the exhibits. The second floor of the museum contains changing exhibits of race and classic cars, concept cars, celebrity and movie cars, and automotive design and technology. A gallery of automotive art is on the third floor. A member of the Natural History Museum of Los Angeles County, the Petersen Museum also offers some educational programs for children.

● Farmers' Market

6333 West Third Street at Fairfax Avenue. (213) 933-9211. Monday–Saturday, 9 A.M.–6:30 P.M. (until 7 P.M. in summer); Sunday, 10 A.M.–5 P.M. (until 6 P.M. in summer). Closed holidays. **All ages.**

The Farmers' Market originated during the Depression when a group of farmers set up stalls on a large vacant field to sell their produce. The market has come a long way from its humble beginnings. Today it is a sprawling complex of some 160 shops, stores, stalls, and outdoor restaurants.

Long a tourist attraction, the market is also a favorite of local families. In addition to the fun of looking around at all the produce and food, families can have a wonderful meal here. Some twenty-six different kitchens sell all sorts of American and international food. Many of the eating places are close together, so it is possible to sample items from more than one restaurant and enjoy them at an outdoor table. For those who like Cajun food, the Gumbo Pot is terrific, as is the Kokomo Cafe, which serves California-style meals in a diner setting. You also can't beat Bob's Coffee and Donuts—well, for donuts.

● Every Picture Tells A Story

7525 Beverly Boulevard, at Gardner. (213) 932-6070. Tuesday–Saturday, 10 A.M.–6 P.M. **All ages.**

Every Picture Tells A Story is both an art gallery of original art from children's books and a children's book store. The art includes original illustrations from award-winning books and illustrators, as well as lithographs from such books as *Charlotte's Web* and *Curious George.* Their exhibits change regularly and the openings are family events.

The store carries about two hundred book titles ranging from infant books and child-rearing topics to fiction and nonfiction at the eighth grade level. Bright, handwoven rugs and kid-size furniture invite children to browse. Book-related merchandise is also sold. The staff is knowledgeable about children's books, as well as art. The store offers gift wrapping and will special order and ship books.

● Silent Movie Theater

611 North Fairfax Avenue, at Melrose Avenue. (213) 653-2389. Wednesday, Friday, and Saturday at 8 P.M. Adults, $6; children, $4. **Ages 6 and up.**

This 250-seat theater screens only classic movies from the silent era. The films, which include comedies by such masters as Keaton, Chaplin, and Laurel and Hardy, are accompanied by live organ music.

Beverly Hills, Century City, and West Los Angeles

● Ed Debevic's

134 North La Cienega at Wilshire Boulevard, Beverly Hills. (310) 659-1952. Monday–Thursday, 11:30 A.M.–3 P.M.; 5:30 A.M.–10 P.M.; Friday and

Saturday, 11:30 A.M.–midnight; Sunday, 11:30 A.M.–10 P.M. **All ages.**

Ed Debevic's is a fifties-style diner with oldies-but-goodies blaring from the jukebox and waitresses who sit at your table when you order. The whole restaurant has an irreverent, life-of-the-party atmosphere that older children and teenagers particularly enjoy. The food is pretty good diner fare—burgers, shakes, blue-plate specials, and the like.

For a different kind of dining experience, **Lawry's** down the street at 100 North La Cienega (phone: 310-652-2827) has been serving families on special occasions since 1938. Their specialty is prime rib served from a large, hooded cart rolled to your table.

● The Museum of Radio and Television

465 North Beverly Drive at South Santa Monica Boulevard, Beverly Hills. (310) 786-1000. Wednesday, noon–5 P.M.; Thursday, noon–9 P.M.; Friday–Sunday, noon–5 P.M. Adults, $6; seniors and students, $4; children under 13, $3. Two hours of free parking is available in the lot underneath the museum. Museum: **Ages 7 and up.** *Television Festival:* **Ages 4–12.**

The exhibits in this state-of-the-art museum are radio and television programs. Downstairs in the stunning two-story building, visitors can slip on headphones in a comfortable listening room and hear selections from the museum's radio collection. Depending on the schedule, you might hear old rock and roll programs, historic newscasts, classic radio dramas, or comedy shows from the golden age of radio. Also downstairs is a plush 150-seat theater that screens special programs and entries from the museum collection. A schedule at the museum entrance desk lets you know what's going on and whether or not the programs are appropriate for children.

The heart of the museum is the **Hubbard Library** upstairs, where the museum's collection of more than 75,000 radio and television programs are cataloged in a bank of Macintosh computers. You sign up to use the library at the downstairs information desk. Upstairs, a librarian will show you how to use the computers. Once you and your children have made your selections, you watch them in a console area. Each console is equipped with a television monitor and headphones that give you control over the playback functions. Two people can sit at a single console.

The museum also sponsors an **International Children's Television Festival** every year with screenings of outstanding children's television programs from around the world. On designated weekends during the festival, television characters are on hand to greet you. Other museum programs include seminars, education programs, and exhibits such as costumes from television programs.

● Museum of Tolerance

9786 West Pico Boulevard, on the corner of Pico and Roxbury Drive, just south of Beverly Hills. (310) 553-8403. Monday–Thursday, 10–4 P.M.; Friday, 10 A.M.–1 P.M., until 3 P.M. April–October; Sunday, 11 A.M.– 5 P.M. Closed Saturdays and religious and national holidays. Adults, $8; seniors, $6; students, $5; children, $3. **Ages 11 and up.**

Far more than just a museum, the Simon Wiesenthal Center Museum of Tolerance seeks to make visitors confront their own bigotry and to understand the connection between modern-day bigotry and the horrors of the Holocaust. The high-tech museum is designed to make visitors interactive participants at every step of the tour. At computerized displays, visitors are challenged on their attitudes toward everything from affirmative action to homosexuality, and throughout the museum they are required to actively make choices.

In the first part of the museum, the Tolerancenter, visitors focus on the major issues of intolerance that are part of our everyday life. Thirty-five hands-on exhibits cover the Los Angeles riots, hate groups in America, the civil rights struggle, and other important issues. Interactive exhibits dramatically engage visitors in real-life situations or feelings. In the Whisper Gallery, for example, visitors are bombarded with racial, ethnic and sexist taunts as they make their way through a fifteen-foot winding tunnel.

In the second half of the tour, visitors are presented with a history of the Holocaust, starting with early 1930s Germany. Each visitor receives a photo passport of a child whose life was caught up in the Holocaust. The passport is updated during the tour, and at end, the child's fate is revealed. At the close of the tour, visitors walk through the barbed gates of a concentration camp and select between doors designated "Able-Bodied" and "Children and Others." No matter which door is selected, visitors end up in the same bunker-like room to hear video testimonies of Holocaust survivors.

Plan to spend about two and a half hours in the museum. It is a powerful experience.

● My Jewish Discovery Place Children's Museum

5870 West Olympic Boulevard, on the lobby level of the Westside Jewish Community Centers of Los Angeles. Parking is available in the structure behind the center or on the street. (213) 857-0036, ext. 2257. Tuesday–Thursday, 12:30–4 P.M.; Sunday, 12:30–5 P.M. Closed national and Jewish holidays. Adults and ages 8 and over, $3; ages 3–7, $2; under 2, free. **Ages 3–10.**

Young children and their families can learn about Jewish culture and history through a variety of hands-on activities in this small, bright children's museum. The exhibits are designed to introduce children ages three to ten to important elements in Jewish life and history. Children can enter a real plane cockpit equipped with an electronic control panel, navigational tools, and pilot's cap and fly off in their imaginations to Israel. Once there, they can make rubbings of artifacts and build their own city of Jerusalem with blocks. A Noah's Ark exhibit includes ship's wheels, dress up, and, naturally, two of each kind of toy animal. An exhibit on Sephardic life includes a family kitchen where kids can prepare for a Shabbat and a wedding celebration complete with costumes. Other exhibits include a dollhouse synagogue, an improvisational theater, a black-light "blast-off" where kids can take off into space, and much more.

The museum gives Jewish children a fun, way to explore their own culture, and gives non-Jewish children an introduction to Jewish culture. School tours and birthday parties are available. Special workshops and family activities also take place regularly.

● Dive!

10250 Santa Monica Boulevard, in the Century City Shopping Center, West Los Angeles. (310) 788-3483. Sunday–Thursday, 11:30 A.M.–11 P.M.; Friday and Saturday, 11:30 A.M.–11 P.M. Meals range from about $8 to $15. Kids' meals are about $5 to $6. **All ages.**

You won't have any trouble recognizing this theme restaurant when you see it. Owned (with help from others) by filmmaker Steven Spielberg, Dive! is fronted by a bright yellow, cartoon-like submarine. The inside looks like a fanciful high-tech submarine—and it even behaves like one. Sirens blare and lights flash as *D.I.V.E.* appears on a 210-foot screen and the restaurant—with the aid of sixty-four video monitors—seems to sink through a flurry of bubbles to many fathoms below. The fare, naturally, is centered around submarine sandwiches. Some twenty-two hot and cold subs are offered, along with barbecue ribs, oven-roasted chicken, burgers, salads, fresh pasta, and children's selections.

● William O. Douglas Outdoor Classroom

Franklin Canyon Ranch. Just north of Beverly Hills. The nature center overlooks the north end of Franklin Canyon Lake. Franklin Canyon Ranch, open to the public from dawn to dusk, is located in the lower canyon. From the intersection of Sunset Boulevard and Beverly Drive, go north on Beverly Drive. Follow the sign to Coldwater Canyon Drive. At the traffic light, go left on

North Beverly Drive. (There is a fire station on the right.) Go one mile to Franklin Canyon Drive. Turn right into the hills for 1.5 miles to the white house on your right. Go past the house 300 feet north to the lower gate. Go through the gates and around the right side of the lake to the nature center parking lot. Or, turn right at the white house and go one mile south on Lake Drive to the Franklin Canyon Ranch. (310) 858-3834. Free. **All ages.**

Located in Franklin Canyon, a pocket wilderness area north of Beverly Hills, the William O. Douglas Outdoor Classroom is a nonprofit environmental education organization serving the people of Los Angeles. The organization offers a number of programs for children and their parents, including family nature hikes, young children's hikes, and hikes for single parents and their kids. There is a nature center with displays, open daily from 10 A.M. to 4 P.M. The center has brochures for a self-guided nature trail and you can picnic in the park.

One gem of a program sponsored by the William O. Douglas Outdoor Classroom is "Babes in the Woods," docent-led nature hikes for children ages two months to three years and their parents. Babies may ride in strollers, Snuglis, or backpacks, or toddle along. The paths are easy, the pace is slow, and there are rest stops for feeding and diapering during the two-hour walks. There are similar programs for children ages two through four and four through seven. You should call ahead to make a reservation for the walks.

● TreePeople

12601 Mulholland Drive (at Coldwater Canyon Road) in Coldwater Canyon Park. Exit the Ventura Freeway (101) at Coldwater Canyon exit and go south to the intersection of Mulholland Drive. Entrance is on the left side of the intersection. (818) 769-2663. The park is open daily, 9 A.M. to dusk. Free. **All ages.**

TreePeople is a nonprofit organization dedicated to planting smog-resistant trees in areas damaged by air pollution. You can take a self-guided tour of their tree nursery in Coldwater Canyon Park. The kiosk in the park has printed guides.

● J. Paul Getty Museum

1200 Getty Center Drive. Located off the 405 Freeway in the Sepulveda Pass. (310) 440-7360. Phone for hours. Free, but fee charged for parking. **Ages 8 and up.**

Scheduled to open in the fall of 1997, the new Getty Museum has more than twice the gallery space of the Malibu museum site. Located on 110 acres in the Santa Monica Mountains above the freeway in the

Sepulveda Pass, the new museum features five two-story pavilions, bridged by walkways, around an open central courtyard. The museum collection of pre-twentieth-century European paintings, drawings, manuscripts, sculpture and decorative arts, and American and European photographs is displayed chronologically in skylight galleries. Among the master works are important paintings and drawings by da Vinci, Michelangelo, Raphael, Rubens, Rembrandt, Renoir, Cezanne, and van Gogh. After parking, visitors take a tram for a five-minute ride up the hill to the museum plaza. The gardens and terraces surrounding the buildings offer sweeping views of the city, the mountains, and the ocean.

The new museum promises to devote significant space to interactive education. Multimedia computer stations, special displays, demonstrations, and hands-on activities are a planned feature of the new museum. A Family Resource Center on the main floor will offer activities to help children get the most from their museum visit. Special viewing hours for school children take place from 9 to 11 A.M. each day. Programs and special events for families are also planned. The new museum includes a full-service restaurant and two cafes.

The original museum, the Roman-style Getty villa in Malibu, will close for renovation when the new facility opens. The villa is scheduled to reopen in the year 2000, displaying the Getty collection of Greek and Roman antiquities.

● Skirball Cultural Center and Museum

2700 North Sepulveda Boulevard. Located off the San Diego Freeway (405) in the Sepulveda Pass just south of Mulholland Drive. (310) 440-4500. Tuesday and Wednesday, 10 A.M.–4 P.M.; Thursday, 10 A.M.–9 P.M.; Friday, 10 A.M.–4 P.M.; Saturday and Sunday, noon–5 P.M. Adults, $6; students and seniors, $4; under 12, free. **Ages 5 and up.**

Located on fifteen acres high in the Sepulveda Pass, the beautiful, new Skirball Cultural Center and Museum focuses on the history and culture of Jewish Americans. The museum uses architectural reconstructions, multimedia presentations, computer displays, and artifacts from a twenty-five-thousand-object collection to trace Jewish history around the globe and, in particular, Jewish life in America.

A young people's museum discovery center explores biblical archaeology through hands-on activities and encounters with genuine artifacts from the Skirball collection. Children aged five and older can log on to interactive computer games for a virtual excavation. In other activities, they can peek into the reconstruction of an ancient rock-cut tomb, create rubbings of ancient alphabets, trace trade routes that brought ancient people together, or play games especially created for the discovery center. Best of all, they can pick up a shovel in an outdoor archaeological dig and, under the guidance of a docent, uncover the simulated remains of an ancient Israeli settlement.

Other activities for families and children at the Skirball include family day workshops, holiday celebrations, concerts, performances, and film screenings. The 125,000-square-foot complex includes an open-air plaza, a 350-seat auditorium, classrooms, a museum store, and a full-service restaurant.

Santa Monica, Pacific Palisades, and Malibu

● Museum of Flying

2772 Donald Douglas Loop North, Santa Monica. Take either the Bundy South or Centinela South exit from the Santa Monica Freeway (I-10). Go two blocks south to Ocean Park Boulevard and turn right; then turn left on Twenty-eighth Street and go to the end of the block. Follow signs to the museum. (213) 392-8822. Tuesday–Sunday, 10 A.M.–5 P.M. Adults, $7; seniors, $5; students, $5; ages 3–17, $3. **Ages 5 and up.**

The shiny, steel-and-glass Museum of Flying is located (appropriately enough) at the Santa Monica Airport. Occupying the site where Douglas Aircraft was originally founded, the three-level museum features some forty historic aircraft, many in flying condition. Among the aircraft suspended from the ceiling and parked on the floor are the 1924 Douglas World Cruiser *New Orleans*—the first aircraft to circle the globe—a World War I–era Curtiss JN-4 *Jenny,* and a World War II Spitfire. Kiosks showing videos of the exhibited aircraft in action are located next to most of the planes. The museum also has a theater that shows films about flying.

Airventure, a large children's interactive area in the museum, includes video displays, model-building stations, and actual plane cockpits to climb into. Workshops for kids take place in a miniature hangar. A first-floor museum viewing area lets you see planes taking off and landing. You can also watch planes from Clover Park, just a short walk from the museum; or you can head for the lawn-covered observation area on top of the airport's Clover Field Terminal.

● Santa Monica College Planetarium

1900 Pico Boulevard, Santa Monica. (310) 452-9223. Shows on Friday at 7 and 8 P.M. Adults, $4 ($7 for both programs). Children are half price. **Ages 6 and up.**

The new John Drescher Planetarium at Santa Monica City College offers two shows a week, on Friday evenings at seven and eight. The first show is generally an introduction to the current sky, and the second is a changing program. There is no minimum age requirement for the shows, although they will be best enjoyed by school-age children and older. On clear nights after the shows, children can go up to the observatory telescope to view the sky. The planetarium is housed on the second floor of the Technology Building on the north side of the campus. (The entrance to the building is on the south, or campus, side.)

● Douglas Park

1155 Chelsea Avenue, Santa Monica. One block west of Twenty-sixth Street, between California Street and Wilshire Boulevard. **Ages 1–10.**

Families with young children will particularly enjoy this lovely small park. The landscaping is very pretty, with rolling green lawns, streams, and a little duck pond. On the California Avenue side of the park is an active playground, with a separate and fair-sized toddler playground. (There are even a couple of swinging benches for the parents.) The playground is separated from the rest of the park by a large oval recessed track (once a wading pool) that is perfect for bike riding. There are public phones and restrooms in the park.

● Nursery Nature Walks

1440 Harvard Street, Santa Monica. (310) 998-1151. $5 donation per family. **Ages infant–8.**

Nursery Nature Walks offers families with young children an opportunity to enjoy gentle, docent-led nature walks in a variety of locations. The volunteer, nonprofit organization specializes in walks for families with young children from infants through eight years old—although older children may come along. Babies can ride in Snuglis, backpacks, or strollers, and older children can join on foot. The pace is slow and the emphasis is on helping children to discover nature. Most walks are about two hours long and include a stop for snack that you bring along. A wonderful feature of the program is that walks take place in parks and mountain areas across much of Los Angeles County. (To find out about walks in Orange County, phone 714-859-3496.) No matter where you live in Los Angeles or Ventura counties, you should be able to find a walk within a thirty-minute drive. Some sites are wheelchair accessible. Nursery Nature Walks also has a training program for parents who wish to become docents. Other programs include a kids' nature festival, environmental workshops for five- through eight-year-olds, a kids leading kids program where four- through eleven-year-olds can share their knowledge, and an annual kids' concert. The organization also publishes a nature activity book for families: *Trails, Tails & Tidepools in Pails.*

● Santa Monica Playhouse

1211 Fourth Street, Santa Monica. (213) 394-9779. Performances: Saturday and Sunday, 1 P.M. and 3 P.M. All seats, $8. Reservations are required. Telephone for workshop schedule and costs. **Ages 3 and up.**

The Santa Monica Playhouse presents children's plays or musicals every Saturday and Sunday afternoon. The programs, which change every three to four months, are recommended for ages three to ninety. Reservations are required. Birthday party arrangements can be made. The playhouse also offers a year-round schedule of theater workshops for children ages four to fifteen. The workshops introduce children to improvisation, scene study, make-up, costumes, music, diction, and live performance.

● Angel's Attic

516 Colorado Avenue, Santa Monica. (310) 394-8331. Thursday–Sunday, 12:30–4:30 P.M. Adults, $4; seniors, $3; under 12, $2. **Ages 6 and up.**

The oldest house in Santa Monica, an 1875 Queen Anne Victorian, has been restored to serve as Angel's Attic, a museum of antique dollhouses, dolls, and toys benefiting autistic children. The house, with its gingerbread trimming and wicker-furniture porch, seems like a giant dollhouse itself. Inside are the real things. Among the most interesting dollhouses are an exact replica of Anne Hathaway's cottage and a 1923 dollhouse from Puebla, Mexico, in the style of a well-to-do Mexican home of that era. Antique toys and miniatures are displayed on a track just below the ceiling. Old-fashioned dolls are displayed upstairs. There is also a small boutique selling dollhouse-related items.

If you phone ahead for reservations, after seeing the museum, adults can have tea and children can enjoy lemonade and cookies at one of the wicker tables on the front porch. The museum, which is very much a "no touch" experience, will be best enjoyed by school-age children, particularly girls.

● Santa Monica Pier

At the western end of Colorado Avenue at Ocean Avenue, Santa Monica. (310) 458-8900. Free. **All ages.**

A $15 million renovation—and an emphasis on family fun—has transformed the historic Santa Monica Pier from an aging, rather downtrodden seaside spot into a bright, old-fashioned family attraction. The renovated pier features a two-acre fun zone called Pacific Park, with eleven rides, including a 1,300-foot steel roller coaster and a nine-story Ferris wheel with red and yellow gondolas. For younger children, there is a mini Ferris wheel, a small bumper car ride, as well as other small rides and some children's midway games.

Also on the pier is a UCLA-sponsored Ocean Discovery Center, and the old, Hollywood music club, the Ash Grove, which offers a program of Saturday morning family-friendly concerts. (For more information on the Ash Grove concerts, phone 310-656-8500.) You can fish, or watch the fishing, on the pier's lower deck fishing balconies. There are also a number of good places to eat on the pier—from fast food to restaurants.

Of course, the highlight of the pier for many is still the 1922 Philadelphia Toboggan Company carousel. The carousel, and the 1916 Hippodrome housing it, have been painstakingly and lovingly restored to their original splendor. Each of the forty-six hand-carved horses is different from the others, and all ride to the merry strains of one of the oldest Wurlitzer organs in the country.

● Santa Monica Heritage Square Museum

2612 Main Street, Santa Monica. (213) 392-8537. Wednesday–Saturday, 11 A.M.–4 P.M.; Sunday, 12–4 P.M. Closed holidays. Adults, $3; seniors, $2; under 12, free. **Ages 6 and up.**

The city of Santa Monica worked for years to preserve, relocate and restore the elegant nineteenth-century home that now serves as the Santa Monica Heritage Square Museum. The downstairs rooms of the house have been decorated to look as they would have in the late nineteenth and early twentieth centuries. The room that will interest children most is the kitchen with its old-fashioned stove and hot-water heater. Off the kitchen is a pantry with a 1920s beehive motor refrigerator that is still working.

Upstairs are changing exhibits that relate to the history of Santa Monica. Past exhibits have included sports, the beach, boats, and even model trains. Perhaps the best time to visit with children is the holiday season, when the exhibits are often playful and the house is decorated for Christmas with a ten-foot tree hung with handmade, old-style ornaments.

● Burton Chace Park

End of Mindanao Way past Admiralty Way, Marina del Rey. (310) 305-9596. Daily, 6 A.M.–9:30 P.M. **All ages.**

Located at the tip of the Mindanao jetty in the Chace Harbor at Marina del Rey, this park is a good place to watch boats, see airplanes (LAX is nearby), fly a kite (there is almost always a breeze), or just play. (The park is very crowded on Sundays, however.) There are picnic tables and barbecues. Free public concerts and other activities frequently take place in the park. Check with the park or the Marina Chamber of Commerce (phone: 310-821-0555) for the current schedule.

● Marina Beach

Along Admiralty and Via Marina ways, between Palawan and Panay ways, Marina del Rey. **All ages.**

This is an excellent beach for children because there are no big ocean waves. In addition to a sheltered surface, the inland beach has a shallow bottom.

● Fisherman's Village

13763 Fiji Way (off Admiralty Way, a half-mile west of Lincoln Boulevard), Marina del Rey. (310) 823-5411. Daily, 9 A.M.–9 P.M. (open until 10 P.M. in the summer). **All ages.**

A replica of a Cape Cod fishing town, Fisherman's Village is a shopping and restaurant complex along the waterfront in Marina del Rey. In the main square is an Orange Julius snack bar in a replica of a lighthouse. Nearby is an old-fashioned red wagon selling popcorn. On Sunday afternoons from 2 to 5 P.M., free concerts take place in the lighthouse plaza.

Two Mississippi riverboat replicas, the *Marina Belle* and the *Showboat,* give regularly scheduled forty-five-minute narrated cruises of the harbor; tours leave the village boathouse at 13727 Fiji Way. Phone (310) 301-6000 for information on the cruises. For information on other companies operating cruises, fishing charters, and boat rentals from the Village, phone (310) 823-5411.

● Will Rogers State Historic Park

14253 Sunset Boulevard, Pacific Palisades. (310) 454-8212. Park is open daily, 8 A.M.–5 P.M. (until 7 P.M. during daylight savings time). House is open 10:30 A.M.–4:30 P.M., daily. Admission is $5 per car. **All ages.**

Will Rogers lived on this 187-acre rustic estate from the 1920s until his death in a plane crash in 1935. Everything in his ranch house is maintained as it was when he lived there. (In the living room, the clock is stopped at 8:17, the time registered on his pilot's watch when their plane crashed.) Kids will appreciate that the famous humorist was also a former cowboy, and the house looks like a cowboy lived there. The stuffed calf that Rogers used to practice lassoing is still in the living room, where he kept it. Next to the house is a little museum that shows a continuous free movie about Rogers.

You can picnic on the large lawn area surrounding the house. Hiking trails wind through the hills above the house, some leading to excellent views of the city, mountains, and ocean.

Rogers was also an avid polo player who installed his own polo field on the estate. Games are still played on the field on Saturday at 2 P.M. and Sunday at 10 A.M. (weather permitting; call the park to make sure the games are being played). The games are great fun to watch.

● Rustic Canyon Recreation Center

601 Latimer Road, Santa Monica. From Sunset Boulevard just south of Will Rogers Park, take Brooktree Road east to the park. (310) 454-5734.
Ages 6 and up.

The Rustic Canyon Recreation Center offers children and teenagers instruction in art, guitar, piano, dance, tennis, swimming, basketball, cooking, and other subjects. Classes generally meet once a week, and fees range from about $20 to $40 per eight-week session. Student artwork is often exhibited at the center, which is located in a lovely glade.

● Malibu Lagoon Museum/Adamson House

23200 Pacific Coast Highway, Malibu. The entrance is located 300 yards west of the Malibu Pier. Parking is in a county lot on the ocean side of Pacific Coast Highway opposite Serra Road. From the parking lot, walk on the sidewalk on Pacific Coast Highway 80 yards east to the entrance. (310) 456-8432. Wednesday–Saturday, 11 A.M.–3 P.M. (Last house tour is at 2 P.M.) House tour: Adults, $2; ages 6–17, $1; under 6, free. Museum: free. Adamson House: **Ages 10 and up.** *Museum:* **All ages.**

In the early part of the century, all of the land that is now Malibu was owned by one family. The daughter of that family built her house on the beach adjacent to the Malibu Lagoon. Her house, the Adamson House, is now operated by the Santa Monica Mountains National Recreation Area and is open to the public. The Moorish-Spanish–style house is quite grand, featuring magnificent tile work. (There is even a colorfully tiled dog shower outside.) The docent-led house tour, which takes thirty to thirty-five minutes, will only be appreciated by older children. However, everyone should enjoy seeing the Malibu Lagoon Museum, located in the former garage. Highlights of the museum for children include Chumash Indian artifacts and displays depicting the history of surfing in Malibu. The grounds include shaded picnic tables with ocean views.

Malibu Lagoon State Beach, adjacent to the house on the west side, is a rich tidal estuary providing haven for some two hundred species of migratory birds and a variety of marine life. You explore the wetlands by walking along boardwalks so as not to disturb the wildlife. Signs along the trail help you to identify the birds you are seeing. The **Malibu Pier,** to the east of the Adamson House, was first built as a landing point for visitors and supplies to Rancho Malibu. Today the state-owned pier is a good place to fish (the bait-and-tackle shop rents supplies) and to watch the local surfers in action.

● Santa Monica Mountains Recreation Area

Visitor Information Center: 30401 Agoura Road, Ste. 100, Agoura Hills, CA 91301. (818) 597-9192, ext. 201. Monday–Friday, 8 A.M.–5 P.M. Saturday and Sunday, 9 A.M.–5 P.M. Free. **All ages.**

The Santa Monica Mountains stretch almost fifty miles across Los Angeles from Griffith Park to Point Mugu. In 1978, fifteen years of effort to protect this resource culminated in the creation of the Santa Monica Mountains National Recreation Area, a new part of the national park system. The area encompasses a variety of mountain parks, as well as the public beaches between Point Mugu and Santa Monica.

The Santa Monica Recreation Area offers a wide range of outdoor programs for families. Families can take easy ranger-led hikes through trails in a number of the parks in the area. Special programs for children have included an early evening hike to learn about nocturnal animals, a look at the special qualities of birds, an introduction to the Native Americans who once lived in the Santa Monica Mountains, and hikes through the woodlands to study the animals of the Santa Monica Mountains. The Visitor Information Center will supply you with a current schedule of activities.

South Bay and Beach Cities

● Sand Dune Park

33rd Street at Bell Avenue, Manhattan Beach. (310) 545-5621 (Manhattan Beach Parks and Recreation Department). Open daily. Free. **Ages 3–10.**

A steep sand dune that kids can climb and slide on is the outstanding feature of this park. The top of the sand dune can be reached climbing the dune or by taking a winding path of steps. (Most kids will get worn out and slide down before they make it to the top.) If your children want, they can bring a large piece of cardboard to slide on. The park has an enclosed small children's playground and play area for older kids. There is a tree-shaded picnic area with tables, barbecues, sinks, and restrooms. The only drawback is that parking is limited to crowded street spaces.

● Lomita Railroad Museum

2135-37 250th Street, Lomita. Go south on Harbor Freeway to Pacific Coast Highway exit. Go west on PCH to Narbonne Avenue, turn right to 250th Street. (310) 326-6255. Wednesday–Sunday, 10 A.M.–5 P.M. Adults, $1; children, 50¢. **Ages 3–12.**

The large train mural at the corner of Pacific Coast Highway and Narbonne Avenue in Lomita will signal to kids that they are near the Lomita Railroad Museum. It's still a great surprise, though, to turn the corner on 250th Street in this ordinary residential neighborhood and see a replica of a nineteenth-century Wakefield, Massachusetts, train depot with a shiny black 1902 Southern Pacific locomotive looming beside it. Kids can climb aboard the locomotive (all the valves and handles in the engine's cab are labeled with explanations of their purpose, but they cannot be touched) as well as a 1910 wooden caboose. Also on the tracks outside are a Southern Pacific tender used for hauling water and fuel oil and a velocipede handcar—a three-wheeled, one-man car used by track inspectors.

Inside the depot are an old-style ticket office, telegraph equipment, a hand-lantern collection, a calliope, train models, a collection of buttons from trainmen's uniforms, and much more. The whole museum is meticulously well kept. Across the street is a grassy annex with a fountain and large red boxcar where you can have a picnic lunch.

● Point Vicente Interpretive Center

31501 Palos Verdes Drive West, Rancho Palos Verdes. (310) 377-5370. Daily, 10 A.M.–7 P.M. Adults, $2; children, $1; under 4, free. **All ages.**

Whales are the focus of this small museum overlooking the ocean on the Palos Verdes Peninsula. Outside is a beautiful site for whale watching, picnicking, or just plain ocean gazing. Inside the center are exhibits on geology, natural history, and marine life. There are some touch exhibits for children, including an assortment of seashells to handle. You can also view a twenty-minute film on whale watching.

● South Coast Botanic Gardens

26300 Crenshaw Boulevard, Palos Verdes Peninsula. Take the Harbor Freeway to Pacific Coast Highway. Go west on PCH to Crenshaw Boulevard, south on Crenshaw. (310) 544-6815. Daily, 9 A.M.–5 P.M. Adults, $5; senior citizens and students, $3; ages 5–12, $1. Free on the third Tuesday of every month. **All ages.**

Kids who are learning about recycling will be especially impressed with the South Coast Botanic Gardens. These lovely gardens were recycled from a trash dump. The eighty-seven-acre site includes a man-made lake inhabited by ducks; a winding stream; and acres of flowers, plants, and trees. Children can bring bread to feed the ducks or buy bags of corn in the gift shop. There are picnic tables on the lawn outside the gardens.

Los Angeles Harbor Area, Catalina, and Long Beach

● Cabrillo Marine Museum
3720 Stephen White Drive, San Pedro. Take the Harbor Freeway south until it ends. Turn left on Gaffey, then turn left on Twenty-second Street. Go two blocks and turn right on Pacific, then left on Thirty-sixth Street, which becomes Stephen White Drive. Bear left past large black anchors. (310) 548-7562. Tuesday–Friday, noon–5 P.M.; Saturday and Sunday, 10 A.M.–5 P.M. Free. Parking, $6.50. **All ages.**

The Cabrillo Marine Museum, on the beach in San Pedro, has long been a favorite of kids. Devoted to the sea life and marine environment of Southern California, the museum includes more than thirty aquariums where children can watch the interaction of sea creatures. Perhaps the most fascinating aquarium is the fourteen-foot-long shark tank containing a variety of small sharks. (The biggest is just two feet long.)

Museum displays cover local habitat settings such as the Los Angeles Harbor, the open ocean, offshore kelp beds, sandy beaches, and mudflats. A colorful tide pool "touch tank" (open at posted or announced times) gives kids the opportunity to feel sea hares, sea cucumbers, urchins, and other sea life under the supervision of a marine expert.

The museum also sponsors whale-watching boat trips and other marine-related activities. Call the museum for their program schedule. School (and preschool) tours of the museum are scheduled throughout the year.

Outside are tide pools that can be explored. There is also a grassy picnic area and a playground adjacent to the museum.

● Point Fermin Park
805 Paseo del Mar at Gaffey Street, San Pedro. (310) 548-7756. **All ages.**

Point Fermin Park, a short distance from the Cabrillo Marine Museum, rests on thirty-seven landscaped acres overlooking the Pacific. The park, which offers an unobstructed view of Catalina, is a great place to watch for ships, harbor seals, and whales. A whale-watching station offers information on the migration of the gray whale. An 1874 wooden lighthouse is located on the point, although you cannot tour inside it.

● Ports O' Call Village

Berth 77, San Pedro. Take the Harbor Freeway south to the Harbor Boulevard exit, turn right for half a mile, and follow the signs to the village entrance. (310) 831-0287. Daily, 11 A.M.–8 P.M. Open until 9 P.M. on weekends. Free admission and parking. **Ages 6 and up.**

Nineteenth-century California and New England seaport villages are simulated in this restaurant and shopping complex at the Port of Los Angeles. Ports O' Call Village, complete with cobblestone streets and gas lamps, aims to give the impression of an early California seaport. Whaler's Wharf is a replica of a New England town with its fish markets and steepled courthouse.

You can watch the ships passing in the harbor, or get a casual, tasty fish dinner from one of the fish markets. Harbor tours are also available from Ports O' Call. **Los Angeles Harbor Cruises** (phone: 310-831-0996) offers daily one-hour fully narrated cruises in the afternoon ($8 for adults and $4 for kids), departing from the Village Boathouse. **Spirit Cruises** (phone: 310-548-8080), departing from Ports O' Call Village, Berth 77, also offers harbor cruises and, in the winter, whale watching.

An electric trolley, stopping at Ports O' Call, operates in the harbor area every forty-five minutes, from 11 A.M. to 7 P.M. The fare is 25¢, and you can take it to the Cabrillo Marine Museum, Los Angeles Maritime Museum, and other harbor attractions.

● Korean Friendship Bell/Angel's Gate Park

Gaffey Street between Thirty-second and Shepard streets, San Pedro. Daily, 8 A.M.–6 P.M. Free. **All ages.**

The largest bell in the United States hangs in a pagoda in Angel's Gate Park. The nineteen-ton Korean Friendship Bell was given to the United States by the Republic of Korea in 1976 to commemorate our nation's bicentennial. It sounds only three times a year: on New Year's Day, July Fourth, and Korea Liberation Day (August 15). The surrounding park offers picnic sites and a magnificent view of the Pacific.

● The Los Angeles Maritime Museum

Berth 84, San Pedro. Take the Harbor Freeway south to Harbor Boulevard exit, turn right to Harbor Boulevard and Sixth Street. (310) 548-7618. Tuesday–Sunday, 10 A.M.–5 P.M. Adults, $1; children, free. **Ages 6 and up.**

The Maritime Museum is dedicated to ships and seafaring. Completed in 1978, the museum is housed in a remodeled ferry building in the Los Angeles Harbor. Among the exhibits are navigation instruments,

the bridge deck from the cruiser *Los Angeles,* wooden ships' wheels
from the two world wars, early navy diving helmets, ships' bells, and
scale models of historical ships such as the USS *Chesapeake.* The museum
is bright and cheery, and the deck offers a good view of the harbor.

● SS *Lane Victory* Memorial Museum

*Berth 94, Los Angeles Harbor, San Pedro. Exit Harbor Freeway (110) or
the Vincent Thomas Bridge at Harbor Boulevard. Cross Harbor Boulevard
to Swinford Street and follow signs to Berth 94. (310) 519-9545. Daily,
9 A.M.–4 P.M. Adults, $3; under 15, $1.* **Ages 6 and up.**

This meticulously restored World War II cargo ship is a national
historic landmark. Now docked in Berth 94 in the Los Angeles Harbor,
the ship served in Korea and Vietnam, as well as during World War II.
You can see most of the ship, including the bridge, crew's quarters,
wheelhouse, navel guns, radio and engine rooms on a self-guided tour.
(Children need to be at least eleven years old to enter the engine room.)
The crew of retired merchant marines are on hand throughout the ship
to answer your questions. There are two museums on board the ship.
One is a museum of vehicles; the other contains memorabilia from the
ship's past.

The ship is not wheelchair or stroller accessible—you will be climbing up and down ladders—and you must wear tennis or other low-heeled,
closed-toed shoes. Since the ship, which is still seaworthy, sometimes
leaves the harbor for excursions, be sure to call before you visit.

● Catalina Island

*Catalina Chamber of Commerce and Visitor's Bureau, Box 217, Avalon, CA
90704. (213) 510-1520. Catalina Cruises (boat service from Long Beach)
phone: (800) 228-2546. Catalina Express (boat service from San Pedro
and Long Beach) phone: (800) 360-1212 or (310) 519-1212. Catalina
Passenger Services (boat service from Newport Beach) phone: (714) 673-5245.
Island Express (six-passenger jet helicopter service from San Pedro and Long
Beach) phone: (310) 510-2525. Island Hopper/Catalina Airlines (air service
from San Diego) phone: (619) 279-4595.* **All ages.**

Once a hideout for smugglers and pirates, Catalina Island still has
natural areas where wild boar, wild goats, cattle, and buffalo roam. (The
buffalo are the descendants of a small herd imported to the island for
the filming of a 1924 movie.) On a day trip Catalina, your visit will
probably be confined to Avalon, the island's only city. Strict legislation
limiting the number and size of cars in the city makes it a pleasure just
to walk there.

Catalina offers a variety of activities for families. One of the most interesting is the glass-bottom boat cruise. Through the windows in the boat's bottom, you see all sorts of fish, including giant saltwater goldfish, as well as waving kelp and sea ferns. Or you could take one of the new semi-submersibles—sixty-foot, fifty-ton vessels with underwater seating and viewing—through Catalina's shallow coastal waters. A more conventional boat cruise takes you to the eastern tip of Catalina, where you can often see seals frolicking. If you are on Catalina in the evening from May through September, take the flying-fish boat trip; the boat's searchlights spot the fish flying up to seventy-five yards through the air. (The fish sometimes even land in the boat.)

On an overnight or longer stay on Catalina, you might want to take a tour of inland Catalina. **Inland Motor Tour** is a three-and-three-quarter-hour trip through the island's beautiful, mountainous interior. (You may even see buffalo, deer, goats, or boars wandering free.) The tour includes a stop at El Rancho Escondido to see a performance of the Arabian horses raised there. Shorter motor and tram tours and other boat tours are also available. You might also want to take a tram from Avalon to see the **Wrigley Memorial and Botanical Garden** filled with native trees, cacti, succulent plants, and flowering trees.

Catalina also offers hiking, camping, picnicking, skin diving, fishing, and horseback riding; swimming and snorkeling in clear, surf-free waters; ocean rafting; and boat, bicycle, and, for sight-seeing, golf cart rentals. On the Pleasure Pier, the Chamber of Commerce has brochures, maps, and information on the island's activities. The Visitors Information Center, a very short walk from the Chamber of Commerce, handles sight-seeing tour tickets. The nearest camping to Avalon is at Hermit Gulch Campground, (310) 510-8368, which has tent sites, tent cabins, and tepees. For camping information elsewhere on the island, call Catalina Island Camping Information and Reservations, (310) 510-2800 or 510-0303.

Outside of Avalon, Catalina's only other real settlement is the tiny, rustic village of Two Harbors. Most of the island remains in a state of rugged, natural beauty, protected by the Santa Catalina Island Conservancy. Ships to Catalina depart year-round.

● Harbor Regional Park
25820 Vermont Avenue, Harbor City. Free. **All ages.**

This lovely 231-acre park contains a large lake for fishing, pedal boating, or duck feeding. Attractive, modern children's play areas are built in sort of a marina style and include nets for climbing. There are picnic facilities.

● Banning Residence Museum and Park

401 East M Street, Wilmington. Take Harbor Freeway south from Los Angeles to Pacific Coast Highway exit. Turn left and go one mile east. Turn right on Avalon Boulevard for two blocks. Turn left on M Street for two blocks to the park. (310) 548-7777. Park is open daily, 6 A.M.–10 P.M. Free. Conducted tours through the house: Tuesday, Wednesday, Thursday at 12:30, 1:30, and 2:30 P.M.; Saturday and Sunday at 12:30, 1:30, 2:30, and 3:30 P.M. Adults, $2 donation; children, free. Museum: **Ages 8 and up.** *Park:* **All ages.**

General Phineas Banning made his fortune developing the transportation networks, including the Port of Los Angeles, that helped link Los Angeles to the rest of the nation. He built his twenty-three-room, showcase mansion in 1864, landscaping the grounds with lovely gardens. Constructed during the Civil War, adjacent to the headquarters of the United States Army of the Southwest, the home was a center for rallies and meetings supporting the cause of the Union in a city with largely Confederate sympathies. The house has been restored to its Victorian splendor with eighteen rooms now open to the public.

Unlike so many historic houses, there is nothing stiff or musty about the Banning Residence. You really have the sensation that the original occupants have departed the rooms just moments before you are seeing them. The guided tour of the house and the stagecoach barn takes about an hour and fifteen minutes.

The Banning Museum has a number of special and seasonal programs, including an 1880s Day for fourth- and fifth-grade students, Victorian kitchen demonstrations, and a recreation of a Victorian Christmas. The residence is surrounded by a twenty-acre park that is open daily. The park has children's playgrounds, picnic facilities, and lovely eucalyptus, giant bamboo, and jacaranda trees.

● Drum Barracks Civil War Museum

1052 Banning Boulevard, Wilmington. Take Pacific Coast Highway east from the 110 Freeway or west from the 710 Freeway to Avalon Boulevard. Take Avalon south to L Street. Turn left on L Street and go three blocks to Banning Boulevard; turn right. Tours depart: Tuesday–Thursday at 10 A.M., 11 A.M., noon, and 1 P.M.; Saturday and Sunday at 11:30 A.M., 12:30, 1:30, and 2:30 P.M. $2.50 per person donation. **Ages 8 and up.**

Only this one building—the former officers' quarters—remains of Camp Drum, a sixty-acre Civil War garrison of some twenty buildings that quartered up to 7,000 men. On a guided tour, you will see a restored barracks bedroom and parlor, as well as displays of Civil War–era documents, furniture, photographs, equipment, and arms, including a rare Gatling gun and a model of the original camp.

● The *Queen Mary*

Pier J, Long Beach Harbor. Take the Long Beach Freeway (710) south to the Queen Mary exit. (310) 435-3511. Daily, 10 A.M.–6 P.M. Extended hours during the summer. Adults, $10; ages 4–11, $6; under 4, free. Combination ticket: Adults, $13; ages 4–11, $7. Parking, $5. **Ages 6 and up.**

The famed British ocean liner *Queen Mary* has been a part of the Long Beach skyline for more years than she sailed the sea. One of the most luxurious ocean liners ever to sail the Atlantic, the *Queen Mary* completed her maiden voyage in 1936. After more than a thousand transatlantic crossings carrying many wealthy and famous passengers, the giant ocean liner was purchased by the city of Long Beach in 1967 for use as a hotel and tourist attraction. Recently placed on the National Register of Historic Places, the *Queen Mary,* under new management, is being restored and refurbished to her former glory.

On a self-guided tour, you'll see areas of the ship that her former passengers never got to see, such as the engine room—complete with boilers and 40,000-horsepower turbines—and the emergency steering station. The propeller chamber, a specially created chamber outside the ship's hull that enables visitors to see one of the ships's giant propellers in the water, should impress the kids.

On the upper decks you'll see replicas of the original staterooms, officer's quarters, gymnasium, children's playroom, and the wheelhouse and radio room. Children should especially enjoy seeing the exhibits that depict the *Queen Mary*'s role as a troop carrier during World War II.

For an additional charge, you can buy a combination ticket that adds a behind-the-scenes guided tour to your visit. The sixty-minute guided tour visits areas you cannot see on your own, such as the first-class swimming pool.

There are a number of places to eat on the *Queen Mary,* ranging from fast food to fine dining. On the dock adjacent to the ship, the Queen's Marketplace is a collection of shops and eating establishments in the style of an English village. Strolling musicians and other entertainers perform during summers, holidays, and weekends.

● Shoreline Village

Off Shoreline Drive at the foot of Pine Street, just south of the Convention Center. Take the Long Beach Freeway to Shoreline Drive. (310) 435-2668. Daily, 10 A.M.–9 P.M. (Open until 10 P.M. during the summer.) Free.
All ages.

Shoreline Village is a shopping, dining, and entertainment complex designed in the fanciful style of a turn-of-the-century beachside village. The top attraction here for children is the beautiful 1906 Charles Looff carousel with sixty-two hand-carved horses—and camels, giraffes, and rams. The carousel operates daily. Dixieland bands and other entertainers frequently perform weekends on an outdoor stage called the Off-Boardwalk Theater. Shoreline Village is adjacent to a marina; it's fun to walk along the wooden boardwalk and look at the boats. Harbor cruises and, in winter, whale-watching cruises are available. (For more information, phone **Spirit Cruises** at 310-495-5884.) Snack food, as well as more substantial fare, is sold in a variety of eating establishments, and there are plenty of places to sit outside. The village is surrounded by grassy park areas where you can picnic.

● *Independent Press-Telegram* Tour

604 Pine Avenue, downtown Long Beach. (310) 499-1489. Tours: Monday–Friday, 10 A.M., during the school year. Reservations required one month in advance. Children need to be in at least the second grade. **Ages 7 and up.**

All aspects of newspaper production—from the editorial to the advertising departments, from the wire room to the presses—are shown on this hour-long tour. A minimum of ten people are needed to take the tour. The best days to take the tour are Thursday and Friday, when the presses are running.

● **Long Beach Firefighters Museum**

1445 Peterson Avenue, Long Beach. (310) 597-0351. Parking inside of gates. Second Saturday of each month, 10 A.M.–3 P.M. Free. **All ages.**

The old Long Beach Fire Station Number 10 serves as the home for a number of antique fire-fighting vehicles, including two horse-drawn steamers. You can see the equipment and watch pumping demonstrations on the second Saturday of every month from 10 A.M. to 3 P.M.

● **Rancho Los Cerritos**

4600 Virginia Road, Long Beach. Take the San Diego Freeway to Long Beach Boulevard. Go north on Long Beach Boulevard to San Antonio Drive, turn left, then go right one block on Virginia Road. (310) 570-1755. Wednesday–Sunday, 1–5 P.M. Self-guided tours: Wednesday–Friday 1–5 P.M. Guided tours: Saturday and Sunday: 1, 2, 3, and 4 P.M. Free. **Ages 8 and up.**

Maybe it's because Rancho Los Cerritos is slightly off the beaten track, but this beautifully restored Spanish hacienda provides a real sense of the past. Built in 1844 around a central patio, the two-story hacienda was made of adobe brick with three-foot-thick walls and redwood beam ceilings.

The house has been meticulously furnished in the style of the period: Antique hairbrushes are arranged on a heavy wood bureau in a bedroom, and an old foot-treadle sewing machine is in the sewing room. Youngsters will appreciate the children's room, where antique toys and dolls are casually placed. You can take a self-guided tour of the rancho Wednesday through Friday. On weekends you can only see the rancho on a forty-five-minute guided tour. The adobe is surrounded by almost five acres of lush gardens. There is a picnic area.

● Rancho Los Alamitos

6400 Bixby Hill Road, Long Beach. From the San Diego Freeway, take the Palos Verdes Avenue exit south to security gate of the walled residential community of Bixby Hill. A security guard will direct you the rancho. (310) 431-3541. Wednesday–Sunday, 1–5 P.M. (Tours are every half hour. The last tour is at 4 P.M.) Free. **Ages 8 and up.**

In 1806, Juan José Nieto built an adobe ranch house on this hill. His ranch was part of a vast Spanish land grant—stretching from San Gabriel to the sea—which had been given to his father, a soldier in the Portolá expedition exploring California. Today all that remains of that vast rancho is seven and a half acres, including five acres of gardens, the original ranch house, and six farm buildings.

On a sixty-minute guided tour of the rancho, which was a working ranch from 1784 into the 1950s, you see the ranch house, furnished with family possessions (including a vintage Edison Graphophone) that span many generations, the blacksmith shop, and the barns, which contain some restored farm equipment. The grounds are lovely and peaceful, but because of the length of the guided tour, a visit here is best made with older children.

● El Dorado Park and Nature Center

El Dorado Park East: 7550 East Spring Street, Long Beach. Take I-605 south to Spring Street/Cerritos exit and go west on Spring Street. (310) 570-1765. East park hours: Daily, 7 A.M.–8 P.M. Nature Center phone: (310) 570-1745. Nature center trails: Tuesday–Sunday, 8 A.M.–4 P.M. Nature Center Museum: Tuesday–Friday, 10 A.M.–4 P.M.; Saturday and Sunday, 8:30 A.M.–4 P.M. Parking at El Dorado Park East: $3 weekdays; $5 weekends. El Dorado Park West: 2800 Studebaker Road. (310) 570-1630. West park hours: Daily, 7 A.M.–10 P.M. Free parking. **All ages.**

El Dorado Park is an eight-hundred-acre recreation area that includes two parks and an eighty-acre semiwilderness nature reserve. El Dorado West City Park (south of Spring Street and west of the San Gabriel River) includes a duck pond, a children's playground, roller-skate rentals, and a number of game courts and ball diamonds. El Dorado East Regional Park (north of Spring Street and east of the San Gabriel River) includes several lakes stocked with fish, a large lake with paddleboat rentals, a train ride, an archery range, open meadows, and bicycle and roller-skating paths.

El Dorado Nature Center, located in the east park, is an eighty-acre forested nature sanctuary. There are two lakes, marshes, meadows, a stream, and miles of soft-bark hiking trails. The area is inhabited by raccoons, weasels, foxes, and other small animals. The Nature Center building, on an island in one of the lakes, has maps for self-guided tours and a museum that houses living and stuffed specimens of the area's animal inhabitants.

The San Fernando Valley

● Universal Studios Tour

Universal City, located just off the Hollywood Freeway at either the Universal Center or Lankershim Boulevard exits. Open daily, except Christmas and Thanksgiving. Summer hours: 7:30 A.M.–11 P.M. (Box office open 7 A.M.–5 P.M.) Rest of the year hours: 9 A.M.–7 P.M. (Box office open 8:30 A.M.–4 P.M. Adults (ages 12 and older), $34; ages 60 and older, $29; ages 3–11, $26; under 3, free. Parking, $6. **Ages 3 and up.**

A tour of Universal Studios gives you amusement attractions and a behind-the-scenes look at a busy movie studio. The Universal Studios tour/entertainment complex has recently undergone a major expansion, and the emphasis now is on big-ticket amusement attractions. The guided tram portion of the tour (which once took two hours) has been revamped into a fast-paced forty-five minute tram ride punctuated by such adventures as *Earthquake*—a simulated 8.3 major temblor—and an encounter with a thirty-foot King Kong. (Most small children will find these encounters terrifying, and there is plenty here to do without taking the tram ride.)

Top among the new attractions is the spectacular *Jurassic Park* ride, billed as the most technically sophisticated attraction ever created. Riders enter the world of Jurassic Park on twenty-five-passenger, free-floating boats to encounter terrifyingly lifelike dinosaurs, some as tall as five-story buildings. The robotic dinosaurs, seeming to respond to the humans, attack almost at the riders' faces. As if all this were not scary enough, the climax of the ride is an eighty-four-foot plunge straight down a water descent. Needless to say, this ride is not for young children or shaky adults.

A ride that everyone can enjoy is the *E.T. Adventure*, in which guests climb aboard starbound bicycles and (through the magic of stunning special effects) fly across the universe with the lovable alien E.T. An attraction geared specifically to young children is the half-acre An American Tail playland with outsize props that double as imaginative play equipment. Kids who watch *I Love Lucy* reruns may also enjoy seeing the walk-through tribute to Lucy.

There are numerous opportunities for children and their parents to see how movies are made and how special effects are done—and kids can participate in many of the demonstrations.

A "starway" people-mover allows visitors to see a portion of the studio that was previously inaccessible to the public. Guests can also view actual live filming of productions through specially designed soundproof viewing areas. An area called Streets of the World offers visitors sets they can walk through, including a fifties American set and the Baker Street of Sherlock Holmes. There are also a number of live, action-packed shows presented—some including daring stunts. (The shows last fifteen to twenty minutes; kids will enjoy any or all of them.)

● Universal CityWalk

Universal Center Drive, next to Universal Studios, Universal City. Exit Hollywood Freeway (101) at Universal Center Drive and follow the signs. (818) 622-4455. Sunday–Thursday, 11 A.M.–9 P.M.; Saturday and Sunday, 11 A.M.–11 P.M. Restaurants may stay open later. Free. Validated parking in Universal Studio lots. **All ages.**

CityWalk is a colorful, three-block, open-air, pedestrian shopping, dining, and entertainment promenade that links Universal Studios, the Universal Amphitheater, and the Universal City Cineplex. The building facades are fanciful versions of famous Los Angeles architecture, giving the impression of sort of a cartoon version of the city. It's fun to pick out the familiar buildings represented in the crazy-quilt facades, and kids will enjoy playing in the miniature version of the Los Angeles Music Center fountains. There are a number of restaurants, almost all of which have some sort of theme, as well as fast food places. Most of the shops have kid appeal, including Wizardz Wonderz, a fascinating magic shop. The Wizardz dinner theater, (818) 506-0066, offers family-oriented, but expensive, dinner and magic shows daily. Strolling street performers add to the atmosphere, and during the winter, CityWalk sets up an outdoor ice-skating rink.

● McGroarty Arts Center

7570 McGroarty Terrace, Tujunga. (818) 352-5285. **Ages 3 and up.**

A former private home now serves the public as an art center for children and adults. Children ages three years and older can select from classes that may include—depending on their age—ballet, ceramics, music, drawing, paintings, arts and crafts, guitar, and other subjects. The ten-week sessions of once-a-week classes cost about $15. A small park with a children's play area adjoins the Arts Center. The Center is accessible to handicapped children.

● Van Nuys Airport Tour

6950 Hayvenhurst Avenue, Van Nuys. (818) 785-8838. School year: Monday–Friday, 9:30 and 11 A.M. Summer: Monday–Friday at 9:30 A.M. Reservations must be made at least a month in advance. Minimum age is 6 years. Free. **Ages 6 and up.**

Van Nuys Airport, one of the busiest general-aviation centers in the nation, offers free tours of its facilities and of some of the aircraft stationed there. To take the tour, however, you must get together a group of at least ten people and all children must be in the first grade or above. (If you can't get together your own group, ask if you can be hooked up with a school group.)

Your group boards an airport bus for the one-hour tour. You'll see aircraft ranging from Air National Guard C-130 cargo carriers to Fire Department and Highway Patrol helicopters. You'll also be able to board one of the aircraft.

● Los Encinos State Historic Park

16756 Moorpark Street, Encino. The park is one block north of Ventura Boulevard, just east of Balboa Boulevard. The entrance is on the south side of the street a few yards from the corner of Moorpark and La Maida streets. (818) 784-4849. Grounds: Wednesday–Sunday, 10 A.M.–6 P.M. Free. **All ages.**

A short distance from the bustle of Ventura Boulevard is a serene and lovely five-acre park containing the San Fernando Valley's first rancho. Gaspar de Portolá's Spanish exploration party camped here in 1769 after finding water on the site. In 1845 Governor Pio Pico gave the site and 4,460 surrounding acres to Vicente de la Osa, who built the nine-room ranch house that is still standing here.

The ranch house suffered serious damage in the 1994 Northridge earthquake and is closed to visitors. However, you can still picnic on the eucalyptus-shaded grounds and feed the ducks in the pond.

● Pages Books for Children and Young Adults

18399 Ventura Boulevard (in Tarzana Square), Tarzana. (818) 342-6657. Monday–Saturday, 9:30 A.M.–5:30 P.M. **All ages.**

Books for children from infancy through high school are carried in this children's bookstore. Pages also has a good selection of books on parenting, books in Spanish, and book-related toys and tapes. The staff all have backgrounds in teaching and are very knowledgeable about helping parents select appropriate books. If they cannot help you find the book you want, they will special order it for you.

Pages has a story hour for children ages three through eight on Saturdays at 11 A.M. The story hours, which last forty-five minutes, generally include craft or dramatic activities relating to the books that have been read. Usually reservations are not needed, but they are required for certain special-event story hours (check with the store or ask to be put on the mailing list for their newsletter).

A story hour for two- and three-year-olds is held during the week. (Check with the store for the schedule.) The store publishes a newsletter four times a year with articles on book-related topics, reviews of new books, announcements of author appearances, and a calendar for the story hours.

● The Enchanted Forest

20929 Ventura Boulevard at De Soto Avenue, Woodland Hills. (818) 716-7202. **Ages 3–11.**

The Enchanted Forest combines creative arts classes for children with a ninety-seat theater where children's plays, concerts, magic, and marionette shows take place. (Telephone for the performance schedule and prices.) The classes include fairy-tale theater workshops, music classes, and mature drama classes. The Enchanted Forest also offers birthday party packages that include puppet and magic shows or helping children put on their own play.

● Reseda Park

18411 Victory Boulevard at Reseda Boulevard, Reseda. (818) 881-3882. Open daily. Free. **All ages.**

The highlight of this thirty-six-acre park is a lake with an assortment of sociable ducks to feed. The park includes picnic areas, children's playgrounds, and huge shade trees.

● The Farm

8225 Tampa Avenue at Roscoe Boulevard, Reseda. The entrance is on Lanark Street, two blocks south of Roscoe Boulevard. (818) 341-6805. School year:

Saturday, Sunday, and holidays, 10 A.M.–5 *P.M. Summer: Daily, 10* A.M.–
6 *P.M. Admission, $3 per person ages one year and up. Pony rides, $2.*
Infants–10 years.

It wasn't all that long ago that this part of the San Fernando Valley
was out in the country. Kids can get a taste of those days at this combination small farm and pony corral. Turkeys, ducks, chickens, kid goats, and
the occasional pig wander around the farmyard. Other animals—including sheep, goats, cows, donkeys, and even llamas—are in pens, and there
are cages of smaller animals, such as bunnies. Bales of hay are stacked in
the yard, and old farm equipment is around to examine. Children can buy
feed for the animals, and there is a separate area for birthday parties.

The pony corral has tracks for slow- and faster-paced riders. The
young people who work in the corral are very good with small children,
and anyone old enough to sit up can find a pony to suit his or her pace.
The Farm is a marvelously low-key place to visit.

● Chatsworth Park South

*22360 Devonshire Street, Chatsworth. Go west on Devonshire Street past
Topanga Canyon Boulevard to the park. (818) 341-6595. Gates close at
10* P.M. *Free.* **All ages.**

Chatsworth Park South has a spectacular setting, with acres of
green lawn spreading against the rugged, red Simi hills. On the right
as you enter, there is a small shady playground with nearby picnic tables.
Straight ahead is a vast expanse of lawn, perfect for Frisbee throwing. You
can bring bikes or hike in the rocky hills.

● Orcutt Ranch Horticulture Center

*23600 Roscoe Boulevard, Canoga Park. (818) 833-6641. Daily (except
holidays), 8* A.M.–5 *P.M. Free.* **All ages.**

Once part of a large private estate, Orcutt Ranch offers a lovely site
for picnicking and strolling. The ranch is surrounded by citrus groves,
and kids can see picking equipment displayed next to the big red barn
in the parking area. A nature trail leads from the rose garden in front of
the ranch house through lush foliage down to a small picnic grove beside
a stream.

Orcutt Ranch is a quiet and uncrowded. On weekdays it is possible
to be the only family there.

● Leonis Adobe

*23537 Calabasas Road, Calabasas. Exit the Ventura Freeway (101) on
Calabasas Parkway, go south to Calabasas Road, and turn left. (818) 222-
6511. Wednesday–Sunday, 1–4* P.M. *Free, but donation requested.* **All ages.**

Once the home of Miguel Leonis, a successful nineteenth-century rancher, this two-story house has been restored to look the way it did in the late 1800s. You can take a self-guided tour of the house, which is furnished with period items. Children probably will be most interested in the grounds where they can see ranch animals, such as horses, sheep, goats, and turkeys, and examine old farm equipment. They can climb stairs to see the old bunkhouse. There is a barn with old wagons and buggies, a blacksmith shop, an original outhouse, and a water pump.

The **Plummer House,** which was the first house built in Hollywood, has been relocated on the grounds and serves as a museum displaying period photographs, clothing, and other items. Wedged between the freeway and a cowboy bar, the Leonis Adobe is a dignified reminder of old California.

● Paramount Ranch

Cornell Road, Agoura Hills. Take the Ventura Freeway (101) to the Kanan Road exit. Go south on Kanan Road for three-quarters of a mile, then turn left at the Cornell Road sign and keep to the right. Go south 2.5 miles; the entrance is on the right. (818) 597-9192. Daily, sunrise to sunset. Free.
Ages 5 and up.

At one time, Paramount Pictures filmed its Westerns here. Later, another owner built a Western town on the site, which became a popular filming location for television Westerns. Today the three-hundred-acre site is operated—like the nearby Peter Strauss Ranch—by the Santa Monica Mountains National Recreation Area. You can see the Western town on a ranger-led hike, or you can walk through it on your own. (Don't enter the buildings though; they are unsafe.) Several picnic tables are scattered under the shade trees in a large grassy meadow adjacent to the Western town.

A bulletin board posted at the foot of the bridge leading to the Western town gives information on the ranch's hiking trails. Family nature programs are scheduled throughout the year, and during the summer silent movies are shown under the stars at the ranch. Telephone for the schedule.

● Peter Strauss Ranch

30,000 Mulholland Highway, Agoura Hills. Take the Ventura Freeway (101) to the Kanan Road exit. Travel south on Kanan Road 2.8 miles to Troutdale Road. Go left on Troutdale Road to Mulholland Highway. Turn left on Mulholland, then right under the arch to the parking lot. Walk back across the bridge on Mulholland and enter the gate into the ranch. (818) 597-9192. Daily, 8 A.M.–5 P.M. Free. **All ages.**

This sixty-five-acre ranch was originally developed as a lakeside resort with a star-shaped dance floor and an outdoor amphitheater. Later the property was owned by actor Peter Strauss; today the site is operated by the Santa Monica Mountains National Recreation Area. You can picnic on the tree-shaded lawn or on the side patio of the charming ranch house. A pleasant 1.6-mile hiking trail loops through oak, eucalyptus, and sycamore trees. Art shows are sometimes held in the ranch house, and there are occasional ranger-led hikes. A family-oriented concert program of folk, bluegrass, and international music is held during the summer. The concerts, which take place in the outdoor amphitheater, are usually held from 2 to 4 P.M. on the first or second Sunday of the month. Every May, the Theater Arts Festival for Youth (TAFFY) takes place at the ranch with performances, craft workshops, and games for kids. (For more information on TAFFY, phone 818-998-2339.)

● **Mission San Fernando Rey de España**
15151 San Fernando Mission Boulevard, Mission Hills. Take the Golden State Freeway (I-5) north to San Fernando Mission Boulevard west. (818) 361-0186. Daily, 9 A.M.–4:15 P.M. Adults, $4; ages 7–15, $3; under 7, free. **Ages 8 and up.**

Founded in 1797, this mission once served as a Butterfield Stagecoach stop. A self-guided tour takes you through the church (reconstructed in 1974 following damage sustained in the 1971 Sylmar earthquake), the workshops, residence quarters, wine vats, and lovely gardens. Across the street from the mission is Brand Park, which features a statue of Father Serra and special plants from the missions.

● **Wildlife Waystation**
14831 Little Tujunga Canyon Road, Angeles National Forest. From the I-210 westbound, exit Osborne Street in Lake View Terrace. Turn right off the ramp. At the first light, turn left. Follow the road five miles up the canyon. You'll see signs. (818) 899-5201. Tours available on the first and third Sunday of every month, 3–6 P.M. Reservations are necessary. Adults, $7; ages 12 and under, $3. **Ages 6 and up.**

The Wildlife Waystation is a working facility caring for injured wild animals. More than three thousand animals are treated yearly, including lions, tigers, leopards, bears, wolves, and birds of prey. Whenever possible, the California wildlife are returned to the wild. Permanent residents of the waystation include a number of great cats that had been in animal exhibits or kept as pets. The Wildlife Waystation offers tours on the first and third Sunday of the month from 3 to 6 P.M. The walking tour takes about forty to forty-five minutes, and you need to phone ahead for a reservation.

Newhall/Valencia Area and Lancaster

● William S. Hart Park

24151 Newhall Avenue, Newhall. Take the 405 Freeway or I-5 north to the Lyons Avenue off-ramp in Newhall. Take Lyons Avenue east to Newhall Avenue and turn right. (805) 259-0855. Park is open daily, 7 A.M. to sunset. Tours of the house: Wednesday–Sunday, 11 A.M.–3:30 P.M. Free. Saugus Train Station, (805) 254-1275, is open Saturday and Sunday, 1–4 P.M. Free. **All ages.**

On a trip to Newhall, children can visit a real cowboy ranch: the former home of silent-movie Western star William S. Hart. Hart willed his 259-acre Horseshoe Ranch to the county of Los Angeles when he died. An old ranch building is filled with saddles and Hart's western gear. Farm animals such as pigs, cows, goats, chickens, and ponies are kept at the ranch, and old horses graze in the corral. From a hiking trail, you can even see a herd of buffalo, donated by Walt Disney. Hart's Spanish-style home is now a museum housing his original furniture and displays of western art, weapons, and Native American artifacts. The tour through the house is guided, but most kids will find it interesting—after all, Hart was a man who designed his bedroom to share with his dogs. The park has barbecues, picnic tables, and wonderful old shade trees.

If your visit to the Hart Ranch is on a Saturday or Sunday afternoon, you can also see the former **Saugas Train Station**, now a museum, which is located next door. Outside are wide benches where passengers used to wait for the trains. Inside, the former station agent's office is furnished as it was in the early part of the century with a safe, kerosene lamps, and telegraph key. In another room of the station are displays of historical items, including pop bottles from the 1950s.

● Placerita Canyon State and County Park and Nature Center

19152 West Placerita Canyon Road, Newhall. Take the 405 Freeway or I-5 north to State Highway 14 (Antelope Valley Freeway) to the Placerita Canyon Road exit. Follow that road about 1.5 miles east to the park. (805) 259-7721. Daily, 9 A.M. to 5 P.M. $3 per vehicle. **All ages.**

Gold in California was first discovered on the site of this park. A sheepherder fell asleep under an oak tree here and dreamed of finding gold—or so the story goes—and when he awoke, he found gold flakes clinging the roots of a wild onion that he dug up to eat. The park is a good place to hike. Eight miles of flat and hilly trails wander through oak woods and brush and along a stream. One of the trails is paved for wheelchair and stroller access. A free pamphlet describes what's alongside the park's half-mile ecology trail. Signs lead the way to the Oak of the Golden Dream, the picturesquely weathered coast live oak under which the sheepherder had his prophetic dream. The park's handsome nature center houses a museum with exhibits on ecology and park wildlife and often offers special activities for children and families. Tortoises, snakes, birds, and other live creatures are in cages outside. There is a large picnic area.

● Vasquez Rocks County Park

10700 West Escondido Canyon Road, Saugus. From Los Angeles, travel north and east via I-5 and Highway 14, left on Agua Dulce Road, and east on Escondido Canyon Road. (805) 268-0840. Daily, 8 A.M. to sunset. $3 parking fee purchased from a machine. **All ages.**

The strange, slanted rock formations in this 754-acre park make ideal climbing for children. Even very small children can find a rock to climb at their level. The park is named for Spanish-California bandit Tiburcio Vasquez, who is said to have hidden from the law here. The area has been used as a set for television and movie Westerns.

● Magic Mountain

Magic Mountain Parkway, Valencia. From Los Angeles, take I-5 northwest and exit at Magic Mountain Parkway. (805) 255-4100 or (805) 255-4111 or (818) 367-5965 or (818) 992-0884. Open daily from April 1 to October 31; rest of the year, open weekends and school holidays. Always opens at 10 A.M., but closing hours vary. Admission covers all rides, attractions, and shows. Adults, $32; seniors, $19; children under 48 inches tall, $15; ages 2 and under, free. Parking, $6. **Ages 3 and up.**

Magic Mountain is one of Southern California's "big attractions." Its much-publicized thrill rides appeal most to teenagers and the almost teenaged. Among the most *awesome* rides are "Superman The Escape," billed as the world's tallest and fastest thrill ride; "Batman The Ride," in which riders fly at intense speeds in suspended cars over hairpin turns, spins, and loops; and "Ninja," a suspended roller coaster with 180-degree side-to-side swinging trains.

However, the park also offers less-publicized attractions aimed at younger visitors. Bugs Bunny World is a six-acre children's park that includes a play area with imaginative equipment and a ride area with gentle, scaled-down versions of the park's rides. There is also a wild animal show, a petting zoo, costumed Looney Tune Characters—such as Bugs Bunny—ice-skating and acrobatic shows, and a restored 1912 carousel.

● Six Flags Hurricane Harbor Water Park

Magic Mountain Parkway next to Magic Mountain, Valencia. Exit I-5 at Magic Mountain Parkway. (805) 255-4111 or (805) 255-4100. Open daily from Memorial Day weekend through Labor Day weekend. Open weekends in May and September. Opens at 10 A.M., but closing hours vary. Adults, $16; children under 48 inches tall and seniors, $10; ages 2 and under, free. Two-park combination ticket with Magic Mountain, $45. **Ages 3 and up.**

Hurricane Harbor is a new water park adjacent to Magic Mountain. Although both are owned and operated by Six Flags, they are separate parks with separate admission fees. (You can buy a same-day combination admission ticket to both parks, but that is a lot of activity for one day.) With a pirate/lost civilization theme, the park includes a large water play area, Castaway Cove, designed exclusively for children under fifty-four inches tall. Chaise lounges in shade surround the pool. Another area surrounded by shaded lounges, Shipwreck Shores contains interactive water activities for both kids and adults.

For families with older children and teenagers, the park has a number of steep-descent, speed, and tube slides. There is also a wave pool, a river raft cruise, and a rafting adventure, as well as food stands.

● Antelope Valley Poppy Reserve

Located fifteen miles west of Lancaster on Lancaster Road (Avenue I). Take the Avenue I exit from the Antelope Valley Freeway (14) and go west about fifteen miles. Avenue I becomes Lancaster Road. (805) 724-1180. Mid-March to mid-May: Daily, 9 A.M.–3 P.M. (Open only during the spring blooming season.) $5 per car. **All ages.**

The state flower, the California Poppy, puts on a spectacular show here during its brief blooming season, usually late March through April. Easy trails lead from the picnic area and parking lot through the fields. The reserve's visitors center, which is burrowed into a hill to conserve energy, has trail maps and exhibits on the flowers and on energy conservation. Be sure to call the reserve before heading out, because the poppy display depends on the weather conditions during the year—if there has been too much or too little rain, for example, the crop can be sparse.

If the blooming season is a good one, the reserve can get extremely crowded on the weekends with a line of cars waiting to enter. In that case, you might want to skip the reserve and just roam around. Poppies—and dozens of other wildflowers—grow everywhere in fields throughout the Antelope Valley. Also, although the visitor center is only open during the poppy season, you can picnic and hike in the reserve any time. There is no parking fee when the visitors center is closed.

● Antelope Valley Indian Museum

15701 East Avenue M, Lancaster. Exit the Antelope Valley Freeway (14) northbound at Twentieth Street; go north to Avenue J. Travel east on Avenue J about seventeen miles to 150th Street, turn right to Avenue M, then left to the museum. (805) 942-0662. Saturday and Sunday, 11 A.M.–3 P.M. Closed early June to late September. Adults, $4; ages 6–17, $2; under 6, free.
Ages 6 and up.

Built into and around the rocks of Piute Butte in the Mojave Desert, the stone and frame chalet-style structure housing the Antelope Valley Indian Museum is quite remarkable. Boulders and natural elements are incorporated into the building, and there are seven roof elevations, as well as two gabled turrets. Originally built as a private house, the building was later purchased and operated for many years as a private museum of Native American culture before being bought by the state of California.

The former living room has kachina dolls painted on the ceiling. Called the Kachina Hall, the room also contains a collection of kachina dolls, as well as Native American textiles, baskets, and pottery. A natural passage through the rocks leads to the upper level, California Hall, where arrowheads, jewelry, stone tools, and other artifacts of early California Indians are displayed. (Because the museum was put together in the 1940s, you may find some of the exhibits and explanatory material dated.) Joshua Cottage on the museum grounds has a table of Native American artifacts and other displays that kids can touch. There is no picnicking on the museum grounds; you might want to combine your visit here with a trip to Saddleback Butte State Park about three miles away. Every year in late September or early October, the museum hosts the American Indian Celebration on Piute Butte, featuring cultural events and special activities.

● Saddleback Butte State Park

17102 Avenue J East, Lancaster. (805) 942-0662. At Avenue J and 170th Street about three miles northeast of the Antelope Valley Indian Museum. From the northbound Antelope Valley Freeway (14), exit at Twentieth Street; go north to Avenue J and east about nineteen miles to the park. (805) 942-0662. Open daily. $5 per vehicle. **Ages 6 and up.**

One of the few places in the Antelope Valley that looks the way it did a hundred or more years ago is Saddleback Butte State Park with its nearly three thousand acres of pristine desert. The park was created to protect Saddleback Butte, the granite mountaintop rising a thousand feet above the valley, and the desert life around it—including forests of Joshua trees. There is picnic area near the park headquarters, with tables, stoves, and restrooms, and a self-guided nature trail nearby. You can also hike a clearly marked two-mile trail to the top of Saddleback Butte where you will have some spectacular views. The best time to visit the park is in the springtime from February through May when the wildflowers are in bloom and the weather is at its best. Summers are hot here, and winters cold.

Burbank and Glendale

● Gordon R. Howard Museum

1015 West Olive Avenue (the main entry is around the corner on North Lomita Street), Burbank. (818) 841-6333. Sunday, 1–4 P.M. Phone to arrange for group tours. Free, but donations appreciated. **Ages 6 and up.**

Devoted to the history of the city of Burbank, the Gordon R. Howard Museum is a surprisingly interesting little museum. The main part of the museum on Lomita Street has historical displays. A series of sets furnished with historical items and costumed dummies depict an early dentist's office, a country store, a 1920s hotel lobby, an old winery, and the filming of the 1927 movie *Jazz Singer*. Each set has an old-fashioned telephone receiver through which kids can hear information about the displays. An exhibit on the history of Lockheed Aircraft include models of hanging aircraft and World War I and II military uniforms. Among the other exhibits are antique dolls and a display on Walt Disney. An adjacent complex houses antique vehicles, including a 1904 Franklin electric car.

Also on the museum grounds is an authentically furnished 1887 house that you can tour. The docents throughout the museum are informative and friendly to children. Next door to the museum is George Izay Park, a small park with a metal maze play structure that is accessible to disabled children.

Warner Brothers Studios VIP Tour

4000 Warner Boulevard, Burbank. Going east on the 101 Freeway to the 134 Freeway, exit at Pass Avenue; turn right on Pass, left on Riverside Drive, right on Hollywood Way, and enter the studio at Gate #4. Going west on the 134 Freeway, exit at Hollywood Way. The ramp actually exits onto Alameda Avenue. Turn left on Alameda and left on Hollywood Way to Gate #4. Going north on the Hollywood Freeway (101), exit at Barham Boulevard. Barham becomes Olive Avenue. Stay on Olive to Hollywood Way and turn right. Monday–Friday, 9 A.M.–4 P.M. Reservations recommended. $29 per person. Children must be at least 10 years old to take the tour. **Ages 10 and up.**

Warner Brothers offers a small-group, information-packed, two-hour tour of its movie and television studios. Twelve people at a time walk and ride in golf-style carts to see whatever is happening at the studio that day. Although it is not guaranteed, the tour tries whenever possible to take visitors onto a working set to watch filming. You might also get to see backlot sets, art and prop areas, wardrobe departments, set construction, and/or postproduction facilities. The tour begins with a fifteen-minute film containing excerpts of famous Warner Brothers films. Children need to be at least ten years old to take the tour.

● NBC Television Studio Tour

3000 West Alameda Street, Burbank. Exit I-5 at Alameda and go west two miles. Traveling on the 101 Freeway to the 134 Freeway, exit at Buena Vista Street, turn left, and follow the signs. (818) 840-3537. Monday–Friday, 9 A.M.–3 P.M.; Saturday, 10 A.M.–2 P.M. Adults, $6; ages 5–12, $3.75; under 5, free. Free parking. **Ages 6 and up.**

A tour of NBC takes you backstage through a giant broadcasting complex. On the seventy-minute walking tour, you'll be taken through the studios by a young page who will answer your questions. You'll see (depending on availability) the *Tonight Show* set, production studios, the wardrobe department, and set construction. There is a video demonstrations on makeup and a sports presentation. Kids will particularly enjoy the special effects set where a member of the tour group is chosen to fly like Superman over Los Angeles.

Tours are taken in small groups and they are completely unstaged—you see exactly what's happening on that day. It's best to arrive early in the day. Tickets are on a first come, first served basis, and they sell out early, particularly during the summer months.

● Brand Park/Brand Library and Art Center

1601 West Mountain Street, Glendale. From I-5, take Western Avenue north through Glendale. Park: (818) 548-3782 or (818) 548-2000 (Glendale Parks and Community Services). Daily, 7 A.M.–10 P.M. Free. Library phone: (818) 548-2051. Art Center phone: (818) 548-2050. Library and Art Center hours: Tuesday, 1–9 P.M.; Wednesday, 1–6 P.M.; Thursday, 1–9 P.M.; Friday and Saturday, 1–5 P.M. Free. **All ages.**

When you first catch sight of Brand Library perched high above the street, you may think you have chanced upon the palace of an Indian rajah or Moorish prince—certainly not a public library and park. The mansion was built by Leslie C. Brand in 1904. Called El Miradero, it was inspired by Brand's visit to the East Indian Pavilion at the 1893 Chicago World's

Fair. The Brands later willed the property to the city to be used as a public park and library.

The library, housed in the mansion, is devoted to art and music. There are no children's books. The interior of the library, although very beautiful, is a no-touch affair. Adjoining the library is an addition, which houses a lovely art gallery. Although the library and art gallery are more for teenagers and adults, children will love the huge grassy park over-looked by a palace. A children's playground is on the east side of the park. The park is also the site of special events throughout the year, including a winter Saturday when snow is trucked in for kids to enjoy.

● Verdugo Park

1621 Canada Boulevard (near Verdugo Road), Glendale. (818) 548-2000. Open daily. Free. **All ages.**

Behind a stone-fence border is the pleasant and shady Verdugo Park. The park has a very nice play area for toddlers, including a miniature slide and horse swings. A playground for older children is next to the toddler yard. Another playground is on the north side of the park. The park's thirty-five acres include some good trees for climbing and lots of shady picnic space.

● Descanso Gardens

1418 Descanso Drive, La Canada. Take the Glendale Freeway (2) north to Verdugo Boulevard, go right to Descanso Drive and turn right again. (818) 952-4400. Daily, 9 A.M.–4:30 P.M. Adults, $5; seniors and students, $3; ages 5–12, $1. Half-price on the third Tuesday of the month. **All ages.**

It's hard to believe, but this flower-filled, 165-acre area was formerly a private residence. The owners, a Los Angeles newspaper publisher and his wife, began planting the gardens shortly after they purchased the place in 1937. Today, visitors to Descanso Gardens can enjoy one of the world's largest camellia gardens, year-round blooming flowers, a section of native California plants, and a native California oak forest.

Although *descanso* means "rest" in Spanish, there are plenty of ways for children to be active here. There are nature trails, open grassy areas to play in, picnic facilities, and ducks that children can feed. A Japanese teahouse serves refreshments from 11 A.M. to 4 P.M. on weekends (closed during August and September) in a Japanese garden setting that features ponds and a flowing stream. Tram tours of the gardens are available Tuesday through Friday at 1, 2, and 3 P.M.; Saturday and Sunday at 11 A.M., 1, 2, and 3 P.M. ($1.50 per person). The Christmas season brings miniature train rides, holiday decorations, and activities for kids.

Pasadena and the San Gabriel Valley and Mountains

● Norton Simon Museum of Art

411 West Colorado Boulevard at Orange Grove Boulevard, at the junction of the 210 and 134 freeways, Pasadena. (818) 449-6840. Thursday–Sunday, noon–6 P.M. Adults, $4; students and seniors, $2; under 12, free. **Ages 8 and up.**

The Norton Simon Museum houses one of the finest art collections in the country. The museum holds European paintings from the fourteenth through the twentieth centuries, one of the finest collections of Indian and Southeast Asian sculpture outside of Asia, an extensive collection of Picasso graphics, and an impressive array of nineteenth- and twentieth-century sculpture. Children may enjoy the Degas gallery downstairs with his paintings and sculpture of ballet dancers and paintings of horses at the races. They should also enjoy the sculpture garden with its fountain, reflecting pool, and monumental sculpture.

● The Armory Center for the Arts

145 North Raymond Avenue, Pasadena. (818) 792-5101. The office is open Monday–Friday, 9 A.M.–5:30 P.M. Gallery hours: Wednesday–Sunday, noon–5 P.M.; Thursday and Friday, 6:30–9 P.M. The gallery is free. **Ages 3 and up.**

The Armory Center for the Arts offers instruction in the arts for children ages three through eighteen and adults. Recent classes for children have included dinosaur art, dollhouse construction, toy making, clowning, film animation, African-inspired masks, improvisational theater, play production, and much more. In addition to spacious art studios, the center includes a gallery that offers regular exhibits of contemporary art. Student artwork is also exhibited. Tuition for art classes is about $50 per seven-week session. Some scholarships are available, and the classes are accessible to disabled children. The center also sponsors free art programs in parks and community centers throughout Pasadena.

● Pacific Asia Museum

46 North Los Robles Avenue, Pasadena. From Los Angeles, take the Pasadena Freeway (110) north until it ends at Arroyo Parkway; continue north on Arroyo Parkway to Colorado Boulevard; turn right on Colorado Boulevard and continue east; turn left on Los Robles Avenue. The museum is on the right. (818) 449-2742. Wednesday–Sunday, 10 A.M.–5 P.M. Adults, $4; seniors and students, $2; under 12, free. **Ages 8 and up.**

In the middle of downtown Pasadena is an elegant Chinese imperial palace courtyard–style building complete with green roof tiles from China and bronze dragons. The building houses the Pacific Asia Museum, which is devoted to the arts and cultures of the Pacific and Asia. The shows, which often feature special effects such as music and fragrant aromas, may include such items of interest to children as costumes, headdresses, saddles, and swords. A special children's gallery includes items such as puppets, toys, dolls, and costumes that relate to the main exhibit.

Younger children who would not get anything out of the exhibits might enjoy seeing the museum building and the magnificent central courtyard featuring a koi pond and Oriental figures and landscaping. Classes and workshops in the arts of Asian and Pacific cultures—such as Japanese clay, Chinese brush painting, Philippine folk dance, and Chinese martial arts—are offered for children and adults. On the third Saturday of each month, the museum holds Family Free Days that include free admission to the museum and special activities in the courtyard.

● Kidspace

390 South El Molino Avenue, Pasadena. From Los Angeles, take the Pasadena Freeway (110) to its end. Go straight on Arroyo Parkway to California Street, then turn right. Go three blocks to El Molino and turn left. (818) 449-9143. School year: Wednesday, 1–5 P.M.; Saturday, 10 A.M.–5 P.M.; Sunday, 1–5 P.M. Summer: Sunday–Thursday, 1–5 P.M.; Friday and Saturday, 10 A.M.–5 P.M. Adults and ages 3 and up, $5; ages 1 and 2, $2.50; seniors, $3.50; under a year old, free. **Ages 2–9.**

Kidspace invites children to activate their senses and use their minds and bodies to explore and, indeed, become part of the exhibits. Every exhibit at this private, not-for-profit children's museum is designed to stimulate a child's imagination, as well as to spark learning. The exhibits, which are geared for children ages two to ten, emphasize arts and culture, the environment, and role playing and skill building.

In the Eco-Beach exhibit, for example, kids can explore a beach environment by crawling inside a sandy-floored exhibit with a large aquarium representing ocean life. In Critter Caverns, they climb into a tree environment and listen to the sounds of animals that inhabit different levels. They can also meet real animals at Kidspace, including a boa constrictor and a python.

Other exhibits give kids the opportunity to shop in a mini supermarket, to deliver the news in a working kid-sized news studio, or to don fire-fighting gear and climb on the back of a fire truck. A little theater area includes props and costumes. There is a padded toddler area with giant balls to roll, a computer lab, and much more.

Kidspace also offers a continuing program of workshops and special events, including puppet shows, storytelling, and art activities. Most workshops and events are free with admission. A number of birthday party packages and age-appropriate school group programs are also available. Kidspace is housed in a former junior high school auditorium, and there are lunch tables outside.

● Eaton Canyon County Park

1750 North Altadena Drive, Pasadena. Take the Altadena Drive exit north from the eastbound I-210. (818) 398-5420. Free. **All ages.**

Almost all of this 184-acre park at the base of the San Gabriel Mountains has been left in its natural state. You will see a wide variety of plants and animals here, and the park is a good place for bird-watching. There are two self-guided nature trails, including one designed primarily for young children. Some of the wildlife you'll observe along the trails are wood rats nesting in the laurel sumac, California legless lizards, Yucca moths and Yucca flowers, white sage, and California sagebrush. Warblers and flycatchers are some of the birds that may be seen along the park's stream.

The park's nature center was destroyed in 1993 in the raging Altadena fire. Plans call for the center to be rebuilt in the very near future.

● Huntington Library, Art Gallery, and Botanical Gardens

1151 Oxford Road, San Marino. From the Pasadena Freeway (110): Continue north from the end of the freeway on Arroyo Parkway to California Boulevard. Turn right and drive two miles to Allen Avenue—the entrance is at the end of Allen. From the 210 Freeway west: Take Hill Street exit and parallel the freeway for two blocks to Allen. From the 210 Freeway east: Take the Allen off-ramp. (818) 405-2100 or (818) 405-2141 (tape). Tuesday–Friday, noon–4:30 P.M.; Saturday and Sunday, 10:30 A.M.–4:30 P.M. During the summer: Tuesday–Sunday, 10:30 A.M.–4:30 P.M. Adults, $7.50; seniors, $6; students, $4; under 12 years old, free. Free the first Thursday of every month. **All ages.**

Millionaire art collector Henry E. Huntington willed this estate—including his art collection, a priceless library, and the two-hundred-acre garden—to the public. On display in the library are a Gutenberg Bible, a first printing of Shakespeare's plays, and George Washington's genealogy in his own handwriting.

The Huntington Gallery was originally the Huntington residence, and many of the works of art are displayed in furnished rooms. Probably the most famous paintings here are Gainsborough's *Blue Boy* and Lawrence's *Pinkie*. The Virginia Steele Scott Gallery for American art, which opened in 1984, displays American paintings from the 1730s to the 1930s. The library and art galleries will probably interest only older children and adults.

If your kids are younger, they'll enjoy a visit just to the Botanical Gardens. Each of the twelve gardens has a separate identity. The most interesting one for children is the Japanese garden, a quarter-mile west of the main entrance. This is a lovely landscaped canyon of five acres with Japanese plants, stone ornaments, an old temple bell, koi ponds, a drum bridge, and a furnished Japanese home.

The Rose Garden cafe serves lunch and snacks. For a special treat, your family can enjoy an English tea served Tuesday through Sunday in a lovely tea room. (Reservations are required; phone 818-683-8131 to make them.)

● Lacy Park

3300 Monterey Road, San Marino. Park entrance is on Virginia Road. (818) 304-9648 or (818) 300-0700. Daily, 6:30 A.M. to sunset. Free on weekdays. On weekends there is a fee of $3 per person to use the park. (Children under four years old are free.) **All ages.**

Lacy Park is one of the most beautiful city parks imaginable. Surrounded by trees and encompassing acres of immaculate rolling lawns, you feel as if you are on a private estate. A pleasant playground in the center of the park includes an old red fire truck to climb aboard. Opposite the playground are a number of picnic tables shaded by sycamore trees. (No barbecuing is permitted.) You can take your kids on a stroll to the rose garden, and there are broad cement paths for bike riding.

The big drawback of Lacy Park is that non–San Marino residents must pay to use the park on weekends ($3 per person ages four and older, which can make a simple family outing to the park rather expensive).

● San Gabriel Mountains

For information and details contact: Angeles National Forest, 701 North Santa Anita Avenue, Arcadia. (818) 574-5200. Office is open weekdays, 8 A.M.–4:30 P.M. **All ages.**

The San Gabriel Mountains, a part of the Angeles National Forest, sit at the back door of Los Angeles. Just a short distance from the city are opportunities for hiking, riding, camping, and picnicking in scenic wilderness areas.

There are hundreds of miles of rivers, eight lakes, and more than five hundred miles of hiking and riding trails. The quiet trails are seldom crowded, and the terrain changes are dramatic: One moment you may be walking in a fern dell or looking at a waterfall and a few moments later you find yourself in a dry chaparral landscape. Although the nicest areas of wilderness must be reached on foot, you can still tour the mountains by car.

● Mount Wilson

East end of Mount Wilson Road, Angeles National Forest, about 19 miles north of Glendale. Take the Glendale Freeway (2) north to Foothill Boulevard and east to Angeles Crest Highway. Or take the I-210 to Angeles Crest Highway (State Highway 2) and go north to Mount Wilson Road. (818) 440-1136. Saturday and Sunday, 10 A.M.–4 P.M. (weather permitting). Free. **Ages 6 and up.**

Located on a crest of the San Gabriel Mountains above Pasadena, Mount Wilson provides spectacular views of Los Angeles. It is also the site of the renowned **Mount Wilson Observatory,** open to the public on weekends. There is a museum with photographs of the heavens and models of the planets on display. During daylight savings time, a guided walking tour leaves the upper parking lot at 1 P.M. You can picnic on the grounds. (But note: There is nowhere here to buy food.)

Mount Wilson Skyline Park, nearby, offers picnicking and three hiking trails leading down the southern slope of the mountain to the valley below.

● Chilao Visitors Center

Angeles National Forest. State Highway 2 located about 27 miles north of the Angeles Crest Highway off-ramp from I-210. (818) 796-5541. Daily, 9 A.M.–4:30 P.M. Closed Tuesday and Wednesday during the winter. Also, the visitors center may be closed for short periods on weekdays when the ranger is leading a school group tour. Free. **All ages.**

The Chilao Visitors Center, located about thirteen miles north of Mount Wilson, offers a variety of indoor exhibits on the forest, and self-guided nature walks on easy trails. Picnic areas and campgrounds are nearby. The Upper Chilao Picnic Area, adjacent to the visitors center, has tables and barbecues. Within the picnic area is a designated snow play area with moderate, brush-free slopes that allow for safe sledding. During the summer, evening campfire programs, ranger-led nature walks, and special children's activities are scheduled. Day visitors to Chilao can purchase food and drinks at Newcomb's Ranch Cafe, (818) 440-1001, just up the road from the center.

Charlton Flats, three miles south of the visitors center on the Angeles Crest Highway, is another good picnic area. There are a large number of tables and barbecues spread out under the tall trees. Charlton Flats also has a self-guided nature trail and an easy hiking trail that is good for families.

● Mission San Gabriel Archangel

537 West Mission Drive, San Gabriel. Exit the I-10 at Del Mar Avenue and go north to Mission Drive. Turn left on Mission Drive, then right on Junipero Serra Drive to entrance. (818) 282-5191. Daily, 9 A.M.*–4:30* P.M. *June 1–September 30, open 10* A.M.*–5:30* P.M.*, daily. Adults, $1; children, 50¢.* **Ages 8 and up.**

Founded in 1771, Mission San Gabriel was the fourth of the California missions. Its location at the crossroads of several well-traveled roads (the mission's original entrance opened onto El Camino Real) made it a busy early California way station. Damaged in the 1987 Whittier earthquake, the Moorish-influenced mission church has been repaired and restored. The bell tower and museum should be restored by late 1997. A small baptistry on the right side of the church near the entrance contains the original domed ceiling, floor, walls, and copper and silver baptismal font.

On the mission grounds, you'll see the anchor of an 1830 schooner (the first ship built in California of native material), an original cannon used by soldiers to protect the mission, a star-shaped Moorish fountain with a lion's head, as well as a horse trough. Off the patio is a replica of the kitchen used in early mission days (note the low doorway). You can see the early mission's soap and tallow vats in the garden. The mission court contains clay models of the twenty-one California missions.

● San Gabriel Municipal Park

Take the San Bernardino Freeway to the Del Mar Avenue exit and go north to Wells Avenue. Turn west and proceed two blocks to the park. (818) 308-2875. Daily, 7:30 A.M.*–10* P.M. *Free.* **Ages 1–9.**

This is an ideal park for families with small children. A Kiddie Korral solely for children six and younger has pony swings, animal- and car-shaped jungle gyms, a little boat, and other playground equipment scaled for preschoolers. In another area, a playground for bigger kids features a rocketship slide and traditional swings, slides, and jungle gyms.

The best part of the park (located behind the baseball diamond) is a colorful zoo of concrete animals to climb on and slide down. Children climb up the arms of a big purple octopus and slide out the mouth of a blue whale. There are dragons to bump down, porpoises to ride, and a half-sunken pirate ship to play on. Nearby, a sea serpent stares at a ten-foot-high snail that doubles as a slide.

There are benches for the old folks and covered tables for birthday parties. The park also has a number of barbecues and picnic tables.

● Los Angeles State and County Arboretum

310 North Baldwin Avenue, Arcadia. Take the Baldwin Avenue off-ramp from the 210 Freeway and go south about a quarter of a mile on Baldwin. (818) 821-3222. Daily, 9 A.M.–4:30 P.M. Adults, $5; seniors and students, $3; ages 5–12, $1; under 5, free. **All ages.**

It's easy to spend the better part of a day enjoying the Los Angeles State and County Arboretum. Once the estate of millionaire E. J. "Lucky" Baldwin, it is now 127 acres of beautifully landscaped public gardens where peacocks roam freely. Palm trees taller than a hundred feet surround a huge lagoon that was once used as a set for Tarzan films. In addition to playing in the thick jungle path surrounding the lagoon, kids can bring bread crumbs to feed the ducks and geese on the lagoon shore.

Following the curve of the lagoon leads you to the reconstruction of the original 1839 adobe ranch house. You can look through windows to see rooms furnished in the original manner. Nearby is the Queen Anne Cottage, built in 1881 by Lucky Baldwin as a lavish guest house. (He lived in the adobe.) You may recognize the house—it was the guest house on the old *Fantasy Island* television show. Looking through the windows, you can see life-size mannequins in Victorian-era rooms. The Coach Barn, nearby, offers interesting displays of old tools and coaches.

The lush grounds include plants from all over the world arranged by continent of origin. There are ponds filled with koi and aquatic plants, footbridges, waterfalls, a walk-through tropical greenhouse, herb gardens, and much more. Tram rides through the park are available for $1.50 from 11 A.M. to 3 P.M. daily. The tram starts at the former Santa Fe Railroad depot building near the entrance. There are picnic tables outside the arboretum.

● Santa Anita Workouts

Santa Anita Park, 285 West Huntington Drive, Arcadia. Take the Santa Anita Avenue exit south from I-210, or north from I-10, to Huntington Drive. Or take the Baldwin Avenue exit south from I-210, or north from I-10. (818) 574-7223. Hours: Wednesday–Sunday, 7:30–9:30 A.M. during racing season (about December 26 to April 22). Free. **Ages 3 and up.**

You can stand at the rail during morning workouts at Santa Anita Park and watch the thoroughbred horses go through their paces any racing day (weather permitting). At the peak of the exercise period, several dozen horses will be on the track at the same time. The practicing horses drill counterclockwise; those finished working out walk clockwise, along the outer rail, back to their barns. A public-address commentary gives the names of the horses and their workout times.

During workout time on Saturday and Sunday, the track offers free tram rides around the track facilities and stable area. A knowledgeable guide points out famous horses and explains about their care. The tram often stops to let you see the stable's pet goats and chickens. Each tour lasts fifteen minutes.

You may want to take your children to see an actual race. Children under seventeen are admitted free with an adult; adults pay $4. You may picnic in the infield during the race, where a fully supervised children's playground, called Anita Chiquita, is also located.

● Whittier Narrows Nature Center

1000 North Durfee Avenue, South El Monte. From the Pomona Freeway (60) going east, exit at Rosemead Boulevard south, turn east on Durfee Avenue. From the Pomona Freeway (60) going west, exit at Peck Road/Durfee Avenue, go left on Peck. At the first stop, turn right on Durfee and go about a quarter mile. (818) 575-5523. The reserve is open daily, 9 A.M. to 6 P.M. The nature center building is open Tuesday–Sunday, 9:30 A.M.–5 P.M. Free. **All ages.**

Along the San Gabriel River is a 127-acre wildlife sanctuary protecting more 150 species of plants and animals. Four lakes, totaling twenty-six acres, attract hundreds of migratory birds each year. There are several miles of self-guiding nature trails where you can sometimes spots rabbits and raccoons. The nature center building has insect, fish, and wildlife displays.

The wildlife sanctuary is part of the 1,092-acre **Whittier Narrows Dam Recreation Area,** which includes a large lake for rowboating and fishing, hiking and equestrian trails, sports fields, children's play areas, and picnic facilities. The phone number for the recreation area is (818) 575-5530.

● El Monte Historical Museum

3150 North Tyler Avenue, El Monte. Exit the I-10 at Santa Anita; go south two blocks to Mildred Street and turn left to North Tyler Avenue. The museum is on the corner. (818) 580-2232. Tuesday–Friday, 10 A.M.–4 P.M.; Sunday, 10 A.M.–3 P.M. Free, but donations appreciated. **Ages 6 and up.**

A plaque outside the El Monte Historical Museum tells you that El Monte was once the end of the Santa Fe Trail; the town was settled by farmers who came west in wagon trains. Inside the adobe-style building, a former WPA library, are historical displays dating from the days of the first pioneers. Many of the exhibits are organized as room settings, such as a Victorian-era parlor complete with mannequins in period costume, and a turn-of-the-century schoolroom. Kids can walk into the settings and even sit among the mannequin children at a schoolroom desk. A special children's section at the museum has old toys that they can play with. Outside in a courtyard are wagons like the ones used by early settlers.

● Pio Pico State Historic Park
6003 South Pioneer Boulevard, Whittier. (310) 695-1217. Wednesday– Sunday, 9 A.M.–5 P.M. Free. **Ages 6 and up.**

Pio Pico, the last Mexican governor of California, built a thirty-room, two-story hacienda here in 1852 as the centerpiece of his nine-thousand-acre ranch. Thirty years later, more the half the mansion was lost when the San Gabriel River flooded. The remaining adobe has been restored and furnished to look the way it did in the 1870s. Although the thirteen-room, U-shaped adobe suffered severe damage in the 1987 Whittier earthquake, it has been repaired and reopened to the public. You can also picnic on the grounds.

● Whittier Museum
6755 Newlin Avenue, Whittier. Take the Whittier Boulevard exit east from the 605 Freeway. Travel on Whittier Boulevard to Philadelphia Street. Go east one block past Pickering Avenue to Newlin Avenue. (310) 945-3871. Saturday and Sunday, 1–4 P.M. Free. **Ages 8 and up.**

A turn-of-the-century Main Street has been recreated inside this historical museum housed in a former telephone company building. There is a Queen Anne–style cottage you can actually enter, a barn filled with farm implements, a newspaper office, and various shop windows filled with old-fashioned items. A docent leads you through the museum; and since this is a looking experience, kids should probably be at least eight years old to appreciate it. Upstairs in the museum are changing exhibits. School group tours are scheduled for weekdays when the museum is closed to the public.

● Heritage Park
12100 Mora Drive, Santa Fe Springs. Exit the I-605 Freeway at Telegraph Road. Travel east to Heritage Park Drive, and turn right to the park. (310) 946-6476. The park is open daily, 7 A.M.–10 P.M. The Carriage Barn Museum is open Wednesday and Thursday, 9 A.M.–4 P.M.; Tuesday, Friday, Saturday, and Sunday, noon–4 P.M. Free. **All ages.**

Heritage Park is a six-acre recreation of the nineteenth-century citrus farm that once occupied this site. Among the reconstructed buildings are a carriage barn, a conservatory, and a windmill/tank house. You can also see the basement and fireplace ruins of the original ranch house. The carriage barn serves as a museum of local history, giving kids an idea of what turn-of-the-century life in Santa Fe Springs was like. The museum includes a hands-on area that is specifically for children. The conservatory is stocked with greenery and seasonal flowering plants. There is also an English-style garden with planters and fountains, and an aviary with doves, finches, and other birds. You can picnic at the park, and a lunchroom sells hot dogs, sandwiches, salads, and other items on weekdays from 7 A.M. to 3 P.M. The park usually holds a Children's Day each year in August or September with old-fashioned games and activities. Heritage Park is a lovely oasis of green in the midst of a highly industrial area.

● Hacienda Heights Youth Science Center

P.O. Box 5723, Hacienda Heights, CA 91745. (818) 965-1494. Telephone for schedule. The museum is located and classes are held at the Wedgeworth Elementary School, 16949 Wedgeworth Drive, Room 8, Hacienda Heights. From the Pomona Freeway (60), exit Azusa south to Pepper Brook Way. Turn right to Wedgeworth Drive. Museum phone: (818) 854-9825. Summers: Monday–Friday, 8:30 A.M.–noon. School year: Wednesday and Friday, 1–4 P.M.; Saturday, 10 A.M.–2 P.M. Free. **Ages 5–12.**

The Youth Science Center is a nonprofit organization dedicated to science education. It operates a museum in Room 8 of the Wedgeworth Elementary School with science exhibits and hands-on experiences. The Youth Science Center also offers science classes and field trips year-round. Past science classes have included model rocketry for ages ten and older; Egyptology for fifth and sixth graders; computer skills for kindergarteners and first graders; and much more. Field trips have included excursions to hospitals, manufacturing sites, and science laboratories, as well as nature outings and stargazing.

Claremont, Pomona, and Vicinity

Raging Waters

111 Raging Waters Drive (Via Verde), San Dimas. (909) 592-8181 or (909) 592-6453. Located in Frank G. Bonelli County Regional Park, near the intersection of freeways 210, 10, 71, and 57. Exit the I-210 at Raging Waters Drive (Via Verde) and drive east to the park. Open weekends, mid-April to June 1 and mid-September to mid-October. Open daily, June to mid-September. Hours vary, but open at least 10 A.M. to 6 P.M. Open evenings in the summer. Adults (over 48 inches), $21.99; seniors, $12.99; children (42–48 inches), $12.99; children under 42 inches, free. General admission for nonparticipants is $12.99. There is reduced admission after 5 P.M. Parking, $5. **Ages 3 and up.**

Covering forty-four acres in Frank G. Bonelli Regional Park, Raging Waters is a combination swimming lagoon, water-slide adventure, and aquatic playground. The park is designed for the whole family. For the daring there are heart-pumping steep-descent and speed slides, as well as hundreds of feet of twisting, curving water slides. A new attraction, Volcano Fantasea, offers a giant smoking volcano towering forty feet over a blue lagoon. Kids and their parents climb through the volcano to glide down slides into a lagoon where there are water-play attractions such as a shipwreck. Another family-oriented attraction is Splash Island, with twelve levels of wet activities such as web crawls and swinging bridges. A popular attraction, called Raging Rivers, offers a quarter-mile of inner-tube rapids, with four separate channels ranging from mild for younger children to wild for the foolhardy. A large, family swimming lagoon, called the Wave Cove, features man-made waves and a beachlike setting. Small children have their own imaginatively designed water playground/pool. There are picnic facilities, as well as a variety of restaurants and snack bars. Dressing rooms and lockers are available. Bring your own beach towels and chairs, and don't forget sunscreen.

Raging Waters has some 250 lifeguards; however you should still keep close watch on your children. For safety, the park maintains a maximum-admission limit. Therefore, if you are coming on a busy weekend, plan to arrive early or after 5 P.M.

● Mrs. Nelson's Toy and Book Shop

1030 Bonita Avenue, La Verne. (909) 599-4558. Monday–Saturday, 9 A.M.–6 P.M. (open to 7 P.M. on Fridays); Sunday, 11 A.M.–5 P.M.
All ages.

This large (six thousand square feet), well-stocked children's book and toy shop features about twenty thousand book titles ranging from board books for babies to young adult titles. There is also a large selection of books on topics for parents. A story hour is held at 11 A.M. on Saturdays throughout the year. (No preregistration is necessary.) The store also offers a Kids Club program for children in the first through eighth grades, with special discounts on books. Other store-sponsored activities include workshops, author signings, and concerts. If you can't find the book you want, they will special order it. The staff is knowledgeable about children's books and almost everyone working in the store is a parent. Mrs. Nelson's also publishes a book-review newsletter five times a year.

The store offers a good selection of high-quality toys, and toys are out where children can examine them. Children's videotapes, musical instruments, and science materials are also sold. The store provides free gift wrapping.

● Kellogg's Arabian Horse Center

Kellogg Campus, California State Polytechnic University, Pomona. Go east on I-10, take the Cal Poly off-ramp near Pomona, and follow the signs. (909) 869-2224. Center open daily, 9 A.M.–4 P.M. Horse shows: first Sunday of the month, October–June, at 2 P.M. Adults, $1.50; seniors, $1; children, 50¢.
All ages.

A splendid herd of Arabian horses lives on this campus. The Arabians are used by students studying horse husbandry and training. On various Sundays during the year, the horses demonstrate their intelligence for the public in an hour-long show. They rock baby carriages, do arithmetic, and even open a cash register and put money into it.

Although the horse show is a lot of fun for everyone, you don't have to attend it to see the horses. You can visit the horses any day, without charge, and even go right up to them and pet them. In the spring, the mares will have their newborn colts by their sides.

● Rancho Santa Ana Botanic Garden

1500 North College Avenue, Claremont. From the I-10, take the Indian Hill exit north to Foothill Boulevard. Turn right on Foothill Boulevard and go east three blocks to College Avenue. Turn left and proceed north to the parking lot. (909) 625-8767. Daily, 8 A.M.–5 P.M. Free, but donation appreciated.
All ages.

The Rancho Santa Ana Botanic Garden is dedicated to cultivating and displaying California's native plants and flowers. The main blooming period of this eighty-six-acre garden is from late February to the middle of June, when the manzanitas, California lilacs, and tree poppies are especially striking. Most of the plants are grouped according to natural associations, such as the chaparral community. Guided school tours and nature classes for families are also available.

● Raymond M. Alf Museum

1175 West Baseline Road, Claremont. (909) 624-2798. Monday–Thursday, 1–4 P.M., and on selected Sundays, 1–4 P.M. (Phone for the Sunday schedule.) School tours: Monday–Thursday, 9 A.M.–noon. Closed June, July, and August. $1 per person; under 6 are free. **Ages 3 and up.**

Located on the campus of The Webb Schools in Claremont, this museum houses the findings of Dr. Alf and his students from their paleontological digs. The findings include thousands of bones, fossil footprints, a fifteen-million-year-old peccary skull, and fossils showing the history of mammals. Among the fossils are an entire fossilized tree, two-hundred-fifty-million-year-old reptile footprints, and the wing of a quetzalcoatlus —the largest flying animal ever known. There are related exhibits of Indian relics and ancient Egyptian artifacts. The museum is quite interesting, and even preschool children can enjoy it.

● Mount Baldy

In the San Gabriel Mountains about 12 miles north of Upland. Exit the I-10 north at Euclid Avenue (Highway 83) in Upland. Continue north after Euclid Avenue becomes Mountain Avenue to Mount Baldy. Continue climbing to Mount Baldy Village. Mount Baldy Information Station Phone: (714) 982-2829. **All ages.**

Less than an hour drive from Los Angeles, Mount Baldy offers families a year-round mountain retreat. During the winter, particularly on weekends, Mount Baldy is crowded with skiers. Manker Flats Campground, situated in a beautiful open pine forest (three miles northeast of Mount Baldy Village on the Mount Baldy Road), offers families a good spot for snow play—although parking is limited. The Mount Baldy Information Station, located in central Mount Baldy Village, can suggest other areas for snow play. They also have maps on hiking trails, and you can call them for weather conditions. The Information Station is open Friday through Sunday from 8:30 A.M. to 4:30 P.M.

During the warmer months, Mount Baldy is much quieter, offering picnicking, uncrowded hiking, clean air, and beautiful scenery. Developed picnic sites with barbecues, tables, vault toilets, and piped water are available at Glacier Picnic Area 2.5 miles north of Mount Baldy Village. Or you can picnic along a stream, or anywhere you like on National Forest land, as long as you pack out. On weekends, sight-seeing chairlift rides are available at the Mount Baldy Ski Area. Trout fishing is offered at various private facilities.

Mount Baldy Village, the mountain's lovely little resort village, has restaurants and a motel. Gasoline and car services are not available.

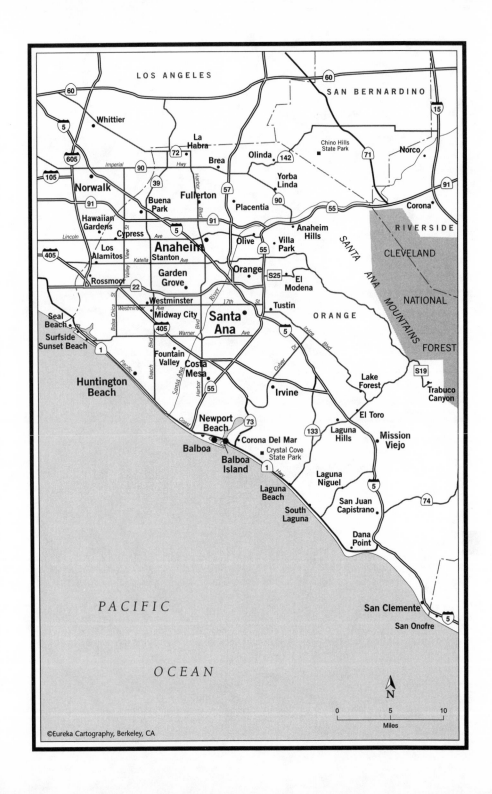

©Eureka Cartography, Berkeley, CA

Orange County

THE CITRUS GROVES after which this county was named have given
way to the greatest concentration of amusement parks and entertainment
attractions anywhere. Yet, impressive as Disneyland and Knotts Berry
Farm may be, there is a great deal more to Orange County than amusement parks.

Orange County boasts miles of beautiful beaches, wonderful harbors,
big green parks with imaginative play areas for children, a famous artists'
colony, and several wildlife sanctuaries. Every year, right on schedule,
flocks of swallows return to their nests in one of the state's loveliest missions. A number of fine museums are located in the county, including
several just for children.

Orange County's public transit system offers extensive service
throughout the county. The OCTA telephone number is (714) 636-7433.
The Los Angeles MTA, (800) 266-6883, has bus and rail service to Orange
County.

Buena Park/Anaheim

● Knott's Berry Farm

*8039 Beach Boulevard, Buena Park. Exit at Beach Boulevard from the 5,
91, or 405 freeways and follow the signs. (714) 220-5200. Summer hours:
Daily, 9 A.M.–midnight. Rest of the year: Monday–Friday, 10 A.M.–6 P.M.;
Saturday, 10 A.M.–10 P.M.; Sunday, 10 A.M.–7 P.M. (Extended hours
during seasonal periods.) Adults, $29.95; ages 3–11 and 60 and over,
$19.95. After 5 P.M., admission is $15 for everyone. Parking, $5.*
All ages.

Those of us who grew up in Southern California remember Knott's
Berry Farm as a recreated Old West ghost town where kids could play all

day for no more than the 25¢ train-ride fare. In the years since that time, Knott's has developed into one of the nation's best-attended amusement parks.

In addition to an expanded Old West section with an exciting log ride, the park now offers five other theme areas with rides and entertainment. Fiesta Village, honoring California's Spanish heritage, features big-ticket thrill rides, including Jaguar, a new roller coaster that zooms high above the park. A new area with a seaside fun zone theme, The Boardwalk (replacing the old Roaring Twenties section), offers more big-ticket thrill rides, as well as the Kingdom of the Dinosaurs, a seven-minute indoor ride that takes you back in time to encounter some twenty-one fully-animated moving and screeching dinosaurs. (The experience may be too frightening for most small children.)

If your children are young, head immediately for Camp Snoopy, a six-acre scenic area of attractions for designed especially for children younger than twelve. In addition to scaled-down rides, Camp Snoopy includes a petting farm, opportunities to be physically active, and old Snoopy himself.

On a hot day especially, the whole family should enjoy a ride on Bigfoot Rapids in the Wild Water Wilderness section of the park. The ride offers guests an exhilarating and very wet ride down a whitewater river. (Many families come prepared with an extra change of clothes or bathing suit for kids to slip into; there are lockers outside the ride.)

A wide variety of live entertainment is offered throughout the park, including big-stage productions in a 2,100-seat theater. Native American culture is celebrated in the Indian Trails area of the park with music, dance, and craft demonstrations and participatory activities for all ages.

Knott's Berry Farm has the most relaxed feeling of all the Southern California amusement parks, and it can be the most enjoyable park for families with small children. There are several reasonably good eating places at Knott's, but by far the best is the old-fashioned chicken dinner restaurant. There is no charge to enter Knott's outside shopping and dining area. Across the street from the park is Knott's replica of Independence Hall, with displays and a multimedia presentation. The Hall is open daily, 10 A.M. to 5 P.M., and admission is free.

● Movieland Wax Museum

7711 Beach Boulevard, Buena Park. From the I-5 or the Artesia Freeway 91, exit Beach Boulevard, south. (714) 522-1155. Daily, 9 A.M.–7 P.M. Adults, $12.95; seniors, $10.55; ages 4–11, $6.95. **Ages 6 and up.**

The spookiness of so many wax museums is completely avoided in this lavish place. Wax replicas of movie and television stars are displayed on individual sets that recreate their famous roles. Most sets include original costumes and props. Laurel and Hardy sit on the running board of an old Model T; Ben Hur is in his chariot pulled by four horses. Special animation, lights, and sound effects enliven the displays.

Children above the age of five should find enough characters they recognize—such as Superman, the crew from *Star Trek*, and Michael Jackson—to enjoy the museum.

● Medieval Times

7662 Beach Boulevard (across the street from Movieland Wax Museum), Buena Park. (714) 521-4740 or (800) 899-6600 (toll-free in California). Performances nightly with a Sunday matinee. Phone for times; reservations required. Admission, including dinner, show, beverages, and tax: Adults, $32.95 ($35.95 for 6 P.M. show Saturday); ages 12 and under, $22.95.
Ages 8 and up.

Medieval Times is an eleventh-century-themed dinner and entertainment complex one block north of Knott's Berry Farm. Knights on horseback parade, joust, sword fight, and engage in games of skill on a sand-covered ring while the audience eats dinner. Each pavilion in the theater has its own knight to root for, and the audience gets into the act with hissing, cheering, and table banging. The horses, Andalusian stallions, are beautiful; the knights are skilled; and the show is exciting. It also gets very loud and boisterous. (Kids in upper elementary school probably have the most fun.) The food, at best, is fair, and the evening is expensive.

● Wild Bill's Wild West Dinner Extravaganza

7600 Beach Boulevard, Buena Park. (714) 522-6414 or (800) 883-1546. Performances nightly with weekend matinees. Phone for show times and reservations. Adults, $32.95 ($35.95 on Saturdays); ages 3–11, $21.95.
Ages 8 and up.

Close to Medieval Times on Beach Boulevard is a similar attraction, different era: Wild Bill's Wild West Dinner Extravaganza. Staged in a rustic dining hall, the two-hour experience includes an all-you-can-eat chicken and rib dinner (beer, wine, and soft drinks included) and a Old West–style variety show. There's singing, dancing, sparkling costumes, and all sorts of acts. Among the highlights are a series of Native American tribal dances and a western roper who ropes over the heads of the audience.

● Printing Museum

8469 Kass Drive, Buena Park. (714) 523-2070. Tuesday–Saturday, 10 A.M.–5 P.M. Adults, $6.50; ages 7–18, $4; under 7, free. **Ages 6 and up.**

Five hundred years of printing history—from handset letters to the hot type of the Linotype machine and the cold type of today—are represented in this fascinating museum. Every piece of equipment is in working order, and you can see some of the presses in operation. A guide dressed in a printer's apron will lead you through the museum (the tour takes about forty-five minutes) and demonstrate how some of the machines work. Kids may even get some freshly printed material to take home.

Among the machines you'll see are an all-metal hand-operated printing press built in England in 1810, a 1900 Midget Reliance Press— valued by frontier printers for its portability—and an 1824 Columbian hand press that's topped with an iron eagle. One corner of the museum is occupied by the Calico Rock Printing Office, an exhibit that depicts a typical country print shop of 1870 when all type had to be handset letter by letter. The experience of this museum is such that children may leave with a new respect for the printed page.

● Ralph B. Clark Regional Park

8800 Rosecrans Avenue, Buena Park. Take the Beach Boulevard exit from either the 91 Freeway or the I-5 and go north to Rosecrans Avenue. (714) 670-8045. October 1 to March 31, open daily, 7 A.M. to 6 P.M. April 1 to September 30, open daily, 7 A.M.–9 P.M. Parking: weekdays, $2; weekends, $4; holidays, $5. **All ages.**

Ralph B. Clark Regional Park rests on a rich prehistoric fossil site. The park was created to preserve the fossil beds, as well as to provide a recreational facility. The developed area of the park, encompassing forty-eight acres, includes a lagoon with an island playground that is reached by crossing a bridge. There are a number of picnic areas with nearby play equipment, three softball fields, a baseball diamond, four tennis and two volleyball courts, and a bike trail.

● Adventure City

1238 South Beach Boulevard, Anaheim. Exit the I-5 at Beach Boulevard and head south. Adventure City is located two miles south of Knott's Berry Farm on the left side of Beach Boulevard at Ball Road. (714) 236-9300. Open daily during the summer. The rest of the year, open Friday–Sunday. Operating hours vary seasonally, so phone ahead. Admission packages range from $2.95 to $9.95 per person. **Ages 2–12.**

In an area rich with theme parks is one just for kids ages two to twelve and their parents. The two-acre park features a mix of rides, hands-on activities, children's theater and puppet shows, a petting zoo, face painting, and other activities. The theme of a visit to an Adventure City is incorporated in the design of the rides and in bright city-scene facades. The rides—including a roller coaster, train ride, a Barnstormer-airplane ride, and an emergency-vehicle ride, where kids can wear firefighter uniforms—all accommodate adults as well as children. The park includes food stands. A particularly nice feature of the park is their flexible admission fee. If your children are too young for rides, or if you don't want to go on the rides yourself, there is a low-price package that includes admission, the children's theater, petting zoo, and face painting. A medium-price package includes three rides, and there is an unlimited ride and attraction package. Birthday party packages are also available.

● Hobby City Doll and Toy Museum

1238 South Beach Boulevard, Anaheim. (714) 527-2323. Daily, 10 A.M.–6 P.M. Adults, $1; children and seniors, 50¢. **Ages 6 and up.**

The Hobby City Doll and Toy Shop is housed in a half-scale replica of the White House as it appeared in 1917. Behind the shop is the museum displaying more than two thousand rare, antique, and collectible dolls and toys. The dolls, ranging from a five-thousand-year-old ancient Egyptian doll to modern Barbies, are arranged chronologically as you go through the museum. Each group from a particular time and place is displayed in a separate glass case with appropriate background and accessories. The dolls are from all over the world; some of the most interesting are from ancient China. The founder of the museum, Mrs. Bea DeArmond, started collecting dolls when she was four years old.

● Disneyland

1313 Harbor Boulevard, Anaheim. Take the Santa Ana Freeway to Anaheim, exit at Harbor Boulevard and follow signs. (714) 999-4565 or (714) 999-4560. Open daily. Summer: 8 A.M.–midnight; winter: Monday–Friday, 10 A.M.–6 P.M.; Saturday and Sunday, 9 A.M.–midnight. (Hours can vary, so it's best to phone ahead.) Admission and unlimited use of attractions: Adults, $34; seniors, $30; ages 3–11, $26; under 3, free. Parking, $6. Discounted two- and three-day passes are also available. Prices usually go up yearly. **All ages.**

Everyone knows about Disneyland. A day spent here can be expensive and exhausting, but it's always memorable. If possible, schedule your visit for the winter months, when the park is much less crowded. If your visit is in the summer, aim for a weekday and come early. In the summer, it's best to get to the park when it opens in the morning.

Go first to the park's most popular attractions, such as the Indiana Jones Adventure, Splash Mountain, Space Mountain, the Matterhorn Bobsleds, and Toon Town. That way you can see them before midday, when the waits can reach two hours. If you have older children you might want to come later in the day during the summer and stay late into the evening when it's cooler, lines are shorter, and there are special entertainments and fireworks. (Try not to miss the Main Street parade.)

One of the best places for families in the park is Frontierland's Tom Sawyer Island. Kids can spend an hour here crawling through tunnels, forts, and mining shafts; running across a barrel bridge; and playing on a teeter-totter rock. Meanwhile, their parents can sit and rest. Fantasyland has the most rides for small children, and Toon Town is designed especially for them. For older children and hardy adults, Space Mountain can compete with scariest of thrill rides anywhere.

Disneyland has a variety of restaurants and snack bars, most with average to good food. If you want to get away from the park to eat, you can take the monorail to the Disneyland Hotel where there are a variety of restaurants. (Disney characters go from table to table at Goofy's Kitchen.) Lockers are available in the park, although you have to arrive early to get one.

● Disneyland Hotel

1150 West Cerritos Avenue, Anaheim. (714) 778-6600. **All ages.**

The Disneyland Hotel is a world of its own. Sitting on sixty acres across the street from Disneyland—and connected to it by monorail—the Disneyland Hotel is one of the largest hotels in the country. In the backyard of the hotel is a freshwater marina with docks, bridges, ramps, and paddleboat rentals. The marina is surrounded by Seaports of the Pacific, a waterfront bazaar featuring shops, artisans at work, restaurants, and displays of marine equipment.

You don't have to be a hotel guest to stroll around the marina or rent a paddleboat (available daily during the summer and on weekends the rest of the year). In the evening there is a "Dancing Water" spectacle produced by lighted fountains, and visitors have a view of Disneyland's fireworks in the summer.

The restaurants in the complex range from full-course continental to casual pantry type; all are accommodating to children and reasonably priced for what they serve.

If you decide to stay at the hotel, double accommodations begin at $180. Special packages that include unlimited admission to Disneyland for up to five consecutive days are also available. On most days, hotel guests are allowed into the park an hour before the general public.

● Anaheim Stadium Tours

Between Katella Street, State College Boulevard, and Orangewood Avenue, Anaheim. For the tour, enter off Orangewood Avenue at Gate 6. Look for the white building with double doors and go to the second floor. (714) 254-3120. Monday–Saturday, each hour on the hour, 11 A.M.–2 P.M. There are no tours on the days of daytime home games or events. Adults, $4; ages 5–16, $2.50; under 5, free. Free parking. **Ages 6 and up.**

This tour takes you behind the scenes at Anaheim Stadium. You'll tour home plate, the locker rooms, the press box, and other areas you would ordinarily not see up close. Tours last between forty-five minutes and an hour. (Groups of ten or more need to make a reservation to take the tour.)

● Anaheim Museum

241 South Anaheim Boulevard across from City Hall, Anaheim. (714) 778-3301. Wednesday–Friday, 10 A.M.–4 P.M.; Saturday, noon–4 P.M. Free, but donations appreciated. **Ages 6 and up.**

Before Disneyland, there were orange groves in Anaheim, and before that, grape vineyards. The Anaheim Museum, housed in a former Carnegie library, is filled with exhibits detailing the city's history. Among the exhibits that children will enjoy are an 1872 horse-drawn fire truck, a horse-drawn carriage from 1852, and displays on Disneyland's 1955 opening. The museum has a Children's Room downstairs with changing hands-on exhibits.

Garden Grove, Santa Ana, and Orange

● Atlantis Play Center in Garden Grove Park

9301 Westminster Avenue, Garden Grove. Exit the Garden Grove Freeway (22) on Magnolia Street, go south about half a mile to Westminster Avenue, and east about a block to Garden Grove Park. (714) 892-6015. Summer: Tuesday–Saturday, 10 A.M.–4 P.M.; Sunday, noon–4 P.M.; School year: Tuesday–Friday, 11 A.M.–4 P.M.; Saturday, 10 A.M.–4 P.M.; Sunday, noon–4 P.M. Admission, $1 per person. Under 2 years, free. **Ages 2–9.**

Garden Grove Park is the home of the Atlantis Play Center, a nicely landscaped, four-acre fenced area where children accompanied by adults can slide down a colorful sea serpent, climb on Stelly Starfish, and enjoy playing on many other outsized concrete aquatic creatures, as well as more traditional play equipment. Picnic tables are available in the play center. The rest of the forty-acre park includes ample play equipment, softball and football fields, and a volleyball court.

● Discovery Museum of Orange County

3101 West Harvard Street, Santa Ana. (714) 540-0404. Wednesday– Friday, 1–5 P.M.; Sunday, 11 A.M.–3 P.M. (Telephone for school, scout, and youth group tour hours, reservations, and prices.) Adults, $3.50; children, $2.50. **Ages 4–12.**

A gabled Victorian mansion serves as the centerpiece of an exciting museum designed to show children what life was like in Orange County at the turn of the century. The mansion—the historic 1898 Kellogg house—has been restored and furnished with period items such as an antique piano. But unlike most other museums in historic houses, kids can touch the exhibits here. They can dress up in Victorian clothing, roll up their sleeves, and do laundry with a scrub board and wooden ringer. They can also try out a hand-crank telephone, operate a telegraph key, use a butter churner, and handle all sorts of other implements from the past. Docents are on hand to explain the exhibits. Outside the house are a rose garden and citrus orchard where kids on school tours can pick fruit.

A different theme—such as transportation or old-time games— offering additional activities is featured each month. Victorian birthday parties also can be arranged for children four to twelve. Centennial Park, adjacent to the museum, offers picnicking and play before or after the museum visit. The Discovery Museum is highly recommended.

● Discovery Science Center

2522 North Main Street, at the intersection of I-5 and Main Street, Santa Ana. (714) 540-2001. Scheduled to be open daily. Phone for hours and prices. **All ages.**

The Discovery Science Center, opening in the fall of 1997, is a major museum dedicated to sparking the interest of children—and people of all ages—in math and science. The one hundred interactive exhibits in the forty-thousand-square-foot facility are designed to encourage children to look at the world through the eyes of a scientist. The museum should interest everyone in the family.

● The Bowers Museum of Cultural Art

2002 North Main Street, Santa Ana. Take the Main Street exit from the Santa Ana Freeway (I-5). The museum is located just south of the exit on Main Street. (714) 567-3600. Tuesday–Sunday, 10 A.M.–4 P.M.; until 9 P.M. on Thursdays. Adults, $6; seniors and students, $4; ages 5–12, $2; under 5, free. Admission is good for both the Kidseum and the Bowers on the same day. **Ages 6 and up.**

Orange County's largest museum, the Bowers Museum of Cultural Art, has an extensive collection of pre-Columbian, African, Oceanic, Asian, and Native American art. The recently expanded and renovated museum also displays artifacts relating to Orange County and California history. Although children will want to spend most of their time at the Kidseum (see the entry below), there is much here for them to look at, including costumes, masks, and dazzling Native American beadwork. The museum also includes a restaurant, the Topaz Cafe, featuring sophisticated food with a multicultural accent for the grown-ups and a low-priced kid's menu. The cafe has both indoor and outdoor seating in a pretty courtyard. (The phone number for the cafe is 714-835-2002).

● Bowers Kidseum

1802 North Main, just down the street from the Bowers Museum, Santa Ana. (714) 480-1520. Wednesday–Friday, 2–5 P.M.; Saturday and Sunday, 10–4 P.M. Open for prearranged school and youth group tours, all day Tuesday–Friday. Adults, $6; seniors and students, $4; ages 5–12, $2; under 5, free. Admission is good for the both the Kidseum and the Bowers on the same day. **Ages 3–12.**

Although children have enjoyed the Bowers Museum for years, they now have their own cultural arts museum in a new eleven-thousand-square-foot facility. Kids cross a creaky bridge to enter the main gallery where the exhibits beckon: masks, costumes, musical instruments, histori-cal artifacts, dolls, and more. The exhibits relate to the multicultural collection of the parent museum—except that everything here is at a child's level and can be touched, played with, worn, and examined. Kids and their parents can check out backpacks containing material that will take them on a special adventure. For example, one kit, "Cracked Pots," encourages kids to become junior archaeologists, providing them with broken pottery to piece together.

The Kidseum also includes a story room where storytellers narrate myths, legends, and stories from around the world. A creative art lab provides the space and material for a range of art projects. Other activities include family festivals of ethnic and cultural celebrations; music, dance, and puppet performances from around the world; and summer adventure camps. A variety of packages is available for children's parties.

● Old Courthouse Museum

211 West Santa Ana Boulevard, in the civic center, Santa Ana. Monday– Friday, 9 A.M.–5 P.M. Free. **Ages 8 and up.**

Children can see what a courtroom looked like at the turn of the century in the Old Courthouse Museum, located in the historic old Orange County Courthouse. Other exhibits detail the history of Orange County. School tours are available.

● Santa Ana Zoo

1801 East Chestnut Avenue in Prentice Park, Santa Ana. Exit the Santa Ana Freeway (I-5) south at Fourth Street; go straight on Mabury Street, left on Chestnut Avenue. Exit the Santa Ana Freeway going north at First Street, then go straight on Elk Lane. (714) 835-7484. Daily, 10 A.M.–5 P.M. (until 6 P.M. on weekends during the summer). Ticket booth closes one hour before the zoo. Adults, $3.50; seniors and ages 3–12, $1.50; under 3, free. **All ages.**

This small zoo contains about fifty species of animals. The highlight is the fairly extensive monkey collection, which includes an unusual group of black-cap capuchins. Other exhibits include a nicely landscaped water-fowl pond and a moated enclosure for alpacas. There is a good petting zoo for children, housing a variety of farm animals. Summer zoo camps, family workshops, school tours, and other educational programs are also available. The zoo has a playground, and there are picnic areas right outside in Prentice Park.

● Rancho Santiago College Planetarium

West Seventeenth Street and North Bristol, in Rancho Santiago College, Santa Ana. Exit I-5 west on Seventeenth Street. (714) 564-6600. Shows are presented October–May. Monday, 9:30 A.M.; Tuesday, 9:30 and 11 A.M.; Wednesday and Friday, 9:30 A.M. $2 per person. Reservations required. **Ages 4 and up.**

The Rancho Santiago College Planetarium offers a one-hour look at the galaxy on Monday, Tuesday, Wednesday, and Friday mornings. The shows are a basic introduction to the planets and stars and are appropriate for preschoolers. You must call ahead to make reservations, since the shows are often booked for school groups.

● Dwight D. Eisenhower Park

Orange. Take the Newport Freeway (57) to the Lincoln Avenue exit. Go west about one-quarter mile, turn north on Ocean View Avenue, and follow the signs to one of four small parking lots. (714) 532-0383 (park information for city of Orange). Daily, 8 A.M.–10 P.M. Free. **All ages.**

Twenty acres of grass, a four-acre lake, ducks to feed, and a two-hundred-yard stream in which children may play help to make this an enjoyable park. There are two play-equipment areas for small children, one of which—Astro City—is an intriguing complex of slides. Picnic tables and barbecues are found throughout the park.

● Santiago Oaks Regional Park

End of Windes Drive, Orange. Take Katella East from the 55 Freeway. Katella becomes Santiago Canyon Road. Go north on Windes Drive to the park. (714) 538-4400. Park: Daily, 8 A.M. to sunset. Nature center: Daily, 8 A.M.–4 P.M. Parking: $2 on weekdays, $4 on weekends. **All ages.**

A few miles east of downtown Orange is a 125-acre wilderness park. The park includes a creek and a pond where kids can fish. The nature center, located in a rustic cottage that was once a private residence, offers trail maps, mounted wildlife exhibits, and special programs. There are a small playground and picnic tables among the coast live oaks.

● Irvine Regional Park

One Irvine Park Road, Orange. Located in Santiago Canyon, six miles east of the city of Orange. Take the Newport Freeway (55) to the Chapman Avenue off-ramp. Go east on Chapman to Jamboree Road, then north to the park. (714) 633-8074 (tape) or (714) 633-8072. November 1 to March 31: daily, 7 A.M.–5:45 P.M.; April 1 to October 31: daily, 7 A.M.–8:45 P.M. Parking: weekdays, $2; weekends, $4; holidays, $5. **All ages.**

Irvine Regional Park is a lovely 477-acre park located in the hill-sides of Santiago Canyon. The park, which dates from an 1897 gift to the county from James Irvine, Jr., contains both beautifully landscaped and wilderness areas. Among the features of the park are five children's play-grounds, two softball diamonds, a paved bicycle path, a nature trail, and a pretty lake where rowboats and paddleboats may be rented. Picnic areas with tables, barbecues, and nearby restrooms and parking are located throughout the park.

The park also contains the **Orange County Zoo,** a small, three-acre zoo with about forty-five species indigenous to the southwest. Many of the animals have been rescued and would not be able to survive in the wild.

Among them are Samson, a six-hundred-pound black bear found relaxing in a backyard hot tub; foxes found on the freeway; a golden eagle wounded by a hunter; and a bobcat raised illegally as a pet. Kids can pet and feed goats and sheep through a fence. The zoo is open daily from 10 A.M. to 3:30 P.M. and costs $1 person. (The zoo phone is 714-633-2022.) Across from the zoo, the **Interpretive Center** (phone: 714-289-9616), open weekend afternoons, has nature exhibits and information on hiking trails and ranger-led hikes.

A highlight of the park for young children is the pony rides, available on weekends and holidays from 10 A.M. to 4 P.M. If your visit to the park is on a weekday, children can still see the ponies grazing in front of their stables. There is also a miniature train that offers rides daily (phone: 714-997-3968). Irvine Regional Park is extremely well-kept and peaceful. It is well worth a day's outing.

Fullerton, La Habra, and Yorba Linda

● Fullerton Museum Center
301 North Pomona Avenue, one block east of Harbor Boulevard between Chapman and Commonwealth avenues, Fullerton. (714) 738-6545. Wednesday–Sunday, noon–4 P.M.; until 8 P.M. on Thursday. Adults, $3; students, $2; under 12, free. **Ages 8 and up.**

The Fullerton Museum Center features changing exhibits in science, history, and the cultural arts. The recently renovated museum is housed in the former Fullerton Public Library, an historic W.P.A. building. Past exhibits have included Tinker Toy creations, Teddy bears, and the history and science of holography. Activities for families and workshops for children ages eight to twelve are scheduled throughout the year.

● Fullerton Arboretum
On the California State University Fullerton Campus, 800 North State College Boulevard, Fullerton. From central Orange County, take the 57 Freeway north to Yorba Linda Boulevard and turn left. Take another left at Associated Road. The arboretum parking lot will be on your left. (714) 773-3579. Daily, 8 A.M.–4:45 P.M. Free. Heritage House tours: Sunday, 2–4 P.M. Donation, $2. **All ages.**

On the campus of Cal State Fullerton is a peaceful twenty-six acre botanical reserve. The reserve is organized into habitats that offer visitors a chance to hike through different climate environments from temperate to tropical to arid. Although the arboretum is relatively young, the grounds are lush enough to offer a lot of shade. There is a duck pond and a stream that opens into a larger pond. Also on the reserve is **Heritage House,** the 1894 Victorian home and office of an early Fullerton physician. If your visit to the arboretum is on a Sunday afternoon, you can tour the house from 2 to 4 P.M. The house, moved from its original downtown site, has been restored and authentically furnished. Among the furnishings are the doctor's pill maker and other antique medical equipment. The house has been surrounded with a garden typical of the 1890s. You are welcome to picnic on the arboretum grounds.

● Craig Regional Park

3300 State College Boulevard, Fullerton. Exit the Orange Freeway (57) at Imperial Highway (90); go west to State College Boulevard, turn left to the park entrance. (714) 990-0271. November–March: Daily, 7 A.M.–6 P.M. April–October: Daily, 7 A.M.–8:30 P.M. Parking: $4 per car. **All ages.**

For kids, a lake with ducks to feed is the highlight of this regional park. A visitors center displays wildlife exhibits. There is also a two-mile nature trail, as well as paved bike paths, children's playgrounds, and covered picnic areas.

● La Habra Children's Museum

310 South Euclid Street, La Habra. From the Orange Freeway (57), exit at Lambert Road and go west. Turn right on Euclid to the museum. From the Riverside Freeway (91), exit at Euclid Street and go six miles north to the museum. (310) 905-9793. Monday–Saturday, 10 A.M.–4 P.M.; Sunday, 1–5 P.M. $4 per person; under 2, free. **Infants–12 years.**

La Habra's 1923 Union Pacific railroad depot is now the home of the La Habra Children's Museum. The station has been restored as closely as possible to its original condition, and retired railroad cars are displayed on the tracks outside. You pay to enter at the old railroad ticket window. The former waiting room houses the nature-walk exhibit: an array of stuffed wild animals—including a bear, mountain lion, deer, possum, and many others—in a natural setting. The animals are out in the open at children's eye level and can be touched and petted. A special touch table in the corner includes such items as a dinosaur knuckle bone, a giant crab shell, and birds' nests. In the bee observatory, kids can see a working beehive behind glass.

Operating in the former baggage room is an elaborate model train and village. Another permanent exhibit is a restored caboose with historical artifacts and a dummy conductor inside. A museum expansion created three new permanent galleries: Kids on Stage, a mini-theater complete with costumes, props, sets, and lighting; Science Station, an area of interactive science exhibits; and Preschool School Playpark, an indoor park with climbing and crawling structures and other activities for children from infants through five years of age. Other permanent exhibits include a sandbox paleontology dig, a real Dentzel carousel to ride, a mini-grocery store, and a working section of an Orange County bus.

In addition to its permanent exhibits, the museum offers a gallery of special changing exhibits. Family workshops, performances, seasonal activities, summer programs, preschool story times, and other special events take place throughout the year. Each spring, the museum sponsors a children's arts festival with workshops and exhibits, food, and special performances. Several birthday party packages are available from the museum. The museum is located in Portola Park, which includes a children's playground and picnic tables.

● The Richard Nixon Library and Birthplace

18001 Yorba Linda Boulevard, Yorba Linda. From Los Angeles, take the I-5 south to the 91 Freeway east, exit at Imperial Highway and follow the signs. (714) 993-5075. Monday–Saturday, 10 A.M.–5 P.M.; Sunday, 11 A.M.–5 P.M. Ages 12–61, $5.95; ages 62 and older, $3.95; ages 8–11, $2; under 8, free. **Ages 8 and up.**

Perhaps the most controversial of the American presidential libraries, the Richard Nixon Library is located in his hometown of Yorba Linda. The grounds include the nine-hundred-square-foot farmhouse in which the thirty-seventh president was born, and as well as the grave sites of the former president and his wife, Pat. The library is really a museum that features a succession of touch-screen presentations and interactive videos on Nixon's life and presidency. For example, kids can "ask" the former president questions and watch him answer. The museum also sponsors exhibits and special events that are not directly tied to the former president. The gardens outside are beautiful.

Huntington Beach, Fountain Valley, and the Newport Beach Area

● Huntington Beach International Surfing Museum

411 Olive Street, Huntington Beach. From the San Diego Freeway (I-405) southbound, exit at Highway 39–Beach Boulevard. Make a right on Beach Boulevard, a right on Main Street, then another right on Olive Street. (714) 960-3483. Summer: Daily, noon to 5 P.M. Rest of year: Wednesday– Sunday, noon to 5 P.M. $2 per person. Ages 5 and under, free. **Ages 6 and up.**

Kids interested in surfing should enjoy this museum. Surfboards from the 1900s through the 1960s are on display, including a 1930 wooden model that weighs 135 pounds and measures more than twelve and a half feet. (Many of today's polyurethane boards weigh less than thirty pounds and measure less than five feet.) Surfing posters, artwork, and historical photos decorate the walls, and surfing music sounds from the museum speakers. Other exhibits include clothing and jewelry popularized by surfers, displays of lifesaving equipment, and a Hall of Fame honoring international surfing legends.

● Huntington Central Park

Golden West and Talbert, Huntington Beach. Take the San Diego Freeway (405) to the Golden West Street off-ramp and drive south about three miles to the park. (714) 960-8847. Free. Park: **All ages.** *Adventure Playground:* **Ages 6–12.**

The outstanding feature of this park for kids is **Adventure Playground,** a shallow, muddy lake where they can slip, slide, and raft. There are inner-tube swings, ropes to climb, and a muddy hill to slide down. Kids are also given wood, nails, and tools to hammer together forts, rafts, clubhouses, or whatever. The result is a child-built village that changes with the whims of young carpenters. Adventure Playground is open only during the summer, Monday–Saturday from 10 A.M. to 5 P.M. Admission is $2; $1 for Huntington Beach residents. Adventure Playground is located near the library in the park. Turn east on Talbert from Golden West and park in the library parking lot. The telephone number for Adventure Playground is (714) 842-7442. You should dress your children in old clothes and bring a change of clothing. Children must wear tennis shoes—no other kind of footwear is allowed. There is an outdoor shower.

The lushly beautiful Central Park also offers fishing in a fifteen-acre lake, six miles of paved bike and walking trails, and three children's playgrounds. There is also a nature center (located on the west side of Golden West) where you can pick up a pamphlet for a one-mile nature walk.

● The Bolsa Chica Ecological Reserve

Off Pacific Coast Highway between Warner Avenue and Golden West Street, Huntington Beach. Main entrance is opposite Bolsa Chica State Beach. Another parking lot is on Warner Avenue. Daily, 6 A.M.–8 P.M. *Free.* **Ages 6 and up.**

This reserve protects a restored salt marsh near the ocean at Bolsa Chica State Beach. A 1.5-mile nature trail loops across a wooden bridge and through the reserve. Children can spot brown pelicans, great egrets, and variety of other migrating birds. This is a walking and viewing experience. There is no bike riding, and visitors may not feed the birds or disturb the wildlife in any way. Bring binoculars and come prepared for a quiet nature walk.

● Mile Square Park

Warner and Euclid streets, Fountain Valley. Take the San Diego Freeway (405) to Euclid Street and go north about a mile. (714) 962-5549. Daily, 7 A.M. to dark. Free. **All ages.**

This park offers two lakes (one for fishing) and ducks to feed. There are four playground areas, including a playground on an island in one of the lakes—kids cross a bridge to reach it. The park also includes paved paths for bike riding and skating, game fields, and picnic areas with barbecues.

● Launch Pad

3333 Bear Street, #332, Costa Mesa. Located on the third floor in the Crystal Court at the South Coast Plaza Shopping Center. Monday–Friday, 10 A.M.–9 P.M.; Saturday, 10 A.M.–7 P.M.; Sunday, 11 A.M.–6 P.M. $5 per person. Under 1 year old, free. **All ages.**

The Launch Pad is a preview and satellite facility of the Discovery Science Center in Santa Ana. The thirty hands-on exhibits here are designed to spark an interest in science in kids of all ages. The interactive exhibits explore human physiology, gravity, momentum, sound, light, and electricity. There is also a room of activities just for toddlers.

● Newport Dunes Aquatic Park

1131 Back Bay Drive, Pacific Coast Highway at Jamboree Road, Newport Beach. (714) 729-3863. Daily, 8 A.M.–10 P.M. $5 per car. **Ages 3 and up.**

The calm, lifeguarded waters of this fifteen-acre lagoon make it an ideal place to take small children to swim. There are large stationary "whales" in the water to play on. Sailboats, kayaks, and paddleboats are available for rent. The park includes a playground, cafe, showers, and barbecues. During the summer, it's best to come here on a weekday when the crowds are thinner. (Newport Dunes is also a tent and recreational vehicle campsite.)

● Newport Harbor Nautical Museum

1714 West Balboa Boulevard (just north of the pier), Newport Beach. (714) 673-3377. Tuesday–Sunday, 10 A.M.–5 P.M. Adults, $4; children, $1. **Ages 8 and up.**

Exhibits relating to the history and activities of Newport Harbor are on display in this nautical museum. Glass cabinets contain a fine seashell collection, model ships, and a nautical medical chest from the 1800s. A fishing dory is out in the open where it can be seen up close. There are a number of historical photographs, including storm photos, and a sixteen-minute videotape on the harbor's history.

● Balboa Island Ferryboat Ride and Fun Zone

Take Pacific Coast Highway to Balboa Boulevard. The ferry is at the foot of Palm Street off of Balboa Boulevard on the Balboa Peninsula near Main Street. Ferry phone: (714) 673-1070. The ferry operates continuously throughout the day, and 24 hours during the summer. Pedestrians ride for 35¢ each way. **All ages.**

One of the few remaining ferries in California crosses the one thousand feet of water that separate Balboa Peninsula from Balboa Island in Newport Harbor. The short trip is fun for kids, and grown-ups love the view. The Fun Zone at the ferry's terminal on the peninsula side has been largely rebuilt. There is a Ferris wheel next to the water, a merry-go-round, bumper cars, and game arcades. Shiny new restaurants and snack places fit in comfortably with the old hot dog and frozen banana stands. At the foot of Main Street, the Balboa Pavilion, still looking much like it must have when it opened in 1905, houses the **Tale of the Whale Restaurant** (phone: 714-673-4633), a good, moderately priced seafood restaurant with children's plates available.

Harbor cruises leave from the dock between the ferry landing and the Pavilion every half hour from 10:30 A.M. to 7 P.M. during the summer and hourly from noon to 3 P.M. during the rest of the year. The cruises, which are narrated, last forty-five minutes. For more information, contact the Fun Zone Boat Company at (714) 673-0240. You can also cruise the harbor aboard the *Pavilion Queen* (phone: 714-673-5245), a double-deck Mississippi-style riverboat that operates daily from the Balboa Pavilion. Newport Landing Sportfishing, just west of the ferry landing at 503 Edgewater (phone: 714-675-0550), offers half- and three-quarter-day fishing trips.

A few short blocks along Main Street from the Pavilion is the **Balboa Pier,** a good vantage point for watching the surfers in action. **Ruby's,** at the end of the pier, is a cute 1940s-style cafe that also has a takeout window.

● Sherman Library and Gardens

2647 East Coast Highway, Corona del Mar. (714) 673-2261. Gardens open daily, 10:30 A.M.–4 P.M. Adults, $2; ages 16 and under, $1. Free to all every Monday. **All ages.**

More than 850 different kinds of flowers and plants grow on this beautiful two-acre garden. There's a temperature-controlled conservatory that includes ferns, orchids, and carnivorous plants. Children will enjoy the touch and smell garden, as well as the koi pond.

Irvine and South Orange County

● Northwood Community Park

4531 Bryan Avenue, Irvine. Exit I-5 at Culver Drive, go northeast to Bryan Avenue and turn right. (714) 552-4350. Monday–Saturday, 9 A.M.–9 P.M; Sunday, 12–6 P.M. Free. **All ages.**

The highlight of this meticulously maintained park is a large two-level concrete castle with a variety of play equipment incorporated into it. Toddlers and young children have their own play areas near the castle. The park's recreation building has balls and other play equipment. There are also picnic tables, barbecues, ball courts, an exercise course, and lots of green lawn.

● Turtle Rock Nature Center

Turtle Rock Community Park, Turtle Rock Drive at Sunnyhill, Irvine. Take Culver Drive south from I-405. Go south on Culver Drive to Bonita Canyon, turn east on Bonita Canyon to Sunnyhill and go north to the park. (714) 854-8151. Monday–Saturday, 10 A.M.–4 P.M. Free. **All ages.**

A five-acre wilderness area within Turtle Rock Community Park gives native wildlife—as well as children—a refuge from the surrounding suburban bustle. Children can walk through the nature center on paved walkways, catching sight of squirrels and other small animals. There is a stream that leads into a duck-inhabited pond. Other animals, including snakes, turtles, rabbits, and raccoons, can be seen every hour on the hour from 11 A.M. to 3 P.M. in a guided animal visit at the nature center building. The animal tour costs fifty cents. The nature-center building also has some displays.

● Adventure Playground

1 Beech Tree Lane, in University Community Park, Irvine. Exit I-405 on Jeffrey Road/University Drive and go west on University Drive to Beech Tree Lane. (714) 786-0854 or (714) 786-0851. Tuesday–Friday, 2:30–5 P.M.; Saturday, 10 A.M.–5 P.M. Free, but there is a fee for organized groups. **Ages 6–12.**

Inside Adventure Playground, kids are given their own plot of land and the tools and materials to build their own forts, clubhouses, or what-have-you. If they don't want to build, they can play in the mud in an unstructured, supervised environment. Adventure Playground is located in University Community Park in a residential neighborhood of Irvine. The playground, open year-round, is situated behind the park recreation building.

Entering Adventure Playground, you really feel as if you are in a different world. Old couches are strewn through the large muddy yard filled with tires, ropes, and hoses. The construction zone to one side is jammed with a wild assortment of kid-built structures. In order to build, kids need to complete a free, one-hour construction course offered Tuesday and Thursday at 3:30 and Saturday at 2 P.M. Children ages six and older may play in the supervised playground alone. Children under six years must be accompanied by an adult. Everyone must wear closed-toed tennis shoes. Birthday party packages are also available.

● Heritage Hill Historical Park

25151 Serrano Road, El Toro. From I-5 south of Irvine, take the Lake Forest Drive exit. Go east on Lake Forest Drive about two miles, then turn left on Serrano Road to the entrance and parking area. (714) 855-2028. Wednesday–Sunday, 9 A.M.–5 P.M. Tours of the historical structures: Wednesday–Friday at 2 P.M.; Saturday, Sunday, and holidays, 11 A.M. and 2 P.M. Free. Park: **All ages.** *Tour:* **Ages 10 and up.**

Heritage Hill is Orange County's first historical park. The park's four acres were once a small part of a 10,688-acre land grant awarded to Don José Serrano in 1842. His adobe, which still stands, is one of four restored historic structures in the park. The others are El Toro's 1890 grammar school, complete with wooden desks and pendulum clock; the 1891 St. George's Episcopal Church, with original stained-glass windows; and the 1908 Bennett Ranch House. You can see the buildings, which all have period furnishings, on a sixty- to ninety-minute free guided tour. Children need to be about ten or older to find the tour interesting.

The park includes a visitors center with exhibits on the county's history from the rancho period to the beginning of the citrus industry. Picnic tables are available, although shade can be limited. There is a children's playground in the adjacent Serrano Creek Park, which also includes picnic areas and hiking trails.

● Tucker Wildlife Sanctuary

29322 Modjeska Canyon Road, Modjeska Canyon. Take the El Toro exit from I-5 in El Toro, south of Irvine. Go left on El Toro Road eleven miles to Modjeska Canyon Road. Turn right and go about two miles to the sanctuary. (714) 649-2760. Daily, 9 A.M.–4 P.M. Admission, $1.50. **All ages.**

This ten-acre sanctuary includes an observation porch where kids can sit on benches and watch the birds as they arrive to get the birdseed put out for them. The sanctuary is most famous for its many humming-birds, although at least twenty-six other kinds of birds make year-round homes here. A naturalist is on duty to explain the types of birds you'll see. Trails lead through the reserve, where, in addition to birds, you can spot frogs, salamanders, snakes, and other small animals. A nature center has wildlife displays.

● Wild Rivers

8800 Irvine Center Drive, adjacent to Irvine Meadows Amphitheater, Laguna Hills. Exit I-405 at Irvine Center Drive in Irvine and go south. (714) 768-9453. Mid-May to early June and mid-September to early October: Open weekends and holidays, 11 A.M.–5 P.M. Mid-June to early September: Daily, 10 A.M.–8 P.M. Ages 10 and older, $18.95; ages 3–9, $14.95; seniors, $9.95; 2 years and under, free. After 4 P.M., $9.95 for everyone. Parking, $4. **Ages 3 and up.**

Wild Rivers is an African-theme water park on the old Lion Country Safari site. The park has three water-attraction areas. Thunder Cove features two large wave-action pools for body boarding and inner tubing, as well as play areas for children. The high-speed slides and water thrill rides appealing to teenagers and young adults are located on Wild Rivers Mountain. The third area, Explorers' Island, caters to children and families. There's a lagoon with scaled-down rides for children under fifty-four inches tall. A separate pool, less than a foot deep, features a gorilla swing and an elephant slide. There is also a pool for adults and a quarter-mile loop for slow-moving inner tubes.

Life vests are available at no extra charge. Lifeguards are stationed throughout the park, although parents should still a keep close eye on young children. Food service is available. (You are not permitted to bring your own food, beach chairs, inner tubes, etc.). Locker rentals and changing facilities are also available. Rates are reduced significantly for people entering the park after 4 P.M.

● Laguna Moulton Playhouse Youth Theater

606 Laguna Canyon Road, Laguna Beach. (714) 494-0743. Telephone for schedule. **Ages 3–12.**

A series of quality plays for children is offered by the Youth Theater of the Laguna Moulton Playhouse. Usually four plays are offered during the season, which runs from late September through June. You can buy season tickets or individual tickets, which are priced from about $9 to about $12. Performances usually take place on weekend afternoons. The Youth Theater also offers drama classes for children, and they have a children's ensemble. Membership to the ensemble is by audition or invitation.

● Mission San Juan Capistrano

Ortega Highway at Camino Capistrano, San Juan Capistrano. Two blocks west of junction of I-5 and SR 74/Ortega Highway. (714) 248-2048 or (714) 248-2049. Daily, 8:30 A.M.–5 P.M. Adults, $4; under 12, $3.
Ages 8 and up.

Founded in 1776, Mission San Juan Capistrano is one of the prettiest of the California missions—and also one of the most tourist-oriented. Sitting in the historic heart of a beautiful city, it gets more visitors than most. The mission is best known for the swallows that return to their nests here every year on or about St. Joseph's Day, March 19, and depart by October 23, the feast day of the mission's patron saint.

The mission has two churches. One, a once-magnificent cathedral, was destroyed in an earthquake in 1812, just nine years after it was completed, and never rebuilt. Scaffolding now supports the ruins of its arched walls. (The new parish church just north of the mission is a copy of the original cathedral.) The other, the Serra Chapel, is one of the oldest structures in California and the only remaining mission church in which Father Serra conducted services.

On a self-guided tour, you'll see the soldiers barracks, the padre's living quarters, and the mission industrial center, excavated in the 1930s, with its tallow ovens, tanning vats, and outdoor kitchen. Children can crawl into a *kitca,* a domed, thatched shelter used by the Juanero Indians and explore other Native American artifacts. The mission museum has exhibits on the Juanero, Spanish, and Mexican Rancho periods, and there are touch tables for children outside.

The lovely mission grounds are full of flowers, shade trees, and rose-covered walls. Children can buy feed or bring their own for the birds that cluster on the grounds. There are picnic tables located on a grassy area behind the soldiers barracks. The mission also sponsors summer concerts, living history days, storytelling, and other programs for children; phone for the schedule.

● The Capistrano Depot

26701 Verdugo Street, San Juan Capistrano. Monday–Thursday, 11 A.M.– 9 P.M.; Friday and Saturday, 11 A.M.–10 P.M.; Sunday, 10 A.M.–9 P.M.
All ages.

Built in 1894 by the Sante Fe Railroad, the red-brick, dome-topped Capistrano Depot is the oldest station of its style in Southern California.

The restored depot is now a pleasant restaurant, as well as an Amtrak station. You can eat outside—and watch the trains—on a pretty patio. Or, you can eat inside in the restored depot. Most of the tables have a view of the arriving and departing trains, and refurbished train cars are part of the bar. The menu ranges from soups, salads, and sandwiches to hearty entrees, and what we sampled was good. There is also a brunch menu.

For a real adventure, you can arrive by train from Los Angeles, North Orange County, or San Diego for your meal here. The mission is just a block away.

● O'Neill Museum

31831 Los Rios Street, San Juan Capistrano. Exit I-5 at Ortega Highway (SR 74) west; turn left immediately on Del Obispo Street, then right on Los Rios Street. (714) 493-8444. Tuesday–Friday, 9 A.M. to noon, and 1–4 P.M.; Sunday, 11 A.M.–3 P.M. Adults, $1; children under 12, 50¢.
Ages 8 and up.

San Juan Capistrano has a very pretty historic district that includes the mission, the depot, and a number of homes and adobes. Within this historic core is California's first neighborhood street, now designated at the Los Rios Historic District. The only house on the street open to the public is a tree-shaded Victorian, the O'Neill Museum. On a guided tour, kids can see what a typical Orange County home was like at the turn of the century. The old-fashioned kitchen includes a Sears and Roebuck Polar Air icebox, and there is an original Singer sewing machine in the bedroom.

● The Jones Family Mini-Farm

31791 Los Rios Street, San Juan Capistrano. (714) 831-6550. Wednesday–Sunday, 11 A.M.–4 P.M. Free entrance; pony rides, $2. **Infants–9 years.**

On historic Los Rios Street—just down from the O'Neill Museum and across the tracks from the depot—is an old-style barnyard. The mini-farm, once part of a 2,500-acre Mexican rancho, offers pony rides for children from eight months to 80 pounds. Young children can pet goats, bunnies, horses, and other barnyard animals, and you can purchase feed for the animals.

● Orange County Marine Institute

24200 Dana Point Harbor Drive, Dana Point. From I-5, take the Pacific Coast Highway/California 1 off-ramp. Follow California 1 north to Dana Point, then go left at Dana Point Harbor Drive. (714) 496-2274. Daily,

10 A.M.–4:30 P.M. The museum is free. There are varying charges for classes and programs. **All ages.**

Dana Point Harbor, a lovely natural cove surrounded by dramatic cliffs, was once the only major port between San Diego and Santa Barbara. Ships anchored here to trade goods from New England to the local ranchers—and the mission at San Juan Capistrano—in exchange for cowhides tossed from the cliffs. In 1835, Richard Henry Dana, a crewman aboard the sailing ship *Pilgrim,* visited the harbor, later writing about his adventures in *Two Years Before the Mast.*

Today, you can see a replica of the *Pilgrim*—owned by the Orange County Marine Institute—in the harbor below their building. Better yet, you can go aboard on one of the Marine Institute's living-history programs.

The Orange County Marine Institute is a nonprofit educational organization dedicated to increasing awareness and understanding of the marine environment. They offer a number of hands-on marine science programs for school groups, including living-history overnights on the *Pilgrim,* wildlife cruises, onshore science labs, and much, much more.

But you do not have to be a part of a school group to participate in their programs. The *Pilgrim* is open to the public for guided living-history tours most Sundays from 10 A.M. to 2:30 P.M. Kids learn knot tying and bell ringing, and join in other hands-on activities aboard the ship. For a real adventure, children ages eight through twelve and their parents can spend the night aboard the *Pilgrim.* Other sea adventures include marine wildlife cruises, nature tours of the harbor, and sailing to Catalina aboard an historic tall ship. A summer program of sea camps is available for children from ages three (with a parent) through fifteen. Weekend tide-pool exploration and other guided activities take place year-round.

The institute building has displays on marine life, including touch tanks and the skeleton of a grey whale. Adjacent to the museum is a beautiful park with green lawns, picnic facilities, and a small beach with a cordoned area for waders.

● Nautical Heritage Museum

24532 Del Prado Boulevard, Dana Point. Exit I-5 at Pacific Coast Highway, go west to Street of the Amber Lantern; turn left to Del Prado Boulevard and left again to the museum. Monday–Friday, 10 A.M.–4 P.M. Free. **Ages 8 and up.**

Housed in a replica of an old New England lighthouse, the Nautical Heritage Museum features dozens of historic ship models. Among them are miniature replicas of the USS *Constitution*, the HMS *Victory*, and *The Golden Hind*, Sir Francis Drake's ship. A corner of the museum has been converted into a model-repair shop, and kids may get see to a model ship-builder work. Other exhibits include shipbuilding tools, scrimshaw (carving done by sailors on ivory, bones, shells, etc.), and original ships' documents. This is mostly a viewing experience, and you will probably want to visit here in combination with a trip to the nearby Marine Institute or to the beach.

● Doheny State Beach Park

25300 Dana Point Harbor Drive, Dana Point. Exit I-5 northbound at Beach Cities Drive, and go southbound at Pacific Coast Highway/Camino Las Ramblas. Park entrance is just seaward of Pacific Coast Highway. Daily, 6 A.M.–10 P.M. Parking, $5. **All ages.**

With over a mile of whitewashed sandy beach fronting blue water, Doheny State Beach Park looks like everyone's dream of a Southern California beach. The water here offers some of the best swimming and surfing in California. The sixty-two-acre state park at the mouth of San Juan Creek includes a five-acre picnic area landscaped with green lawns and shady trees. There are plenty of tables, grills, fire rings, and lots of nearby parking. At low tide, tide pools form in a rocky area at the beach's western end.

A beachside snack bar, open 11 A.M.–4 P.M. on weekends and daily in the summer, rents bikes, Rollerblades, umbrellas, volleyballs, boards, and other equipment. A small visitors center near the entrance has nature displays, including a simulated tide pool and fish tanks. Overnight camping is available in 121 developed campsites.

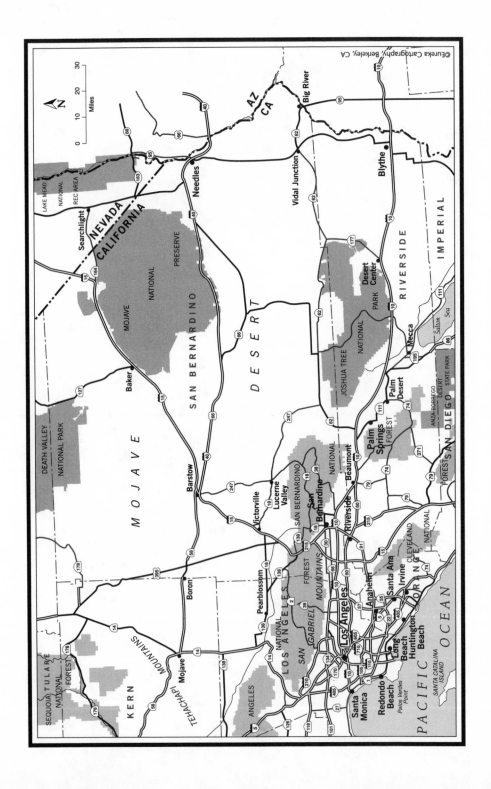

©Eureka Cartography, Berkeley, CA

Riverside and San Bernardino Counties

TWO GREAT DESERTS, splendid mountain ranges, spectacular lakes, famous resorts, and large urban areas all come together in Riverside and San Bernardino counties.

The San Bernardino Mountains, stretching fifty miles across, are the highest of the mountain ranges surrounding Los Angeles. Popular mountain-resort areas built around two beautiful lakes—Arrowhead and Big Bear—offer summer camping, hiking, fishing, and water sports; wintertime brings snow sports and activities. The less well known Crestline resort area offers families activities centered around Lake Gregory. Silverwood Lake, north of Crestline, is a relatively new state recreation area offering scenic picnic sites, swimming beaches, fishing, and boating. The San Jacinto Mountains to the south (both ranges are included the San Bernardino National Forest) include the lovely resort area of Idlewild.

Adjacent to the San Jacinto Mountains, the Palm Springs area offers children an introduction to the wonders of the Colorado Desert. Usually thought of as a playground for adults, this famous resort area offers a number of fascinating adventures for children, including the Palm Springs Aerial Tramway's breathtaking ride up the face of San Jacinto Mountain.

The vast Mojave Desert can be explored from a base in Barstow. Among the attractions for families in the Barstow area is the restored 1880s Calico Ghost Town.

The urban areas of Riverside and San Bernardino also offer their share of enjoyable destinations: great parks, historical attractions, and museums housing everything from mounted birds to trolley cars.

Riverside, San Bernardino, and Vicinity

● Riverside Art Museum

3425 Seventh Street, Riverside. From Riverside Freeway (91) south, exit at Seventh Street; going north, exit at University Avenue and turn west on Seventh Street. (909) 684-7111. Monday–Saturday, 10 A.M.–4 P.M. Adults, $2; children, free. **Ages 3 and up.**

The Spanish Revival–style building housing the Riverside Art Center and Museum was originally designed as a YWCA in 1929 by Julia Morgan, the chief architect of Hearst Castle. Downstairs is a lovely lobby with a tile fireplace and several galleries hosting changing exhibits and displaying the work of Southern California artists. In galleries upstairs, kids can see art created by children in the museum's art classes. The classes, available for children ages three and older, are taught by professionals and are geared to the children's age levels. In a recent session, children ages eight and older learned printmaking techniques, while five- through seven-year-olds created castles of clay, and preschool children experimented with a variety of mediums. Tuition for the classes averages about $40 for a ten-week session of weekly classes.

Lunch is served in the museum's courtyard (or by the fireplace on rainy days) on weekdays from 11 A.M. to 2 P.M. Kids are welcome. For lunch information, phone (909) 682-9566.

● Riverside Municipal Museum

3720 Orange Street, at Seventh Street, downtown Riverside. (909) 782-5273. Monday, 9 A.M.–1 P.M.; Tuesday–Friday, 9 A.M.–5 P.M. Saturday and Sunday, 1–5 P.M. Free. **All ages.**

Once the downtown post office, this pleasant museum contains exhibits on the human and natural history of the region. There are displays of area wildlife, local Native American artifacts, guns and tools of early settlers, and—especially interesting—the skeleton of a saber-toothed cat in a case on the floor, where it can be easily examined by children.

● Mission Inn

3649 Seventh Street, between Main and Orange streets, downtown Riverside. From Riverside Freeway (91) south, exit at Seventh Street; going north, exit at University Avenue and turn west on Seventh Street. Museum: (909) 788-9556. Daily, 9:30 A.M.–4 P.M. Free. Tours: (909) 781-8241, weekdays; (909) 784-0300, ext. 5035, weekends. Monday–Friday at 10 A.M., 10:30 A.M., 1:30 P.M., and 2 P.M.; Saturday and Sunday, 10 A.M.–3 P.M. Adults, $8; children under 12, free. **Ages 8 and up.**

Built in several phases between 1902 and 1932, and recently restored, the Mission Inn is both a hotel and a national historic landmark. The Spanish Mission–style structure covers a city block with its arches, belltowers, wrought-iron balconies, gargoyles, fountains, sculptures, Spanish paintings, antiques, and Tiffany windows. The original owner, Frank Miller, used the hotel to showcase the art and antiques he acquired on his world travels, and many of the items are still in the hotel or displayed in the first-floor museum. Interested families with older children (school group tours start at the third grade) can take a ninety-minute guided tour of the hotel (reservations suggested). Highlights of the tours for older kids are the more than seven hundred bells on display, the garden fountains, the Flyer's Wall containing mementos of famous aviatiors, and the music room.

You do not have to take the tour, though, to get the flavor of the inn. The free first-floor museum has displays on the inn and exhibits of inn treasures. Among the exhibits are instruments from the music room collection, antique bells, and barber chairs and paraphernalia from the old hotel barber shop.

● California Museum of Photography

3824 Main Street, corner of University Avenue on the pedestrian mall, downtown Riverside. (909) 784-3686. Wednesday–Saturday, 11 A.M.–5 P.M.; Sunday, noon–5 P.M. Adults, $2; seniors and students, $1; under 12, free. Free on Wednesdays. **Ages 7 and up.**

A facility of the University of California at Riverside, this museum presents changing exhibits of contemporary photography and related media. Housed in a renovated dime store on Riverside's very pleasant pedestrian mall, the museum also features a permanent collection of historic photographs ranging from early daguerreotypes to contemporary prints. Also on display are cameras and equipment dating from the invention of photography to current models and an impressive collection of stereoscopic cards. Family programs with special activities for kids take place on selected first Sundays of the month throughout the year. The museum closes for installation of exhibits, so phone before heading out.

● Heritage House

8193 Magnolia Avenue, about ten minutes south of downtown, between Adams and Jefferson boulevards, Riverside. (909) 689-1333. Tuesday and Thursday, noon–2:30 P.M.; Sunday, noon–3:30 P.M. During the summer, open only on Sunday, noon–3:30 P.M. Donation requested: Adults, $1; children, 50¢. **Ages 8 and up.**

This marvelous-looking Victorian house was completed in 1891 for the family of a citrus grower. It is now owned by the Riverside Museum, and you can see the inside on a tour. Outstanding features of the home include a beautiful staircase, gas lamps (the house was one of the first in Riverside to have them), and tile fireplaces in every room. The house is furnished with period pieces, some of them original. Since you must see the house on a tour—where you may hear about the legend of a ghost who sometimes haunts the house—and since there is obviously no touching, a visit here is best appreciated by older children.

● California Citrus State Historic Park

Van Buren Boulevard at Dufferin Avenue, Riverside. Exit the Riverside Freeway (91) at Van Buren Boulevard and go south to Dufferin Avenue. (909) 780-6222. Daily, 8 A.M.–6 P.M. Free. **All ages.**

From the 1880s through the 1940s, Riverside was famous for its lush groves of navel oranges, considered some of the best in the world. The California Citrus State Historic Park pays tribute to the industry for which Riverside was famous. The park features hundreds of navel orange trees and a demonstration grove of about eighty varieties of citrus, land-scaped as groves would have been at the turn of the century. The visitors center is constructed in the Craftsman/California Bungalow–style popular in the early 1900s. There are grassy, shaded picnic areas and interpretive walking trails around the site. The park is in an early stage of develop-ment. Future plans call for the recreation of a complete citrus-producing community circa 1880-1935.

● Jensen-Alvarado Ranch Historic Park

4307 Briggs Street, Riverside. From the 60 Freeway, two miles west of Riverside, take the Rubidoux exit south one mile to Tilton Avenue. Turn right and go three blocks to Briggs Street; turn left to the park. (909) 369-6055. Saturday, 10 A.M.–4 P.M. Closed July to mid-September. Adults, $3; children, $1.50. **All ages.**

This historic park was once the prosperous ranch of a former Danish sea captain and his *Californio* wife. The family built a brick two-story home, a winery, livery stable, and barn, and successfully developed five hundred acres. Although the house is closed for renovations, its bedroom, parlor, and kitchen have been recreated in the winery, using original fur-niture and items from the 1880s. Wine-making equipment, including a grape crusher, is also on display. But this is more than just a looking experience. Children are invited to try doing laundry with a washboard, churning cream for butter, and feeding the chickens. Afterwards, they can try their hands at a hoop race. Docents in period costumes add to the ambience. You are also welcome to picnic on the grounds.

● University of California at Riverside Botanic Gardens

900 University Avenue, Riverside. The Botanic Gardens are on the east side of the campus. Exit I-215 at University Avenue and go east to campus. Follow Campus Drive to Parking Lot 13, then follow signs through the lot to Botanic Gardens parking area. Botanic Gardens phone: (909) 787-4650. Daily, 8 A.M.–5 P.M. Free, but donations appreciated. **All ages.**

Extending across thirty-nine hilly acres, the botanic gardens at the University of California, Riverside, feature more 3,500 plants from around the world. Kids will see many varieties and shapes of cactus and other desert plants. They'll also see herb gardens, rose and iris gardens, and a fruit orchard. The cool and shady Alder Canyon is filled with azaleas, camellias, ferns, and buddleias. A geodesic lath dome houses a special collection of cycads and palms. The gardens are also a wildlife sanctuary with some two hundred species of birds spotted within its borders. There are four miles of scenic trails and plenty of benches. A paved pathway through the garden accommodates strollers and wheelchairs.

● March Field Museum

Intersection of I-215 and Van Buren Boulevard, adjacent to March Air Force Base, Riverside. Exit I-215 at Van Buren Boulevard. The museum is on the east side of the freeway, the only building between March Air Force Base runway and the freeway. (909) 655-3725. Daily, 10 A.M.–4 P.M. Adults, $3; children, $1. **Ages 6 and up.**

March Field, established in 1918, is the oldest Air Force base in the western United States. Exhibits on display inside and around the hangar-style museum building depict the evolution of air power and the history of the base. Starting with World War I uniforms and artifacts, the history of the Air Force is traced to the present. One exhibit lets you listen in on a recorded mission briefing for a World War II bombing run. More than forty-five historic planes are displayed, including bombers, fighters, and trainers from World War II through the Vietnam era. Among the planes are a B-13 Valiant, a B-17 Flying Fortress, a B-29 Superfortress, an F-14 Tomcat, and an SR-71 Blackbird.

● Lake Perris

On Ramona Expressway off I-15E, southeast of Riverside. (909) 657-0676. Daily, 6 A.M.–8 P.M. (open until 10 P.M. summer). Day use, $6 per vehicle. **All ages.**

Lake Perris is a large man-made lake offering boating, swimming beaches, fishing, and picnicking. The picnic areas include tables and grills. There are also playgrounds, restrooms, hiking and bicycle trails, and a snack bar. Because the park is relatively new, the trees are still small. Facilities are available for recreational vehicles, and there are also boat-launching areas and a boat supply shop. Lake Perris is a popular recreation spot, so you may find a line at the entrance during summer.

● Orange Empire Railway Museum

2201 South A Street, Perris; just south of Riverside on I-215. Exit I-215 at Highway 74 west; go west one mile to A Street and turn left. (909) 657-2605. Grounds open daily, 9 A.M.–5 P.M. Trains and trolleys operate Saturday, Sunday, and holidays, 11 A.M.–5 P.M. Grounds free. All-day train pass: Adults, $6; ages 6–11, $4; under 6, free. **All ages.**

In the late 1950s, as the last streetcar and interurban rail lines were closing in Southern California, a group of young men dedicated to preserving this passing technology founded the Orange Empire Railway Museum. Since then, a large number of cars have found their way to the museum, including steam locomotives and wooden passenger trolleys; freight, maintenance, and construction cars; and even an old Los Angeles funeral car. Museum members restore the cars and lay all the tracks.

The outdoor museum is the size of a small town, and it is a wonderful place for kids. Construction is constantly in progress. On a weekend visit, children can see the actual work of building and maintaining a railroad. They may see crews laying rails, setting poles, stringing trolley wire, or restoring an old train or trolley car. In addition to seeing the trains, children can wander around and see a variety of off-rail equipment and old trucks.

Best of all, they can ride the old cars. Several different streetcars and trolleys—and sometimes the steam locomotive—are usually running on a weekend. An all-day pass allows you to go from one to another, riding as many times as you wish. The old cars, which still have their original advertising posters above the seats, are staffed by uniformed volunteer motormen and conductors who are wonderfully serious about what they do.

The museum has a shaded picnic ground. Dress for warm weather, wear old clothes, bring lunch, and plan to spend some time here. Special events and excursion train rides happen throughout the year.

● Temecula Museum

Front Street and Moreono Road, Temecula. Located on the I-15 in southern Riverside County just north of the San Diego county line. Exit I-15 at the Rancho California exit; go one block west to Front Street. (909) 676-0021. Wednesday–Sunday, 11 A.M.–4 P.M. Free. **Ages 8 and up.**

During the Old West days in California, the frontier town of Temecula was a stop on the Butterfield Stage route. You can still see some of that frontier town today in Old Town Temecula. A number of the original buildings have been preserved in the historic Old Town, and the newer buildings have Western-style fronts. While most of Old Town is given over to antique shops, kids can sip a cold drink in the deli located in a former frontier store/saloon and wander over to the old jail.

The Temecula Museum, recently moved to this brand new building, has displays on the history of the valley from Native American times through the frontier era. Particularly interesting, if you plan on strolling through Old Town, is the detailed miniature town depicting Temecula around 1914.

● Prado Regional Park

16700 South Euclid Avenue, Chino. From I-10, take Euclid Avenue south; or take Highway 71 north from the Riverside Freeway or south from the Pomona Freeway. (909) 597-4260. Daily, 7:30 A.M. to dusk. $5 per car. **All ages.**

This 2,200-acre park is nestled in a rural area dotted with cattle and dairy farms. From the car window kids can see the cattle grazing along Highway 71 (leading to the park from the Pomona Freeway), and you can smell the farms from the park. The park has a number of large grassy areas surrounding a central, fifty-six-acre lake. Fishing is offered, and paddleboat and rowboat rentals are available. (A fishing permit is $5 for ages seven and older; $2 for children under seven. A license is also required for ages sixteen and above. You can buy a license at the park.) There are individual and group picnic areas with tables and grills, and several small, attractive playgrounds. The park also has riding stables and trails and a well-equipped recreational-vehicle camping area.

● Planes of Fame Air Museum

7000 Merrill Avenue, Chino. Located at the Chino Airport. From the Pomona Freeway (60) take the Euclid Avenue exit (Highway 83) south to Merrill. The air museum is in the northeast section of the airport. (909) 597-3514. Daily, 9 A.M.–5 P.M. Adults, $7.95; ages 5–11, $1.95; under 5, free. **Ages 6 and up.**

A large collection of rare aircraft from the beginning of aviation to the space age is housed in hangars and on the ground at the Planes of Fame Air Museum at the Chino airport. Among the aircraft you'll see are an 1896 hang glider, a Japanese Zero—the only flyable one still in existence—an M-109, a B-17, and many more planes in flyable condition. Veterans from World War II who actually flew the big B-17 bombers are frequently on hand to share their experiences and answer kids' questions.

● San Bernardino County Museum

2024 Orange Tree Lane, Redlands. From eastbound I-10, take the California Street exit, turn left on California Street, and go about two blocks to the museum. (909) 798-8570. Tuesday–Sunday, 9 A.M.–5 P.M. Adults, $5.75; ages 2–12, $3.75. **Ages 3 and up.**

Located in a bright geodesic-domed building, the San Bernardino County Museum houses a remarkable mounted-bird exhibit and the world's largest display of birds' eggs. More than twenty-thousand eggs are exhibited, as well as nests from all over the world. Other displays cover California's prehistoric people, Native Americans, and rancho life, and the area's geological and fossil history—including some dinosaur tracks. Specimens of local wildlife are also on display. There is a hands-on **Discovery Hall** where—in addition to other activities—children can meet and pet a variety of live animals, including snakes, lizards, toads, guinea pigs, bunnies, and a pot-bellied pig. The Discovery Hall is open Tuesday through Thursday, 10 A.M.–1 P.M.; Friday and Saturday, 10 A.M.–4 P.M.; and Sunday, 1–4 P.M.

● Oak Glen Apple Farms/Oak Tree Village

Oak Glen Road, Oak Glen. From Los Angeles, take I-10 past Redlands to the Yucaipa Boulevard exit. Take Yucaipa Boulevard east to Oak Glen Road and turn left. Oak Tree Village is about five miles up the hill. (909) 797-4020. Daily, 10 A.M.–5 P.M. **All ages.**

Oak Glen, a mile into the foothills of the San Bernardino Mountains, is the Southland's largest apple-growing region. Indeed, during a fall visit, when the air is crisp and the leaves are in vibrant color, you'll feel as if you have been transported to New England.

Most of the apples grown here are sold directly to the public; many of the orchard owners sell their apples in roadside stands. A few of the orchards—including Linda Vista Orchards, Riley's Farm and Orchard, and Apple Creek Orchard—will allow you to pick your own apples. Apple cider is made daily at some of the orchards, and visitors can watch the presses in action. Most of the orchards have shaded picnic areas. Riley's Farm also offers hayrides and other old-fashioned activities for kids.

Oak Tree Village, an area of restaurants and shops near the center of Oaks Tree Road, offers children a small animal park where, for 25¢, they can see deer, peacocks, hens, and other small animals. Mountain Town, another group of shops near Oak Tree Village, offers kids a small nature museum containing a variety of stuffed wildlife. Another interesting stop along Oak Glen Road is the old schoolhouse, which contains historical displays and information on apple growing. Near the schoolhouse, kids can see an old wagon and early apple-farming equipment.

Apple harvest season lasts from September to December. You will want to schedule your visit for a time *other* than a weekend in October, when Oak Glen gets very crowded. Visits to Oak Glen are also enjoyable in the winter when snow may fall—the roads are kept cleared—and during the spring (mid-April through mid-May), when the apple trees are in blossom. If you come in the spring, you might want to combine the visit with a trip to nearby Cherry Valley, where some of the farms permit you to pick cherries.

● Gilman Ranch Historic Park and Wagon Museum

Wilson and Sixteenth streets, Banning. From I-10, take the Sunset exit east of Highway 79. Go north to Wilson Street and turn right. (909) 922-9200. Sunday, 10 A.M.–4 P.M. Tours at 11 A.M. and 2 P.M. Closed the month of January. Adults, $3; ages 12 and under, $1.50. **Ages 6 and up.**

Once a stagecoach stop and a successful ranch, the Gilman Ranch is the most recent addition to the Riverside County Park system. The highlight of this very new park is its wagon museum. Among the wagons on display are an overland stagecoach, a "prairie schooner," a chuck wagon, and a covered wagon. Many carry original hardware. The Riverside County Parks Department plans to add trails and interpretive programs in the future. For now, the park is a low-key place where you can picnic and get a sense of the Old West.

● A Special Place Children's Hands-on Museum

1003 East Highland Avenue, San Bernardino. (909) 881-1201. Tuesday–Friday, 9 A.M.–1 P.M.; Saturday, 11 A.M.–3 P.M. Reduced admission and extended hours for groups by appointment. $2 per person. Under a year old, free. **Ages 2–10.**

An outstanding feature of this hands-on children's museum is its regard for disabled children. The museum is a part of Easter Seals, and all of the exhibits and activity areas in the museum have been designed to accommodate wheelchairs. Children can increase their awareness of what it is like to be disabled by trying out wheelchairs, crutches, braces, and walkers. A wheelchair swing and a wheelchair maze is on the patio. In a shadow room, kids moving in wheelchairs and on their own can see their shadows freeze on the wall.

An old-fashioned schoolroom set up in the museum gives kids a chance to see how things were in the "olden days." They can work at the old-fashioned desks or shovel real coal into the pot-bellied stove. Other exhibits include a mini Kaiser clinic, a puppet theater, a bubble center, and a western dress-up area. A pair of cockatiels reside at the museum, as well as toads and turtles. The museum also offers craft activities, changing exhibits, and much more. Birthday parties are held in the afternoon.

Lake Arrowhead, Big Bear, and Vicinity

Within a thirty-minute drive from San Bernardino—and a two-hour drive from Los Angeles—are two mountain resorts built around man-made lakes, Lake Arrowhead and Big Bear Lake. Lake Arrowhead is smaller and more pristine (only property owners or guests at local lodges can swim or boat on the lake) while the higher-altitude Big Bear is larger and more city-like. Big Bear offers a range of accommodations and restaurants, skiing, and public use of the lake. The more scenic Lake Arrowhead has fewer accommodations. For a list of places to stay in Big Bear, phone the chamber of commerce, (909) 866-7000. For Lake Arrowhead area accommodations, phone (909) 337-3715.

● Lake Arrowhead Resort and Village
27984 Highway 189, Lake Arrowhead. Resort phone: (909) 336-1511 or (800) 800-6792. Village phone: (909) 337-2533. Village hours: Daily, 10 A.M.–5:30 P.M. Open until 6 P.M. on weekdays in the summer and 8 P.M. on weekends. **All ages.**

Lake Arrowhead Resort is a child-friendly, 261-room resort fronting Lake Arrowhead. The resort includes a swimming pool, a private beach on the lake, comfortable rooms, a family restaurant, and supervised activities for children ages four to twelve. It is on the expensive side, however, and there are certainly other places to stay in the area. The adjacent Lake Arrowhead Village, fronting the lake, is a tri-level shopping mall with an Alpine theme. In addition to stores and factory outlets, the village contains the Lake Arrowhead Children's Museum, the *Arrowhead Queen* dock, and a number of restaurants, fast-food places, and an ice-cream shop. The Village is also site of special events for children and families throughout the year. For special events information, phone (909) 336-3274.

● Lake Arrowhead Children's Museum
28200 Highway 189, Suite T100, Lake Arrowhead. From Highway 18, take the Lake Arrowhead turnoff two miles to the Lake Arrowhead Village. Go straight at the light into the lower village. The museum is located at the end of the peninsula. (909) 336-1332. Summer: Daily, 10 A.M.–6 P.M. Winter: Wednesday–Monday, 10 A.M.–6 P.M. Ages 2–59, $3.50; ages 60 and over, $2.50; under 2, free. **Ages 1–12.**

Fronting the lake in Lake Arrowhead Village, this small children's museum features its own play village complete with a bank, post office, veterinary office, photo shop, and fire department. A camping area includes a tent, a fire ring, cooking equipment, and a boat for fishing. In another area of the museum, called the "Inventors' Workshop," kids use low-temperature glue guns and a variety of material stored in assorted bins to create their own widgets and gadgets.

Among other exhibits are a theater area, a bubble center, an ant-hill-like crawling maze, and a toddler area that includes a Peter Pan–style pirate ship. Weekly activities for children ages three through twelve are scheduled on a regular basis. Family memberships and birthday party packages are also available.

● Arrowhead Queen

On the waterfront in Lake Arrowhead Village. Tickets sold at LeRoy's Sports in the Village. (909) 336-6992. Summer: Departures daily on the hour, 10 A.M.–6 P.M. Rest of year: Daily, 11 A.M., 12:30, 2, and 3:30 P.M. Adults, $9.50; seniors, $8.50; ages 12 and under, $6.50. **Ages 6 and up.**

The *Arrowhead Queen* offers one-hour narrated cruises of Lake Arrowhead. Although not a paddle wheeler, the ship is outfitted to resemble one, and the captain, who does the narration, is friendly to kids. The scenery on the lake is beautiful year-round, and the tour should hold the interest of kids ages six and older.

● Blue Jay Ice Castle

Highway 189 and North Bay Road, Blue Jay, about a mile west of Lake Arrowhead on Highway 189. (909) 337-5283. Phone for hours. Admission and skate rental, $7 per person. **Ages 6 and up.**

The Blue Jay Ice Castle is an exceptionally nice ice-skating rink. Covered on top but open to the trees on the sides, skating here is as close as you can get to skating outdoors on a frozen pond. The skate-changing area includes a fireplace.

● Santa's Village

Skyforest. From San Bernardino, take I-215 north from the I-10. Go about four miles to Highway 30/Mountain Resorts turnoff. Continue on Mountain Resorts Freeway to Waterman Avenue exit. Turn left on Waterman, which is Highway 18; the village is on Highway 18, two miles past the Lake Arrowhead turnoff. (909) 337-2481. Mid-June to mid-September and mid-November through December: open daily, 10 A.M.–5 P.M. Closed March 1 to Memorial Day weekend. Rest of year: open weekends and holidays, 10 A.M.–5 P.M.,

*weather permitting. Ages 3–adult, $11; 2 and under, free. Admission
includes unlimited rides.* **Ages 1–11.**

Children can visit Santa Claus year-round at Santa's Village in the
San Bernardino Mountains. The village is essentially designed for small
children. Kids can pet and feed Santa's reindeer and other tame animals.
There are a number of rides for young children, including a Cinderella's
pumpkin coach ride, train and antique car rides, a bumblebee monorail,
a merry-go-round, a Ferris wheel, bobsleds, and pony and burro rides.
The rides are all old and slow, but small children seem to love them.
Other attractions include a puppet theater, a tree-house slide, a bird
sanctuary, and toy and doll shops. The village includes a pantry, a bakery,
a candy shop, and snack bars, and there is gift-shop browsing for the
grown-ups. Children's birthday party packages are also available. Santa's
Village is rather worn and old-fashioned, but it is absolutely charming to
young children. The village, which is located in a spectacular mountain
setting, gets very crowded on weekends between Thanksgiving and
Christmas.

● Heaps Peak Arboretum

*Highway 18, 2.5 miles east of Lake Arrowhead. (909) 337-2444. Open
daily during daylight hours. Free.* **All ages.**

Heaps Peak Arboretum offers an easy (although not stroller-accessible)
.7 mile trail through thirty-three acres of native mountain plants and
trees. A pamphlet at the entrance has information on the trail. You'll see
wildflowers in bloom from April through October, trees changing color in
the fall, and, of course, snow in the winter. In addition to some beautiful
mountain views, you'll be able to catch sight of the Mojave Desert. If your
walk is early in the morning, you may spot a variety of wildlife, including
deer, bobcats, and foxes.

● The National Children's Forest

*Keller Peak Road, off Highway 18. From the intersection of Highways 173
and 18 outside of Lake Arrowhead, travel east 8.3 miles to just past the Deer
Lick Forest Service Station turnoff, a mile east of Running Springs. Trail
maps and other information are available at the Arrowhead Ranger Station,
28104 Highway 18, in Skyforest. (909) 337-2444. Open May through
October.* **All ages.**

The National Children's Forest is a 3,400-acre site in the San Bernardino National Forest dedicated to the efforts of the many children who
helped replant here after a devastating fire in 1970. The **Trail of the
Phoenix** is a half-mile, paved, wheelchair- and stroller-accessible trail

designed for, and with the input of, children at the entrance of the
Children's Forest. Located at the end of a four-mile paved road off Highway 18, the Trail of the Phoenix includes benches for resting and observ-
ing and trail signs composed by kids.

The Children's Forest Association sponsors outdoor education programs for families in the Children's Forest. During the winter, they take
families into the forest on top-quality snowshoes for naturalist-led hikes.
During the summer, they offer a full schedule of programs for families.
For information on their programs, contact The Children's Forest Association, 1824 South Commercenter Circle, San Bernardino, CA 92408;
phone: (909) 884-6634, ext. 3121.

● The Alpine Slide at Magic Mountain

*800 Wildrose Lane, off Highway 18, one-quarter mile west of Big Bear
Lake. (909) 866-4626. Alpine slide: Summer: daily, 10 A.M.–6 P.M.; until
9 P.M. weekends. Fall: weekends, 10 A.M.–6 P.M.; Monday, 11 A.M.–4 P.M.
Winter: weekends, 10 A.M.–dusk; Monday–Friday, 11 A.M.–4 P.M. Spring:
weekends, 10 A.M.–5 P.M. $3 per ride; ages 6 and under ride free with an
adult. Water Slide: Open daily mid-June to mid-September, 10 A.M.–5 P.M.
Day pass, $10; under 6, free. Snow play: Daily, November through Easter,
weather permitting, 10 A.M.–4 P.M. $10 per person; ages 6 and under, free.*
All ages.

The Alpine Slide at Magic Mountain offers families opportunities for
year-round play. On the alpine slide, family members pilot their own
toboggans down a concrete track, controlling their speed with a hand
lever. The slide is reached by chairlift, and there are two tracks, one fast
and one slow. Grandma—or for that matter, Mom—can take it nice and
easy, while kids zoom down the mountain. Younger children can ride
with adults. In winter, there is snow play that includes a rope tow and
sledding down the hill on rubber tubes. In the summer, a water slide is
in operation. There is also a miniature golf course here.

● Moonridge Animal Park

*43285 Moonridge Road at Goldmine Drive, across from Bear Mountain Ski
Resort, Big Bear Lake. Take Moonridge Road from Highway 18/Big Bear
Boulevard until it reaches Bear Mountain. (909) 866-0183. Open daily,
mid-May through October, 10 A.M.–5 P.M. Ages 11 and over, $2; ages 3–10,
$1; under 3, free.* **All ages.**

This small zoo houses animals native to the San Bernardino Mountains. Among them are the endangered wood bison, wolves, mountain
lions, coyotes, foxes, bears, and a bald eagle.

In and Around Palm Springs

● Dinosaur Gardens

5800 Seminole Drive, Cabazon, off the I-10, just before Highway 111, eighteen miles northwest of Palm Springs. (909) 849-8309. Daily, 9 A.M.– dusk. Free. **All ages.**

A giant brontosaurus and a fifty-five-foot-high tyrannosaurus rex looming beside the highway make an amazing sight as you travel along the I-10 just west of Palm Springs. Built by the late designer Claude Bell, the dinosaurs are located next to the Wheel Inn Truck Stop and Cafe. There is a small museum/gift shop inside the brontosaurus, displaying guns, arrowheads, and other Southwestern memorabilia. The cafe serves meals and snacks twenty-four hours a day (phone: 909-849-7012). Even if you don't stop, the sight gives kids something to look for on the boring stretch of freeway.

● Palm Springs Aerial Tramway

From Los Angeles, take I-10 to Highway 111 to Palm Springs city limits and Tramway Road. The tramway's valley station is 3.5 miles from High- way 111. (619) 325-1391. Monday–Friday, 10 A.M.–9:45 P.M. Saturday and Sunday, 8 A.M.–9:45 P.M. Cars depart at least every half hour. The last car up to Mountain Station is at 8 P.M. (During daylight savings time, the last car up to Mountain Station is at 9 P.M. and the last car down the mountain is at 10:45 P.M.) Adults, $16.95 round trip; ages 5–12, $10.95. Free parking. **Ages 3 and up.**

In eighteen minutes, an eighty-passenger car on the Palm Springs Aerial Tramway carries you safely up the side of Mount San Jacinto, from cactus and desert sand to the cool air and evergreen trees of 8,516-foot Mount San Jacinto State Park. The ride up is breathtaking. At times, the car heads directly into the jutting face of the mountain and then rises around it in a sharp uplift. The view of the valley below and the changing terrain is spectacular. (Try to be near the head of the line boarding the tram so you can find your children a place next to the window. You must stand on the tram ride, but there are benches next to the window where kids can stand to see out.)

At the San Jacinto Station are a restaurant, a snack bar, a game room, snow equipment rentals, and observation decks that provide a view of the entire valley, extending to the Salton Sea, forty-five miles away. The top of Mount San Jacinto is a six-mile hike from the tram station. Behind the station is a walkway leading to a recreation area; the walkway is heated in the winter to keep it free of snow. Picnic facilities are available in summer; in winter months there is a play area where toboggans and snow saucers can be rented.

● Palm Springs Desert Museum

101 Museum Drive, Palm Springs. From Palm Canyon Drive in downtown Palm Springs turn west on either Andreas Road or Tahquitz-McCallum Way and go two blocks to the museum. (619) 325-7186. Tuesday–Sunday, 10 A.M.–4 P.M.; open until 8 P.M. on Friday; closed every Monday and during the summer. Adults, $5; seniors, students, and ages 6–17, $3; ages 5 and under, free. Free (except for special exhibits) the first Friday of the month. Free parking. **Ages 6 and up.**

Housed in a beautiful seventy-five-thousand-square-foot, split-level, cantilevered building, the Palm Springs Desert Museum is devoted to art, natural science, and performing arts. The art galleries feature constantly changing exhibitions from collections around the world. The museum gives art classes for local schoolchildren and frequently displays their work. There are also two lovely sunken sculpture gardens and a main-level sculpture court that children might enjoy seeing.

It is the museum's natural science galleries, however, that will impress children most. One particularly appealing exhibit is a long diorama of the desert life by day and by night. It's out in the open and at children's eye level. They can activate the display by pushing a button to see animals such as a roadrunner, a coyote, and a bobcat in their daytime and night-time environments. A button-activated desert wildflower exhibit, Cahuilla Indian dioramas and artifacts, a display of Salton Sea birds, and a self-activated desert slide show also invite exploration.

The museum's staff conducts nature field trips every Friday, from the first Friday in October to the last in May. The trips, which vary in length and subject, leave from the museum's north parking lot at 9 A.M. Call the museum for information.

● Village Green Heritage Center

221 South Palm Canyon Drive, Palm Springs. (619) 323-8297. Wednesday and Sunday, noon–3 P.M.; Thursday, Friday, and Saturday, 10 A.M.–4 P.M. Closed June to mid-October. Adults, 50¢ per home; children, free. **Ages 8 and up.**

The Village Green Heritage Center is a grassy plaza containing Miss Cornelia White's House, the 1893 home of a pioneer Palm Springs woman, and the McCallum Adobe, the first house built by a white settler in Palm Springs. The McCallum Adobe features changing exhibits of local historical artifacts. Displays that should interest children include an antique doll carriage and doll, a spinning wheel, an early typewriter, costumes, and toys from the early 1900s.

Miss Cornelia White's House, built from railroad ties, was the home of a remarkable woman who wore pants and boots long before it was acceptable dress for women and who taught political science, carpentry, and plumbing. The house has been extremely well kept. Inside you'll see an old-fashioned hand-crank telephone (the first phone in Palm Springs); the delightful old kitchen with its antique stove, charcoal iron, and original water pump on the sink; and the bedroom, where the chamber pot is visible under the bed.

● Ruddy's 1930s General Store Museum

221 South Palm Canyon Drive, Palm Springs. (619) 327-2156. October–June: Thursday–Sunday, 10 A.M.–4 P.M. July–September: Saturday and Sunday, 10 A.M.–4 P.M. Ages 12 and over, 50¢; under 12, free. **Ages 6 and up.**

Sharing the Village Green with Miss Cornelia White's House and the McCallum Adobe is an authentic recreation of a 1930s general store. Vintage shelves, counters, and showcases contain rows of original products, from groceries and medicines to clothing and hardware. Household products such as boxes of Lux detergent and tins of Chase & Sanborn coffee sit on oak shelving above a long grain merchandiser filled with beans, flour, and other grain. Patent medicines, long-ago beauty aids, hats, high-topped shoes, and tobacco tins fill other shelves, while vintage advertising signs—such as one for Cleo Cola—cram the walls. Of course, there is a gumball machine. In all, the museum boasts one of the largest and most complete displays of unused antique store products in the country.

● Agua Caliente Cultural Museum

219 South Palm Canyon Drive, Palm Springs. (619) 323-0151. Wednesday–Saturday, 10 A.M.–4 P.M.; Sunday, noon–3 P.M. Summer: Friday and Saturday, 10 A.M.–4 P.M.; Sunday, noon–3 P.M. Free. **Ages 6 and up.**

The Agua Caliente Cultural Museum is the newest resident of the Village Green Historical Plaza. The museum is devoted to the Agua Caliente Band of Cahuilla Indians, the indigenous residents of the Palms Springs area. Exhibits include ancient artifacts, pottery, basketry, photographs, and a diorama of the desert environment of the Cahuilla. Kids should enjoy seeing the recreation of a *ki-sh,* an early Cahuilla dwelling, in the patio garden. The museum sponsors the **Agua Caliente Indian Heritage Festival,** held every year in April. The event features traditional and modern Indian music and dances, storytelling, pottery firing, crafts, food, and more.

● Moorten's Botanical Gardens

1701 South Palm Canyon Drive (two blocks south of East Palm Canyon Drive), Palm Springs. (619) 327-6555. Monday–Saturday, 9 A.M.– 4:30 P.M.; Sunday, 10 A.M.–4 P.M. Adults, $2; ages 7–16, 75¢; under 7, free. **All ages.**

More than two thousand varieties of cactus and other desert plants from every desert in the world are arranged according to region in this botanical garden. Kids will enjoy picking out personalities in the cacti. Some even have names, such as the Bearded Grandfather. Rabbits, chipmunks, and other small animals live on the garden's four acres and can often be seen scurrying through the grounds. There are also displays of rocks, petrified wood, and a real dinosaur's footprint. Kids can climb on the wooden wagons on display, and they'll enjoy watching the live turtles.

● Palm Springs Air Museum

745 North Gene Autry Trail, at the Palm Springs Regional Airport, Palm Springs. Take Gene Autry Trail (Highway 111) south from the I-10 or north from East Palm Canyon Drive. (619) 778-6262. Wednesday– Monday, 10 A.M.–5 P.M. Ages 13–65, $7.50; over 65, $5.95; ages 6–12, $3.50; under 6, free. **Ages 6 and up.**

The new Palm Springs Air Museum at the Palm Springs Airport features a large collection of propeller-driven World War II fighters, bombers, and trainers in flying condition. You can climb up and look in the cockpits of such legendary planes as a Grumman Wildcat, Hellcat and Tigercat, a Curtis Warhawk, a Douglas Invader, and a Boeing Flying Fortress. You can see the planes in action during fly-overs and aviation celebrations on Memorial Day, Veterans Day, Armed Forces Day, Pearl Harbor Day, V-E Day, V-J Day, and other times. Call the museum for schedules and details. Other museum exhibits include photographs and World War II aircraft memorabilia.

● Oasis Waterpark

1500 Gene Autry Trail, between Ramon Road and Highway 111; six miles south of the I-10, Palm Springs. (619) 325-7873. Mid-March to early September, open daily, at least 11 A.M. to 5:30 P.M. Early September through October, open weekends, at least 11 A.M. to 5:30 P.M. Ages 12 and over, $17.95; children 40 to 60 inches, $11.50; under 4 years, free. **Ages 3 and up.**

This twenty-one-acre water park in the desert offers thirteen slides of various configurations and speeds. There is a very large wave pool with waves of up to four feet for inland surfing. For a more relaxing time, you can float in a slow-moving inner tube along a six-hundred-foot loop.

A play area for young children, called Creature Fantasy, features oversize aquatic creatures to climb, little water slides, and a shallow pool. Lifeguards are on duty, but plan to keep a close eye on young children. Body boards and lockers are available to rent. No food or drink may be brought into the park.

● Palm Springs Bicycle Trails
Ages 8 and up.

Palm Springs has more than thirty-five miles of bicycle trails, clearly marked by blue and white signs. A free bike trails map is available at the Leisure Center in the Sunrise Park complex (bounded by Sunrise Way, Ramon Road, Baristo Road, and Pavilion Way; phone: 619-323-8272). Bike rentals are available at Palm Springs Cyclery, 611 South Palm Canyon Road (phone: 619-325-9319), and at most other Palm Springs bicycle shops.

● Horseback Riding/Smoke Tree Stables
2500 Toledo Avenue, Palm Springs. (619) 327-1372. Phone for hours and prices. **Ages 8 and up.**

Smoke Tree Stables rents horse to riders of all abilities. Miles of bridle trails provide adult riders and kids with wonderful views of the desert and plenty of fun. Guides are available and overnight pack trips can be arranged.

● Palm Springs Swim Center/Sunrise Park
Sunrise Park: Bounded by Sunrise Way, Ramon Road, Baristo Road, and Pavilion Way, Palm Springs. Open daily. Free. Swim Center: Located in Sunrise Park. (619) 323-8278. Daily, 11 A.M.–5 P.M. Adults, $3; ages 12 and under, $2. Season passes are available. **All ages.**

The Palm Springs Swim Center features a fifty-meter, Olympic-size public swimming pool with two one-meter diving boards and one three-meter board. There is a separate swimming section for children, as well as spacious lawns and a sun deck. Swimming instruction for children and adults is also given.

The Swim Center is located in Sunrise Park, a lushly landscaped thirty-eight-acre park complex that includes a large playground, the main branch of the Palm Springs public library, the Palm Springs Parks and Recreation headquarters, the Palm Springs Angels Baseball Stadium and practice field, as well as picnic facilities. Organized activities for children, summer concerts and family film series, and Fourth of July fireworks are also held in the park. (Phone the Palm Springs Parks, Recreation, and Library Department at 619-323-8272 for the schedule.)

● Indian Canyons

Five miles south of Palm Springs. From Palm Springs, take the toll road at the end of South Palm Canyon Drive. (619) 325-5673. Daily, 8 A.M.– 6 P.M. Adults, $5; ages 6–12, $1. **Ages 6 and up.**

The Native American residents of the Palm Springs area still own and control large sections of land here. The Agua Caliente Indian Reservation comprises thirty-two thousand acres in and around Palm Springs. The tribal council has reserved a portion of the reservation south of Palm Springs, including three magnificent canyons, for visitors to see. **Andreas Canyon** offers many unusual rock formations, a hiking trail that follows a stream, and picnic facilities. **Palm Canyon** stretches for fifteen miles and contains more than three thousand Washington palm trees, some as old as two thousand years; you can see the trees by taking a steep walk into the valley. **Murray Canyon** is less accessible than the other two, but it contains spectacular rock formations. Bring water with you.

● Coachella Valley Preserve

Located ten miles east of Palm Springs near Thousand Palms. Take Ramon Road over the I-10; turn left on Thousand Palms Canyon Road, and watch for signs. (619) 343-1234. Daily, sunrise to sunset. Free, but donations accepted. **All ages.**

Thirteen thousand acres of clear springs, sand dunes, bluffs, mesas, palm oases, and rare animals, including the fringe-toed lizard, are preserved in this sanctuary managed by the California Nature Conservancy. The preserve includes a visitors center, picnic area, and hiking trails.

● Children's Museum of the Desert

Temporary: Palm Desert Town Center, Highway 111 between Monterey and Palm Desert Town Way. Permanent (under construction): Gerald Ford Drive, off Bob Hope Drive, Rancho Mirage. (619) 346-2900. Phone for hours and prices. **Ages 2–12.**

At press time, ground was being broken for a new seven-thousand-square-foot, four-million-dollar building in Rancho Mirage to house the Children's Museum of the Desert. The museum hopes to be on the cutting edge of a new generation of children's museums. The goal is to offer kids activities that will help them adapt to an ever-faster changing world. One planned area, the Attic, is blueprinted to contain suitcases and trunks that—in addition to offering the usual dress-up clothes—will contain videos and multimedia activities on how life used to be in the past and may be in the future. Another planned area, Make It/Take It Apart, will offer safety-proofed appliances that kids can take apart and put back together. Other plans call for a rock-climbing wall and a rope maze. The Children's Museum of the Desert will remain open in its temporary facility until the new museum is complete.

● Living Desert Reserve

47-900 Portolo Avenue, Palm Desert. From I-10, take the Thousand Palms–Ramon Road exit and follow the signs to Palm Desert, traveling south on Bob Hope Drive to Highway 111 and east to the reserve. (619) 346-5694. Open daily, October–June: 9 A.M.–5 P.M. September and July: daily, 8 A.M.–noon. Closed August. Adults, $7.50; seniors, $6.50; ages 3–15,$3.50; 2 and under, free. **All ages.**

One thousand acres of beautiful California desert are set aside and protected from development in the Living Desert Reserve. The reserve is home to a wide variety of desert plants and animals. You'll see animals such as rabbits, roadrunners, and hummingbirds roaming freely on the reserve. Other animals from desert habitats around the world, including bighorn sheep, Arabian oryx, coyotes, zebras, gazelles, meerkats, and great horned owls, reside in naturalistic habitats. You enter one of the newest exhibits, Eagle Canyon, through an aviary housing golden eagles to reach a realistically simulated desert canyon populated with more than thirty animal species, including mountain lions, bobcats, Mexican wolves, and javelina. Acres of botanical gardens throughout the reserve recreate different deserts of the world.

The Pearl McManus Center, through which you enter the reserve, has exhibits of small live animals in natural habitats. Especially interesting is the "Desert at Night" exhibit, a dark room where you can watch the nighttime activity of desert animals. A **Discovery Center** offers kids (accompanied by an adult) hands-on exhibits and activities, such as a chance to construct a giant cactus or make animal footprints in sand. The Discovery Center is open weekends and school holidays, 10 A.M. to 4 P.M.

The reserve has an excellent trail system with more than six miles of self-guided trails, permitting you to choose from walks of varied length. There is a shaded picnic area, and there are water fountains and shaded areas throughout the grounds. The reserve also has a cafe.

● Lake Cahuilla

Located south of Indio, at the intersection of Jefferson and Fifty-eighth streets, nine miles south of Highway 111. From Palm Springs, take Highway 111 southeast to Jefferson Street outside of Indio and turn south. (619) 564-4712. Friday–Monday, 6 A.M.–7 P.M. Picnics/swimming: $4 per vehicle (add 50¢ per person after the fourth person). Fishing: Adults, $5; ages 10–17, $3.50; under 10, free. **All ages.**

In the brilliant desert sun, Lake Cahuilla shimmers a cool, inviting turquoise. Surrounded by date trees, this huge (135-acre surface) lake is operated by Riverside County Parks. There is swimming in the lake from 11 A.M. to 6 P.M. and a special play area for children on the beach. Striped bass, channel catfish, and (in winter) rainbow trout can be caught in the fishing areas of the lake (license required). Picnic tables and barbecues are available, and there are grassy, shaded areas around the lake. There are hiking trails for those who want to explore the desert. Family campsites and RV hookups are available. (Phone 800-234-PARK for reservations.)

● Shields Date Gardens

80-225 Highway 111, Indio. (619) 347-0996. Daily, 8 A.M.–6 P.M. Summer: daily, 9 A.M.–5 P.M. Free. **All ages.**

The Coachella Valley is known as the date capital of the world. Many varieties of dates are grown here, packaged, and shipped all over the world. You can take a self-guided tour of the Shields Date Gardens to see the cultivation process. Inside their sales building are booths and a large, old-fashioned counter where you can sample a date shake or some of their black date ice cream. In an auditorium, they show a continuous, free, but dated (no pun intended) slide show on the romance and sex life of the date.

● Jensen's Date and Citrus Gardens

80-653 Highway 111, Indio. (619) 347-3897. Daily, 9 A.M.–5 P.M. Free. **All ages.**

From the highway, Jensen's pink-walled gardens resemble the Garden of Allah. The gift shop is situated in a lovely garden with roses and fruit trees. It's a nice stop for children because it is an opportunity to see a variety of fruit-laden trees up close. Big Grapefruits hang from one, blood oranges from another. There are date trees, of course, with the ladders used for gathering the fruit. The trees are all labeled, and the date-growing process is explained. Inside the gift shop you can enjoy date shakes or fresh citrus juice.

● El Dorado Polo Club

50-950 Madison Street, Indio. (619) 342-2223. Games played November through April: Tuesday–Sunday (telephone for schedule). Practice matches are free. Tournament matches are $6 per person. **Ages 6 and up.**

Polo is played on ten fields at this large club, and visitors are welcome. Practice matches, generally held during the week, are free. On weekends, when top players often compete in tournament matches, there is usually an admission charge. (Telephone the club for the schedule.)

You are free to picnic, either on the grass under the trees or at the tailgate of your car as you watch the games.

● Cabot's Old Indian Pueblo and Museum

67-616 East Desert View Avenue, Desert Hot Springs. Desert Hot Springs is just north of Palm Springs. Take Palm Drive north to Desert View Avenue and turn east. (619) 329-7610. Wednesday–Sunday, 10 A.M.–3 P.M. Closed July and August. Adults, $2.50; seniors, $2; ages 6–16, $1; under 6, free. **Ages 6 and up.**

At the age of sixty, Cabot Yerxa began building this thirty-five room Hopi-style pueblo by hand, using material he found in the desert. When he died twenty years later in 1965, he was still building. Yerxa was an unusual man who sold tobacco in Alaska during the gold rush, traveled widely, lived with the Native Americans of the Southwest, and came to live in the desert. His idea to build a pueblo for his home came from his affection for the Hopi Indians. One of the reasons for building it was to make the Hopis who visited him feel at home.

The pueblo, built out of the side of the mountain, is similar to that of the Hopis, except Yerxa did not use ladders as the Indians did. Instead he built narrow, twisting staircases that go up from room to room. The structure is four stories high and contains 150 windows and sixty-five doors. The pueblo has been preserved and kept open to the public; you can see it on a guided tour.

You'll go through Yerxa's kitchen with its water pump and wash basin, the Hopi prayer room, and the living room with its dirt floor. You can climb the narrow stairs to his wife's quarters on the next floor. Some of the pueblo's rooms are used as a museum where you will see Native American headdresses, Geronimo's wristband, Kit Carson's money belt, Buffalo Bill's chair, and a 1914 Troy motorcycle. Many other things are also displayed, including tools and animals skins used by the Alaskan Eskimos. (Yerxa lived with the Eskimos in Alaska. Their treatment of his frostbitten hands left him with a deep affection for the Eskimo people.) Other displays include desert animal traps, pack saddles, and pictures taken during the gold rush.

● Whitewater Trout Farm

Whitewater Canyon Road, Whitewater. Take the Whitewater turnoff from I-10 northwest of Palm Springs. (619) 325-5570. Wednesday–Sunday, 10 A.M.–5 P.M. 50¢ per person aged 2 and over. $2.50 for pole and bait. **Ages 3 and up.**

You can catch your own dinner in this pleasant, tree-shaded picnic area. The water is packed with trout, so you are virtually assured of catching one. Cleaned and packaged, the trout cost $2.72 a pound. There are barbecue areas where you can grill your fish, and running water is usually available.

● Morongo Wildlife Reserve

Morongo Valley. Take I-10 to Highway 62. Turn right on East Drive from Highway 62 in the town of Morongo Valley. (619) 363-7190. Daily, 7:30 A.M. to sunset. Free, but donations appreciated. **All ages.**

A well-known wildlife sanctuary, Morongo is home for more than 200 hundred species of birds and 150 varieties of plant life. Kept in its natural state so as not to disturb the wildlife inhabitants, the preserve is an ideal spot for nature study. There is a good system of hiking trails ranging from an easy one-third-of-a-mile trail with wheelchair access to a strenuous five-mile trail running the length of the canyon bottom. No dogs are permitted.

● Hi-Desert Nature Museum

57116 Twentynine Palms Highway, Yucca Valley. Turn north on Dumosa Street from Route 62 in the city of Yucca Valley. The museum is located in the Community Center Complex just off Route 62. (619) 369-7212. Tuesday–Sunday, 10 A.M.–5 P.M. Free. **Ages 6 and up.**

This small, well-kept museum has a fine collection of nature displays. Among them are an extensive collection of butterflies from around the world, live reptiles and small desert animals, birds' nests and eggs, fossils, petrified wood, a fascinating display of insects, and an unusual collection of pine cones. There is also a fluorescent display of rocks and minerals. In addition to the regular exhibits, the museum has changing exhibits, such as a wildflower display in the spring. Everything is well lit and attractively displayed. Information about nearby nature trails can also be obtained from the museum.

● Joshua Tree National Monument

The north entrances to the monument are off Highway 62 (take the I-10 east from Los Angeles to Highway 62) at the towns of Joshua Tree and Twentynine Palms. The south, or Cottonwood Springs, entrance is twenty-five miles east of Indio on I-10. There are visitor centers at the Cottonwood Springs and Twentynine Palms entrances. (619) 367-7511. Open daily all year. Monument headquarters, located near Twentynine Palms, is open daily, 8 A.M.–5 P.M. The Cottonwood Springs visitors center is open daily, 9 A.M.–4 P.M. (may be closed at lunchtime). Free. **All ages.**

Two great deserts—the low Colorado and the high Mojave—come together at the dramatically beautiful 870-plus-acre Joshua Tree National

Monument. If there has been enough rain, spring is the best time to visit, because then the desert blooms with wildflowers. The western half of the monument is dominated by Joshua trees—actually not trees at all, but giant desert lilies. With their thick, matted trunks, and limbs stuck together at all sorts of odd, twisted angles, the trees (named by pioneer Mormons who thought they resembled Joshua raising his arms to heaven) have been known to grow as tall as forty feet.

Some areas of particular interest in the monument are the Fortynine Palms Oasis, a beautiful California fan palm oasis reached by a 1.5-mile hiking trail; Hidden Valley, whose picnic facilities and trail system lie in a stunning area of massive boulders; the Geology Road Tour, an eighteen-mile nature tour that you take in your car through some of the monument's most fascinating terrain; and Cottonwood Springs, a man-made palm oasis noted for its bird life and easily accessible by road.

The visitors center in Oasis of Mara (Twentynine Palms) and Cottonwood Springs have maps and other information. There is also a small museum at the Twentynine Palms visitors center. If your visit to the monument is during warm weather, be sure to carry plenty of drinking water for your family.

● General Patton Memorial Museum

Chiriaco Summit. Located 30 miles east of Indio via the I-10. Take the Chiriaco exit. (619) 227-3483. Daily, 9 A.M.–5 P.M. Adults, $4; seniors, $3.50; children under 12, free. **Ages 6 and up.**

If you are traveling on the I-10 between Indio and Blythe, the General Patton Memorial Museum makes an interesting stop. The museum is at the entrance to the former Camp Young, which was established during World War II to train troops for desert combat in North Africa. Outside the museum are some equipment and vehicles, including a Patton Tank. Inside are military memorabilia and displays on the career of General Patton. Among the exhibits are a silk map of France—the maps were carried by paratroopers dropping into Normandy on D day; Civil War, World War I and II uniforms; and a vintage jukebox.

Barstow, Victorville, and Vicinity

● California Desert Information Center

831 Barstow Road, Barstow. Take the Central Barstow exit from I-15 and go north one block. (619) 256-8313. Daily, 9 A.M.–5 P.M. Free. **Ages 6 and up.**

Barstow lies in the heart of the fascinating high desert. A former mining center and frontier town, Barstow is a booming city today. It is also a good base for exploring the surrounding Mojave Desert. Depending on your family's interests, you can explore caverns, drive or hike into lovely canyons, rock hunt, see the remains of ancient volcanic activity, visit a restored ghost town, and much more.

Your first stop in the area should be the California Desert Information Center, operated by the Bureau of Land Management. The center is staffed by friendly personnel trained to assist you in planning your explorations. They supplement their information with free maps, brochures, and current weather information.

The Desert Information Center is also worth visiting for its displays. Kids should enjoy the Desert IQ display where they can test their knowledge of the desert by pushing buttons that light up explanations of correct and incorrect answers. Other displays inform about desert hazards and where desert animals are located during the day and at night. A display of plant medicines includes a touch table. Outside the center is a short nature trail with a pond where you might catch sight of a desert tortoise.

● Mojave River Valley Museum

270 East Virginia Way (corner of Barstow Road), Barstow. (619) 256-5452. Daily, 11 A.M.–4 P.M. Free, but donations appreciated. **Ages 6 and up.**

This small, two-room museum houses rock and mineral displays, including phosphorous rocks, Native American artifacts such as arrowheads, and local wildlife displays, including a stuffed coyote and wildcats. There are also local history displays, such as the organ from the original Calico saloon. A corner area features displays kids can touch. A park across the street has grassy areas, picnic tables, and playground equipment.

● Calico Ghost Town

Located ten miles northeast of Barstow via I-15, then four miles north on Ghost Town Road. (619) 254-2122. Daily, 8 A.M. to dusk. Closed Christmas. Adults, $5; ages 6–15, $2. **Ages 3 and up.**

Calico Ghost Town is a restored 1880s silver-mining boomtown located beside the ore-filled Calico Mountains. Founded in 1881 as a result of one of the West's richest silver strikes, the town enjoyed a colorful heyday and then declined rapidly when the price of sliver dropped dramatically at the turn of the century. Walter Knott, the founder of Knott's Berry Farm, worked in the camp as a youth. Years later he decided to restore the town as accurately as possible. The area was eventually deeded to San Bernardino County, which now operates it as a regional park.

Many of the buildings you will see in the town are original; you'll notice that they were built with a crude form of cement, using the local dirt, which gives the buildings a reddish hue. There is a museum with exhibits such as a blacksmith's shop and an old barber shop that doubled as a dentist's office, complete with appropriate-looking dummies. The rails around the exhibits are very low, so it is easy for children to get a close look.

Everyone except claustrophobics will enjoy a walking tour of the Maggie Mine, which includes an opportunity to look deep into the shaft. Children will also enjoy a ride on the Calico-Odessa Railroad and a visit to the Mystery Shack, which seems to defy the laws of gravity. The town's old schoolhouse has an ancient teeter-totter and a swing kids can use. The town also includes a shooting gallery, a theater, shops, and places to eat. Camping is available near the town in shaded canyons; telephone for reservations.

One of the best times to visit is during one of the old-time celebrations: Calico Hullabaloo, held on Palm Sunday weekend; Calico Spring Festival, held on Mother's Day weekend; or Calico Days, on Columbus Day weekend. Visitors come dressed in Old West costumes, and there is music and a lot of family fun.

● **Rainbow Basin**

Eight miles north of Barstow. From the Desert Information Center, take Barstow Road north to Main Street. Go left on Main and turn right on First Street. Take First Street across two bridges and turn left on Fort Irwin Road. Go six miles north to Fossil Bed Road. Turn left on this unpaved road and follow the signs to Rainbow Basin Loop Road. Rainbow Basin Loop Road is narrow and impassable for vehicles larger than campers. Open daily. Free.
Ages 10 and up.

Rainbow Basin was formed some ten to thirty million years ago on lake beds now long gone. Over the years, erosion of the multicolored sedimentary layers has produced a panorama of vividly colored and wildly shaped rock formations. The scenery on the four-mile drive around the Rainbow Basin Loop Road is dazzling and rather unlike anything else. The richly colored rocks tower in wondrous formations over the narrowest of dirt roads, giving you the feeling you are not quite on this earth.

● **Calico Early Man Archaeological Site**

Fifteen miles northeast of Barstow via I-15. From the Minneola Road exit, follow the signs north about 2.5 miles along graded dirt roads to the site. (619) 255-8760 (California Desert Information Center). Wednesday, noon– 4:30 P.M.; Thursday–Sunday, 9:30 A.M.–4 P.M. Free. **Ages 10 and up.**

In 1942 an amateur archaeologist recognized what he thought were prehistoric stone tools here. An excavation of the site began in 1964 under the leadership of famed archaeologist Dr. Louis Leakey. Since then more than twelve thousand stone tools dating back about two hundred thousand years have been unearthed. (Apparently this area was once a sort of stone-tool factory; very early nomadic hunters stopped here to fashion tools from the silica rocks.)

You can take a guided or self-guided tour of the site to see what a real archaeological dig looks like. A very small museum displays some of the artifacts found. For most families, a self-guided look around is sufficient. It is very hot out here, and there are limited facilities.

● Roy Rogers–Dale Evans Museum

Seneca Road and Civic Drive, Victorville, off I-15. Exit I-15 at Roy Rogers Drive. (619) 243-4547. Daily, 9 A.M.–5 P.M. Adults, $5; seniors and ages 13–16, $4; ages 6–12, $3; under 6, free. **Ages 6 and up.**

Here's old Trigger, the smartest horse in the movies, stuffed and on display along with Bullet the dog, the jeep Nelly, and the other mementos of former cowboy stars Roy Rogers and Dale Evans. While adults may find the museum somewhat peculiar (especially its displays of the sort of family relics most people keep in a box in the garage—if at all), kids seem to have a good time in the fort-like building. Kids will probably enjoy seeing Rogers's collections of guns, animal trophies, and old cars. There is also a considerable selection of photographs from the couple's movies and television shows, as well as a lot of costumes.

● Mojave Narrows Regional Park

Two miles south of Victorville via I-15. From I-15, take Bear Valley cutoff east to Ridge Crest Road and go north to the park. (619) 245-2226. Wednesday–Monday, 7:30 A.M. to dusk. Closed Tuesday. Day use: weekdays, $4 per car; weekends, $5 per car. **All ages.**

There is no better description of this park than the one the San Bernardino County Regional Parks people give: It's Huck Finn country. Lush and pastoral, this is a wonderful park with creeks, ponds, broad meadows, cottonwood patches, willow thickets, a marsh, and two lakes. The larger lake, Horseshoe Lake, offers some of the finest fishing in the area. (Fishing licenses and bait are available at the boathouse and entrance station.) Pedal boats can be rented for a ride on the lake.

There are miles of hiking and horseback-riding trails, a wildlife area, a nature trail, and a specially designed paved nature trail for the disabled. Picnic facilities with barbecue grills are available. The park is bordered by pasture land, so you will even see cows grazing, a silo, and bales of hay. Overnight camping is available in an eighty-seven-unit campground complete with hot showers, adjacent to Horseshoe Lake. The park is the site of the **Huck Finn Jubilee,** held every year on Father's Day weekend. Events include raft-building contests, fence painting, clog dancing, blue-grass music, and much more.

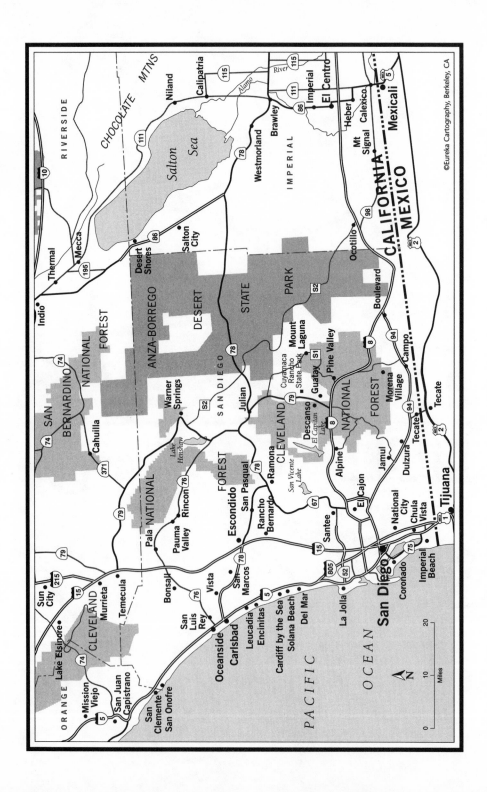

©Eureka Cartography, Berkeley, CA

San Diego County

CALIFORNIA HISTORY BEGINS in San Diego. The first Europeans to discover California landed at Point Loma in 1546, and the Spanish made their first West Coast settlement at Mission San Diego de Alcala, on Presidio Hill. The chain of missions that the Spanish used to settle California led north from San Diego.

Today, San Diego is California's second-largest city. It is a major commercial center and seaport, the home of the U.S. Navy's largest fleet, and, many believe, the best vacation destination in Southern California.

There is a belief that it never rains in Southern California. Well, it may rain in *some* places in Southern California, but it never rains in San Diego—or so it seems. The area is blessed with one of the world's most equable climates; temperatures average seventy degrees and humidity is low year-round. On top of its weather, San Diego boasts a stunning natural beauty with lush vegetation, miles of shoreline, and one of the world's prettiest natural harbors. San Diego's Spanish heritage and close proximity to Mexico result in a Spanish-flavored lifestyle that adds to the area's charm.

Families will find a variety of memorable experiences here, many of them free. San Diego's history is preserved in its Old Town section, in its mission, and on Presidio Hill. The city boasts one of the world's finest zoos, one of the country's most interesting city parks, and one of the largest oceanariums in the world. There are a number of fine museums here, too, and countless water activities.

But there is far more to San Diego County than just the city of San Diego. Nearly the size of Connecticut, San Diego County stretches from the Pacific to include foothills and mountain ranges, a national forest, and a great desert. A wild-animal park, a giant telescope, and a charming old mining town are just a few of the places that can be reached in a short jaunt or an all-day tour up the coast or into the backcountry.

The excellent San Diego Convention and Visitors Bureau offers all sorts of information and assistance to visitors. The Visitor Information Center is located in the Horton Plaza shopping center at First Aveune and F Street in downtown San Diego (phone: 619-236-1212). The Mission Bay Visitors Information Center (phone: 619-276-8200) off I-5 at the end of the Claremont-Mission Bay off-ramp provides a similar service.

Downtown San Diego

● Balboa Park

Entrances at Sixth Avenue and Laurel Street and along Park Boulevard, San Diego. From I-5, take Exit 163. General parking is available in several lots off Park Boulevard. (619) 239-0512. Open daily. Free. **All ages.**

In the heart of San Diego is one of the country's prettiest and most interesting city parks. In addition to lovely green spaces, this 1,158-acre park holds most of the city's major museums, a Shakespearean and two other theaters, an artist's colony, sports facilities, the world's largest outdoor organ, and one of the world's best zoos. It is impossible to see all of this park in a day. If you can spend only one day here, see the zoo and the children's zoo first. If you have any energy left after that, you might visit either the Natural History Museum or the Reuben H. Fleet Space Theater and Science Center.

The park's information center, located in the House of Hospitality on El Prado, has maps and information on the park. You can also purchase a discount pass to all the park museums, good for one week, at the information center. A free tram with eleven stops throughout the park operates everyday from 10 A.M. to 4 P.M. During the summer, its hours are 9:30 A.M. to 5:30 P.M.

Two playgrounds are located in the park. One is at the north end of Balboa Drive; the other is at the Pepper Grove Picnic Area. Younger children will also enjoy the **miniature train** and the **merry-go-round,** both located beside the zoo parking lot. The train operates from 11 A.M. to 4:30 P.M. on weekends and school vacations. The carousel operates 11 A.M. to 5:30 P.M. summers, weekends, and school holidays.

On Sundays, mid-March through October, from 2 to 3 p.M., the House of Pacific Relations sponsors free lawn programs of ethnic music and dance. Free concerts featuring the historic 4,445-pipe Spreckels organ are presented Sundays rain or shine from 2 to 3 P.M.

Tours of the Old Globe Theater take place most Saturdays and Sundays at 11 A.M.; group tours are by reservation (telephone 619-231-1941). Docent tours are available at most of the museums by request.

Balboa Park also offers an exciting variety of summer classes for children. Special programs are offered at the Museum of Man, the Aerospace Museum, the Natural History Museum, the Reuben H. Fleet Center, the Museum of Art, the Old Globe Theater, and the zoo. Contact the park or the individual institutions for more information.

The park has a number of restaurants, cafes, and concession stands. And, of course, you can always bring a picnic.

● San Diego Zoo

Balboa Park, off Park Boulevard. (619) 234-3153. Open daily at 9 A.M.; closing times vary by season. Adults, $15; ages 3–11, $6; under 3, free. Various combination ticket packages are also available. **All ages.**

One of the world's largest collections of wild animals resides at the San Diego Zoo in a hundred-acre tropical garden. Instead of bars and cages separating animals from visitors, most of the zoo's four thousand animals roam freely behind moats and low walls in habitats that resemble their homes in the wild. In addition to the popular favorites—lions, tigers, elephants, and the like—the zoo is home to many rare and exotic species, including koalas, long-billed kiwis, pygmy chimps, New Guinea tree crocodiles, and rare Sichuan takins. A new exhibit, the Polar Bear Plunge, features underwater viewing of the bears as they dive, wade, swim, and fish in a chilled 125,000-gallon pool. A similar exhibit, "Hippo Beach," allows visitors to observe hippopotamuses above and below the water.

Above Hippo Beach is a replica of an African rain forest housing a pygmy chimpanzee habitat. The nearby Gorilla Tropics is a two-and-a-half-acre simulation of an African rain forest, complete with four aviaries of African birds, six gorillas, thousands of African plants, and a special sound system recorded in the real African rain forest. Another attraction, Tiger River, contains more than a hundred animals—including tigers, crocodiles, and tropical birds—in an environment that simulates a tropical rain forest.

A highlight of the San Diego Zoo is its **Children's Zoo.** Everything in the zoo, including drinking fountains and benches, is scaled to the size of a four-year-old. In addition to the exhibits, which are all at a young child's eye level, is a paddock where kids can pet baby sheep, goats, deer, and other gentle animals. There are two baby animal nurseries.

A guided forty-minute bus tour covers most of the zoo. An aerial tramway called the Skyfari gives an exciting overhead view and is also a shortcut from the front of the zoo to its outer exhibits. Cameras, strollers, and wheelchairs are available to rent. The zoo also has free animal shows, several restaurants, a gift shop, snack bars, and shaded picnic areas. It is open evenings during the summer.

● San Diego Museum of Man

1350 El Prado (west end of El Prado), Balboa Park. (619) 239-2001. Daily, 10 A.M.–4:30 P.M. Closed Thanksgiving, Christmas, and New Year's Day. Adults, $4; ages 13–18, $2; ages 6–12, $1; under 6, free. Free on the third Tuesday of the month. **Ages 6 and up.**

The California Building in Balboa Park, designed to look like the Cathedral of Mexico in Mexico City, houses a fine anthropology museum. The emphasis is on the cultures of the western Americas, particularly Mexico and the Native Americans of the Southwest. The changing exhibits downstairs often include demonstrations such as a tortilla making or weaving. The permanent exhibits upstairs include life-size models of prehistoric humans in various stages of evolution, ancient Egyptian mummies, and artifacts of the Kumeyaay, San Diego's original residents. Also upstairs is the excellent Life Cycles and Ceremonies exhibit, examining the biological and cultural elements of the human life cycle, including reproduction and birth. The exhibit includes life-size models of babies in the womb, as well as a hands-on high-tech lesson in biology and reproduction.

● San Diego Museum of Art

1450 El Prado, Balboa Park. (619) 232-7931. Tuesday–Sunday, 10 A.M.–4:30 P.M. Adults, $7; seniors, $5; ages 6–17, $2; under 6, free. Permanent exhibit free on the third Tuesday of the month. **Ages 6 and up.**

The San Diego Museum of Art offers parents and teachers an excellent way to introduce children to the pleasures of looking at art. The museum is home to the nation's most advanced museum computer system, the Interactive Multimedia Art Gallery Explorer (IMAGE), an interactive computer catalog of more than three hundred of the most significant artworks from the museum collection. In the IMAGE Gallery, located on the first floor, visitors can sit in front of a high-resolution computer screen and make their own personalized tour of the museum. A child interested in dogs, for example, could call up museum artworks featuring dogs and print out a map to locate them. Or, you and your children can come here after your tour of the museum to learn more about the paintings or artists who interested you.

The museum has a fine collection of European and American masterworks, as well as Asian art. Kids may particularly enjoy seeing the swords and sixteenth-century armor in the Japanese art gallery. The museum is stroller and wheelchair accessible.

Outside the museum is a sculpture garden and cafe. The **Sculpture Garden Cafe** (619-696-1990) serves lunch from 11 A.M. to 2 P.M. and during the Old Globe season, dinner from 5–8 P.M. The fare is salads, sandwiches, and California cuisine–type entrees. For more of a kid's lunch, there's a food cart selling hot dogs and other items in front of the cafe.

● Botanical Building

Balboa Park. (Behind and to the right of the Museum of Art.) Friday– Wednesday, 10 A.M.–4 P.M. Free. **All ages.**

This enormous lath building houses a vast array of tropical and sub-tropical plants, fern, and flowers. The plants are all labeled, and the building is very pleasant to wander through. A lily pond is outside, and on weekends you will usually find musicians, magicians, and other entertainers performing beside the pond.

● Timken Museum of Art

1500 El Prado, Balboa Park. (619) 239-5548. Tuesday–Saturday, 10 A.M.–4:30 P.M.; Sunday, 1:30–4:30 P.M. Closed Mondays, holidays, and the month of September. Free. **Ages 10 and up.**

The small Timken Museum, next door to the San Diego Museum of Art, contains works by European masters, including Rembrandt, Rubens, and Cezanne, eighteenth- and nineteenth-century American paintings, and a collection of Russian icons—beautiful and elaborate altar screens.

● Mingei International Museum of World Folk Art

House of Charm, across from the Museum of Art, Balboa Park. (619) 239- 0003. Tuesday–Saturday, 11 A.M.–5 P.M.; Sunday, 2–5 P.M. Adults, $5; ages 6–17, $2; under 6, free. **Ages 8 and up.**

Mingei combines the Japanese words for people (*min*) and art (*gei*) to mean arts of the people. Formerly tucked away in the corner of a shopping center, this museum of international folk art now has a new, much larger home in Balboa Park. Children's interest in the museum will, of course, vary with the exhibits. Past exhibits with family-wide appeal have included dolls and folk toys of the world, Dentzel carousel pieces, wearable folk art, dance costumes from Ecuador, Mexican folk art, the horse in folk art, and art relating to American expressions of liberty.

● Museum of San Diego History

1649 El Prado, in Casa de Balboa, Balboa Park. (619) 232-6203. Wednesday–Sunday, 10 A.M.–4:30 P.M. Adults, $4; seniors, $3; ages 5–12,

$1.50. Open and free on the second Tuesday of the month. **Ages 8 and up.**

The Museum of San Diego History is devoted to bringing the city's history to life—from its incorporation in 1850 to the present. The changing exhibits use photographs, videos, costumes, and artifacts to trace an aspect of the city's history, such as San Diego in World War II or changing swimsuit fashions. In the foyer is a Concord Stage that transported mail and passengers between San Diego and El Cajon from 1866 to 1910.

● Museum of Photographic Arts

1649 El Prado, in Casa de Balboa, Balboa Park. (619) 239-5262. Daily, 10 A.M.–5 P.M. Adults, $3.50; under 12, free. Free on the second Tuesday of the month. **Ages 10 and up.**

The Museum of Photographic Arts is one of a small number of museums in the country that is devoted exclusively to photography. The museum features changing exhibits of the work of important artists such as Ansel Adams, Henri Cartier-Bresson, and Alfred Stieglitz. The museum will appeal primarily to older children and adults, although it is not difficult to visit here with small children. Check to see if there is a family activity sheet for the exhibit you are seeing.

● San Diego Model Railroad Museum

1649 El Prado, in Casa de Balboa, Balboa Park. (619) 696-0199. Tuesday–Friday, 11 A.M.–4 P.M.; Saturday and Sunday, 11 A.M.–5 P.M. Adults, $3; under 15, free. **All ages.**

Working scale models of historic California train routes are on display in this museum founded by three San Diego model-railroad clubs. All the routes are authentically landscaped. The San Diego and Arizona Eastern route, for example, includes a model of downtown San Diego and a ride over a wooden trestle spanning the steep Carriso Gorge. A toy-train gallery features hands-on buttons, interactive throttles, and enhanced viewing for children. Elsewhere, small children will have to be lifted up to see some of the trains. Work on the exhibits is ongoing.

● San Diego Hall of Champions

1649 El Prado, in Casa de Balboa, Balboa Park. (619) 234-2544. Daily, 10 A.M.–4:30 P.M. Adults, $3; seniors, $2; ages 6–17, $1; under 6, free. Free on the second Tuesday of every month. **Ages 8 and up.**

The San Diego Hall of Champions honors San Diego's outstanding athletes, including Ted Williams, Bill Walton, Archie Moore, Florence Chadwick, and Marcus Allen. All the major sports are covered, even motorcycle racing and surfing. Exhibits include photographs, equipment, uniforms, computerized team records, and video displays. A bass fishing exhibit features live bass. Continuous, free sports films are shown in a small theater.

● Natural History Museum

Corner of El Prado and Village Place, opposite the fountain, Balboa Park. (619) 232-3821. Daily, 9:30 A.M.–4:30 P.M. Half-price and extended hours on Thursday, 4:30–6:30 P.M. Adults, $6; ages 6–17, $3; under 6, free. Permanent collection free the first Tuesday of every month. **All ages.**

A favorite of kids, the San Diego Natural History Museum displays permanent exhibits on the animal, vegetable, and mineral life of our planet, with an emphasis on the southwestern United States and Mexico. The museum's traveling shows, often featuring robotics and hands-on displays, are usually the big draw.

Among the highlights of the permanent collection are a skeleton model of an *Allosaurus fragilis*—one of the top carnivores of the latter Jurassic—and the Foucault Pendulum, a 185-pound brass bob suspended on a forty-three-foot cable that demonstrates the rotation of the earth. There are displays on whales, birds, plants, minerals, mammals, reptiles, shells, prehistoric animals, and ecology. The Hall of Desert Ecology illustrates the evolution and adaption of plants and animals to the environment of the southwestern deserts. Children will want to visit the Desert Discovery Lab where they can touch living desert animals. The Hall of Mineralogy features a mock mine tunnel and hands-on learning centers. Other interesting exhibits include the seismograph and the Hall of Shore Ecology, which features a tide pool and other seashore exhibits.

● Reuben H. Fleet Space Theater and Science Center

1875 El Prado (east end of El Prado, at the Plaza de Balboa), Balboa Park. Call (619) 238-1233 for details on the shows, starting times, and prices. Prices vary depending on show. Admission to Science Center: Adults, $2.50; ages 5-15, $1.25; under 5, free. Science Center only free on the first Tuesday of every month. Theater: **Ages 6 and up.** *Science Center:* **All ages.**

The Space Theater is a combination Omnimax theater and planetarium. Seating accommodates 350 people, all facing the same direction (as opposed to the usual full circle in a planetarium). The screen itself is a hemisphere, seventy-six feet in diameter and tilted at twenty-five degrees. Depending on the schedule, the shows feature Omnimax films, planetarium shows that give the audience the sensation of sitting in space, and summer evening laser light shows. (Projected onto the dome screen, Omnimax films give viewers the sensation of being in the center of the action, as if they were actually flying into the eye of a hurricane or surfing that thunderous wave in Hawaii.) The shows are best for school-age children and older.

The Space Theater ticket also admits you to the Science Center across the hall, which is a great place for kids. All the exhibits are visitor-activated, encouraging the kids to touch and participate. Many of them are at children's height. For example, you might telephone your image from one station to another, or bounce a whispered conversation from one side of the room to the other.

● Aerospace Museum

Aerospace Historical Center, 2001 Pan American Plaza, Balboa Park. (619) 234-8291. Daily, 10 A.M.–4:30 P.M. Adults, $5; ages 6–17, $1; under 6, free. **All ages.**

The history of aviation in our country from the dawn of flight to the age of space travel is excitingly depicted in the San Diego Aerospace Museum. You'll see early gliders, a replica of the plane flown by the Wright Brothers at Kittyhawk, World War I planes, early barnstorming planes, the first airmail planes, and an exact flying replica of Charles Lindbergh's *Spirit of Saint Louis*. Aircraft from World War II are on exhibit, as well as modern fighter planes, a "Blackbird" spy plane, and a NASA space capsule. Many of the planes are colorfully displayed within a surrounding exhibit. There are a number of push-button displays and a platform to climb for a bird's-eye view of planes hanging from the ceiling.

Also in the Aerospace Historical Center is the International Aerospace Hall of Fame, which features memorabilia of the heroes of aviation and space history; don't miss the exhibit honoring the contribution of women to aviation. The museum also offers tours of its basement workshop.

● The San Diego Automotive Museum

2080 Pan American Plaza, Balboa Park. (619) 231-2886. Daily, 10 A.M.–4:30 P.M. Summer hours: 9 A.M.–5 P.M. Adults, $5; seniors, $4; ages 6–17, $2; under 6, free. Free admission on the fourth Tuesday of every month. **Ages 6 and up.**

Located next to the Aerospace Museum, the San Diego Automotive Museum features more than sixty gleaming vehicles in its permanent collection, ranging from horseless carriages to future prototypes. Among them are a 1906 Cadillac, a 1910 Pierce Arrow motorcycle, a 1915 Ford Model T, a 1948 Tucker, and a 1981 Delorean. In addition to the core collection, the museum displays vehicles in special shows organized throughout the year, such as a recent one on cars of the American drive-in era.

The museum is housed in a building once used as San Diego's first convention center, and there is kind of a convention center feel to the layout. The cars are behind ropes, and there is obviously no touching.

Marie Hitchcock Puppet Theater

Palisades Building, Balboa Park. South of El Prado between the Balboa Park Club and the Automotive Museum. (619) 685-5045. Showtimes: Wednesday–Friday, 10:30 A.M. (and sometimes at 11:30 A.M.); Saturday and Sunday, 11 A.M., 1 P.M., and 2:30 P.M. Adults, $2; ages 2–14, $1; under 2, free. **Ages 2–11.**

The Marie Hitchcock Theater presents puppet and marionette shows the whole family can enjoy. The performances are put on by various groups of the San Diego Guild of Puppetry, and different shows are presented each week. Telephone to find out what is playing.

● Japanese Friendship Garden

Pan American Plaza, adjacent to the Spreckels Organ Pavilion, Balboa Park. (619) 232-2721. Tuesday, Friday, Saturday, and Sunday, 10 A.M.–4 P.M. Adults, $2; ages 7–18, $1; under 7, free. Family tickets, $5. Free on the third Tuesday of every month. **All ages.**

The Japanese Friendship Garden is a small, half-acre meditation garden. (Plans call for an eventual expansion of the garden to 11.5 acres.) The garden encompasses an entry garden, a sand and stone garden, an exhibit house, and a wisteria arbor with benches. In the style of a Japanese teahouse, the exhibit house has displays on the future development of the garden and special exhibits. Although not a traditional destination for kids, the garden makes a nice place to be peaceful for a while in the bustle of Balboa Park.

● San Diego Junior Theater

Casa del Prado Building, Balboa Park. Theater office: Room 208. (619) 239-1311. Box office: (619) 239-8355. Box office hours: Tuesday–Sunday, 10:30 A.M.–4 P.M. Ticket prices: $6–$8. **Ages 4–18.**

The oldest children's theater in the United States is headquartered at Casa del Prado in Balboa Park. The theater group produces five children's plays—such as *Anne of Green Gables*—a year, performing in the 680-seat Casa del Prado Theater. The San Diego Junior Theater also offers classes and summer programs for children ages four through eighteen.

● Villa Montezuma Museum

1925 K Street. Coming south on I-5, take the Imperial Avenue exit; go left on Imperial to Twentieth Street and left on Twentieth Street to K Street. Coming north on the I-5, take the J Street exit, go right on J Street to Twentieth Street, and go right on Twentieth to K Street. (619) 239-2211. Saturday–Sunday, noon–4:30 P.M. Last tour is at 3:45 P.M. Adults, $3; under 13, free. **Ages 8 and up.**

If you visit just one restored old home in Southern California, it probably should be this one. Built in 1887 (during San Diego's land boom) for Jesse Shepard, a celebrated musician of the era, the Villa Montezuma was (according to the December 17, 1889, *San Diego Sun*) "the most ornately finished and artistically furnished house in the city."

The house is so unique and so lavish that it should interest everyone above the age of six or so. It is filled with brilliant stained-glass windows, which include portraits of Shakespeare and Goethe. The redwood music room contains, in addition to a piano and other furniture, an antique doll collection. Ask to see the downstairs kitchen, which has been restored as a typical turn-of-the-century townhouse kitchen, complete with spices in the spice rack and hanging laundry.

● The Old Spaghetti Factory/Gaslamp Quarter

Fifth Avenue at K Street. (619) 233-4323. Lunch: Monday–Friday, 11:30 A.M.–2 P.M.; Dinner: Monday–Thursday, 5–10 P.M.; Friday, 5–11 P.M.; Saturday, noon–11 P.M.; Sunday, noon–10 P.M. **All ages.**

At the turn of the century, the 16.5-block area bounded by Fourth and Sixth avenues and Broadway and Harbor Drive was San Diego's main business district. But like the old downtowns in so many cities, the once-thriving area deteriorated into a slum. Restoration of the historic district —known as the Gaslamp Quarter for its picturesque gas lamps— began in the mid-1970s. Although the Gaslamp Quarter still retains elements of its skid row past, today it is a lively area of restaurants, shops, businesses, and nightspots inhabiting restored Victorian buildings.

A pioneer among the Gaslamp Quarter restaurants, the Old Spaghetti Factory opened in 1973 in a commercial building built in 1898. Although there was nothing much surrounding it then, the restaurant was an immediate hit with families. It continues to be just as popular today. Decorated with a bright jumble of Tiffany lamps, stained glass, and Victorian couches, the cavernous restaurant offers an unusual assortment of eating arrangements. You can dine in an old streetcar in the middle of the restaurant or at table set between the headboard and footboard of an antique bed. Dinners start at $4.35; a child's dinner is available for $2.95.

For a more upscale Italian restaurant, or a different kind of restaurant, just take a look up the street—Fifth Avenue is jammed with places to eat.

● Horton Plaza

Located between Broadway and G Street and First and Fourth avenues, downtown San Diego. (619) 238-1596. Store hours: Monday–Friday, 10 A.M.–9 P.M.; Saturday, 10 A.M.–6 P.M.; Sunday, 11 A.M.–6 P.M. Restaurants, theaters, and some shops have extended hours. Extended hours during the summer and holidays. First three hours of parking are free with validation. Free. **Ages 6 and up.**

The brightly hued, multitiered Horton Plaza, with its distinctive architecture, is as much a tourist attraction as it is a shopping center. Even if you don't want to shop, Horton Plaza merits a look around. The plaza has a couple of major department stores, some 140 shops—including kid favorites such as Disney and Warner Brothers Studio stores—a multiplex cinema, and lots of places to eat. The open-air top level, where the restaurants and fast-food places are located, is the most fun for a stroll. Most of the places are done in a bright, California-funky style with tables outside. Here, you'll find the pleasant **Galaxy Grill,** a fifties-style soda fountain—with outdoor, indoor, and fountain seating—serving burgers, sandwiches, salads, fountain dishes, and a kid's menu. On the street level is a **Planet Hollywood** restaurant, well liked by kids, tolerated by parents. Kids might enjoy seeing the movie-star handprints in the cement on the wall outside the restaurant.

● Children's Museum/Museo de Los Niños of San Diego

200 West Island Avenue, corner of Island Avenue and Front Street, downtown San Diego. (619) 233-5437. Tuesday–Saturday, 10 A.M.–4:30 P.M.; Sunday, 11 A.M.–4:30 P.M. Adults and children ages 2 and over, $4; seniors, $2; under 2, free. **Ages 3–12.**

Located in a brightly painted warehouse a block from the Convention Center, the Children's Museum of San Diego is an outstanding participatory museum for kids. The spacious, colorful museum includes both indoor and outdoor space, permanent and changing exhibits, and high- and low-tech displays. All signs and exhibits are labeled in both English and Spanish.

On a visit to the museum, children might play virtual reality basketball, wheelchair basketball, or a game of giant checkers. They could make their own puppets and put on a show in a puppet theater or act on a large stage with a red velvet curtain. In another exhibit, they might spend time in a rainhouse, listening to the sound of rain on a metal roof. A preschool play pod gives children ages three to five their own area for jumping, crawling, climbing, and exploring. An indoor/outdoor art studio provides kids with a variety of art experiences—possibly the best is the chance to splash paint on an old pickup truck.

The museum offers special monthly programs and weekend workshops. Group rates and birthday party packages are also available. A new children's park is across the street from the museum.

● Seaport Village

West Harbor Drive at Kettner Boulevard. (619) 235-4014. Daily, 10 A.M.–9 P.M. Shops open until 10 P.M. during the summer. Restaurants have extended hours. Parking, $2—validated if you buy something. **All ages.**

Built on the site of the old Coronado Ferry landing on San Diego Bay, Seaport Village is an enjoyable waterfront complex of shops, restaurants, and family amusements. Three plazas—designed to look like Victorian San Francisco, nineteenth-century Monterey, and old Mexico—front eight acres of parkland on the bay. The architecture is fun, with a lighthouse, a Victorian clock tower, and a boardwalk. The pleasant landscaping includes a lake and a koi pond.

The highlight of the village for young children is the **Broadway Flying Horse Carousel,** a beautifully restored 1890s Charles I. D. Looff merry-go-round with forty-six hand-carved wooden animals, each with its own leather reins. Rides on the carousel, which goes around at a good clip, are $1.

Musicians, mimes, jugglers, clowns, magicians, and other entertainers stroll through the complex. There is also a monthly schedule of special events that includes shows and activities for kids and live music. If you feel like splurging, **Cinderella Carriages** (phone: 619-239-8080) offers horse-drawn carriage tours along the embarcadero or through downtown. They operate noon–11 P.M., departing from their stand next to the Harbor House restaurant.

As well as a variety of shops, there are number of places to eat in Seaport Village, from bay-view restaurants to food stands. A good choice is the **San Diego Pier Cafe** (phone: 619-239-3968), overlooking the water. They serve breakfast, lunch, dinner, and good seafood in a relaxed, family-friendly atmosphere.

Marina Park is adjacent to Seaport village, with a view of Coronado Bridge and Island on one side and the San Diego skyline on the other. It is a great spot for watching sailboats and navy ships, for flying kites, and for picnicking.

● Navy Ships' Open House

U.S. Navy Pier, off Harbor Drive, near Broadway on the Embarcadero. (619) 532-1430. **Ages 6 and up.**

You can tour a submarine, an aircraft carrier, a destroyer, or other naval craft most weekends between 1 and 4 p.m. when U.S. Navy ships hold open house for the public. (You need to make special arrangements, however, to tour an aircraft carrier.) At least one ship is usually shown each weekend. The Navy guide will take you through the entire ship and patiently answer any questions.

● San Diego Harbor Excursion

Foot of Broadway at Harbor Drive. (619) 234-4111. Daily. Two-hour cruise: Adults, $17; ages 3–12, $8.50. One-hour cruise: Adults, $12; children, $6; under 3, free. **Ages 4 and up.**

Pleasant excursion ships with sundecks, glass-enclosed cabins, and galley snack bars offer one- and two-hour cruises in the San Diego Harbor. A tour guide singles out and explains the points of interest over a clear public address system. The one-hour, twelve-mile cruise passes by the *Star of India* sailing ship, the Naval Air Station, and San Diego's ship-yards. The fishing fleet, aircraft carriers, merchant vessels, and Coronado Bridge are some sights the guide will point out to you. The two-hour, twenty-five mile trip covers the same territory plus the Cabrillo National Monument.

For most children's attention spans, the one-hour cruise is probably best. There are cruises daily, with frequent departures during the summer; telephone for the schedule. In the winter, whale-watching cruises are offered. Even in the summer, it's a good idea for everyone to bring a sweater.

● The San Diego Bay Ferry/The Old Ferry Landing

Ferry service provided by San Diego Harbor Excursion, 1050 North Harbor Drive (foot of Broadway on the Embarcadero), San Diego. (619) 234-4111. Departures begin from Broadway Pier at 9 A.M. daily, and from Coronado at 9:30 A.M. daily. $2 each way per person. 50¢ per bicycle. The Old Ferry Landing is located at 1201 First Street at B Avenue on the Bayfront, Coronado. (619) 435-8895. Shops open daily. **All ages.**

Of course you can drive across the bridge to **Coronado Island,** but taking the ferry is a lot more fun. Departures begin from San Diego's Broadway Pier at 9 A.M. daily, continuing every hour on the hour. Heading the other way, departures begin from the Old Ferry Landing in Coronado at 9:30 A.M., continuing every hour on the half-hour. Last

sailings leave San Diego at 9 P.M. (10 P.M. on Friday and Saturday) and
Coronado at 9:30 P.M. (10:30 P.M. on Friday and Saturday). The trip across
the bay, which takes fifteen minutes, is smooth and pleasant. The ferry
disembarks at the Old Ferry Landing in Coronado, which is actually a new
Victorian-style shopping/eating complex. Bike and roller-skate rentals are
available, and you can bike along waterfront paths. There is also a fishing
pier, a small beach, grassy lawns, and plenty of snack food. If your family
would like to see the **Coronado Hotel,** you can take the 904 bus from the
Ferry Landing for fifty cents. (The walk down the length of Orange Grove
Avenue to the hotel is too far for most families.)

● San Diego Trolley

*Santa Fe Depot, Broadway and Kettner, downtown San Diego. (619) 231-
8549 or (619) 233-3004.* **All ages.**

The bright red electric San Diego Trolley operates along two routes
that originate in downtown San Diego. One route travels south to the
Mexican border at San Ysidro, the other runs east to Santee. Most children
who live in Southern California have so little experience with public
transportation that just riding on the trolleys can be a kick for them. You
can take a longer trip or ride just a few stops. The lines run from early
morning until midnight, with fifteen-minute service most of the day. The
fares range from $1 to $1.75, depending on the distance; children under
five travel free. You purchase tickets from machines at the trolley stops.
The trolleys stop for only thirty seconds at each stop—to board, push the
lighted green button beside the doors. Stations are announced as the trolleys approach them. Push the lighted white button beside the door to exit
the car.

A fun trip is to take the trolley to visit the Chula Vista Nature
Center (see page 166). From San Diego, you ride seven miles to the
Bayfront/E Street station in Chula Vista, where a free shuttle bus takes
you and brings you back from the Nature Center.

● Maritime Museum

*1306 North Harbor Drive, one mile south of San Diego Airport on the north
Embarcadero between Ash Street and Broadway. (619) 234-9153. Daily,
9 A.M.–8 P.M. Adults, $5; seniors and ages 13–17, $4; ages 6–12, $2. One
ticket provides admission to all three ships.* **Ages 6 and up.**

A fully rigged iron windjammer, an 1898 ferryboat, and a World
War I vintage yacht make up San Diego's Maritime Museum. By far
the most interesting of the three vessels is the *Star of India,* an 1863 merchant sailing vessel. The ship's keeper directs you first to the main deck,
where the captain and first-class passengers slept and ate. The cabins are

furnished in detail; old uniforms hang in the captain's closet; a chamber pot is near the bed. There is a children's cabin with toys and a small rocking horse. (The half-gates across the cabins have wide posts, so small children can see without being lifted.) At the other end of the main deck are the cramped bunks of the crew.

Between decks on the *Star of India* is a museum with photos of ships, displays of rope knots and old tools, and some interesting odds and ends, such as a doctor's medical saddlebag. Young children will probably enjoy standing behind the ship's wheel and playing on the poop deck.

The *Berkeley*, docked next door, is a propeller-driven ferryboat. She is much less engaging than the *Star,* and you'll probably want to spend less time here. The *Medea*, built is 1904, is an old English yacht with a colorful history. The yacht itself is not that interesting, but what is fun is crossing the gangplank to her from the *Berkeley.* You might not want to try it with small children, but kids ages six and older will love jumping onto the small ship from the narrow gangplank.

● Firehouse Museum

1572 Columbia Street, corner of Cedar. (619) 232-FIRE. Thursday and Friday, 10 A.M.–2 P.M.; Saturday and Sunday, 10 A.M.–4 P.M. Adults, $2; ages 13–17 and seniors, $1; 12 and under, free. Free the first Thursday of every month. **All ages.**

The Firehouse Museum is an old fire station now housing major pieces of antique fire-fighting equipment. One of the most interesting is the Metropolitan Steamer, built in 1903. Weighing ten thousand pounds, it used coal to operate the water pump. In addition to hand-drawn, horse-drawn, and motor-driven vehicles, you'll see—among other things—the original firehouse pole and spiral staircase, an old dispatcher's console, and the speaking trumpets, through which the chief would shout his orders. Lanterns, old hats, pictures, axes, hoses, and badges are displayed on the walls and other surfaces. The retired firefighter on duty will show you around, answer any questions, and give you a demonstration of how the old system of fire bells worked.

● Cabrillo National Monument

At the tip of Point Loma, San Diego. Take Highway 209 to its south end at the monument. The monument is approached through the gates of the Naval Oceans System Center. (619) 557-5450. Daily, 9 A.M.–6 P.M. Admission, $4 per car. **Ages 6 and up.**

Commemorating the European discovery of the West Coast by Juan Cabrillo, this national monument on the tip of Point Loma offers an unparalleled view of the city and the bay. The visitors center shows films and has exhibits on Cabrillo—and the other Pacific Coast explorers—and on the grey whales. (The monument includes a whale-watching lookout.) A walkway leads uphill to the old **Point Loma Lighthouse,** which has been restored and furnished to look the way it did a century ago. A tape recording tells kids what life was like for the lightkeeper and his family. (The light from the lighthouse was often obscured by low-flying clouds, and in 1891 the lighthouse was abandoned for one on lower ground.)

You can also take a walk along a nature trail that winds through the chaparral along the bay side of Point Loma. A guide to the trail is available at the visitors center. (Warn children to stay on the path and away from the edges of the cliff.) Tide pools are located on the rocky coast. (You can ask for directions at the visitors center, and again, watch your footing.)

● Whale Watching

Ages 6 and up.

Every year more than ten thousand California gray whales make the five-thousand-mile migration from their summer feeding grounds north of Alaska and Siberia to their winter mating and calving grounds in the warm lagoons of Baja California. The migration passes by Southern California from about mid-December to about mid-February. As many as eighty whales per day can be spotted off San Diego's coast during the height of the migration in January. You can actually see the whales from land at the free whale-watching station at **Cabrillo National Monument** on the tip of Point Loma (see previous entry). But for a closer look, you'll want to join one of the whale-watching excursions. These usually last a couple of hours, and sightings are almost certain. Among the companies offering whale-watching excursions are: **San Diego Harbor Excursions,** phone (619) 234-4111; **H & M Landing,** phone (619) 222-1144; and **Invader Cruises**, phone (619) 234-8687.

● Pier Fishing

Ages 6 and up.

The ocean off San Diego is one of the finest areas for catching fish along the Pacific Coast. Many companies operate half-day sportfishing boats out of San Diego. However, you don't have to take your children out on a boat to have a good day fishing: perch, bonito, and barracuda can be caught off San Diego's piers. No fishing license is required, you won't get seasick, and what's more, it's free. The following piers are open daily and do not charge for fishing:

Crystal Pier is located at the foot of Garnet Street in Pacific Beach. Fishing is open to the public daily from 7 A.M. to sunset on this privately owned pier. (There is no fee, but children must be accompanied by an adult fisherman.) There is a bait house on the pier.

Oceanside Pier is located at the foot of Third Street in Oceanside. As the story goes, a thirty-five-pound yellowtail was once caught off this 945-foot pier. The bait house next to the pier will take care of your bait and tackle needs.

San Diego Public Fishing Pier, located at the foot of Niagara Street in Ocean Beach, is a section of San Diego city. Built in 1966 at a cost of $3 million, this pier stretches 2,150 feet into the ocean. The bait house rents tackle and will advise you on a selection of bait. Yellowtail have been caught off this pier.

Shelter Island Fishing Pier, on Shelter Island, is smaller than some of the others, but catches are often made here. It is also the prettiest pier. A bait house rents tackle, and there is a snack bar.

Old Town San Diego, Hillcrest, and Mission Valley

● Old Town/Old Town San Diego State Historic Park

Located just southeast of Interstates 5 and 8. From I-5, take the Old Town off-ramp. Park headquarters: (619) 220-5422. Park hours: Daily, 10 A.M.–5 P.M. Shops open until 9 P.M. Free. **Ages 3 and up.**

Old Town is the heart of old San Diego. The city began near here on Presidio Hill in 1769; from the 1820s to the 1870s, Old Town was the commercial, political, and social center of the city. Today it is a hodge-podge of homes, businesses, restored historical buildings, grassy areas, restaurants, and shops. Families can easily spend an entire afternoon exploring the area.

Within the Old Town district, the Old Town San Diego State Historic Park (bounded by Wallace, Juan, Twiggs, and Congress streets) is a six-block area of historic structures, restaurants, and shops that is closed to automobile traffic. The park's visitors center, located in an 1853 two-story adobe, the Robinson-Rose House (4002 Wallace Street), is a good place to begin a self-guided tour. You can purchase a brochure for your tour, and there is an interesting, scale-model of Old Town as it appeared in the 1870s on display. (Families with older children may want to take the guided tour that leaves the visitors center most days at 2 P.M.) The grassy plaza in the center of the park has an old cannon that kids love to climb. Places of interest within the park include:

Mason Street School (on Mason Street between San Diego Avenue and Congress Street; daily, 10 A.M.–4 P.M.; free), built in 1865, was the first public school in San Diego. It has a potbellied stove, old-fashioned desks, and books. The blackboard has an assignment on it, and there is a dunce's hat on a high stool next the blackboard.

Casa de Machado y Stewart (on Congress Street, near the school; daily, 10 A.M.–4 P.M.; free), a two-room adobe, is one of the few structures remaining from San Diego's earliest days. Built in 1835, the walls of the house still contain the original adobe bricks. Inside, you can peer behind wire mesh to get an idea of how the adobe looked when it was originally inhabited.

In 1868 the **San Diego Union Building** (on San Diego Avenue across from the Squibob Square; Tuesday–Sunday, 10 A.M.–5 P.M.; free) became the home of the *San Diego Union* newspaper. The *Union* has since restored the frame building to look the way that first office did. You can see the old press, an ancient typewriter, and the bins full of lead type.

Seeley Stables (Calhoun Street between Mason and Twiggs streets; daily, 10 A.M.–5 P.M., when staffing permits; adults, $2; children, $1; under 6, free; the same ticket admits you to the Casa de Estudillo) houses an extensive collection of wagons and stagecoaches, including a Wells Fargo mail coach and the old Julian-to-San Diego stagecoach. Upstairs are displays of saddles, branding irons, and cowboy photos. Of interest to kids is a display of nineteenth-century children's toys and an old-fashioned telephone that can be touched.

Casa de Estudillo (Mason Street between Calhoun Street and San Diego Avenue; daily, 10 A.M.–5 P.M., when staffing permits; adults, $2; children, $1; under 6, free; the same ticket admits you to the Seeley Stables), a beautifully restored and refurnished adobe home, was built by a wealthy rancher in 1827. (You look over half-doors into the rooms of the house, so small children will have to be lifted.) Of special interest is the floor-warmer in the living room where hot rocks were placed to warm the room; at that time there were no trees for firewood. Also note the children's room with its old dolls and the outdoor oven where all the baking was done.

Vintage blacksmithing techniques are demonstrated at **Black Hawk Smithy & Stable** (corner of Mason and Juan streets; free) every Wednesday and Saturday from 10 A.M. to 2 P.M.

Among the exhibits at the **Wells Fargo History Museum** (2645 San Diego Avenue; 619-294-5549; daily, 10 A.M.–5 P.M.; free), a small museum dedicated to Wells Fargo history, are a shiny Abbot-Downing Concord stagecoach and a replica of a nineteenth-century Wells Fargo stage office.

● Whaley House

*2482 San Diego Avenue, corner of Harney. (619) 298-2482. Daily,
10 A.M.–5 P.M. (The last tour is 4:30 P.M.) Adults, $4; seniors, $3; ages
5–18, $2; under 5, free.* **Ages 6 and up.**

Built in 1856, the Whaley House is the oldest brick structure in
Southern California. Once the center of social life for old San Diego, the
house also served—at different times—as a theater, granary, school, city
hall, and courthouse, as well as a home for the Whaley family. Today the
house, including the courthouse, has been restored to its original state and
is open to visitors.

Kids will enjoy seeing the old courtroom, with its furnishings authentic down to a spittoon. The downstairs rooms include the furnished
parlor and the kitchen with its metal bathtub. You can also see the rooms
upstairs, which include a child's bedroom that is full of dolls. The house is
one of the most interesting and least musty historic homes I have seen. If
your children are old enough for ghost stories, ask one of the docents to
tell you about the ghosts who allegedly haunt this house. It's delightfully
spooky.

● Heritage Park

*Corner of Juan and Harney streets just above Old Town; signs point the way.
Doll shop open daily, 10:30 A.M.–5:30 P.M. (619) 291-1979. Free.* **Ages 6
and up.**

Heritage Park was created as a preserve for some of San Diego's
endangered Victorian buildings. Once threatened with demolition, the
buildings have been moved to this park from other sites and restored. The
park looks like a picture-book page, with a half-dozen brightly painted
Victorian structures and an historic synagogue sitting on a grassy hill.
The interiors of the homes have been leased to businesses. There is one
shop that some children should enjoy seeing—Ye Olde Doll Shoppe.
Dolls, dollhouses, stuffed animals, and collector trains fill room after room
of the restored Victorian. Other children will enjoy seeing the outside of
the buildings and playing in the park, which has a grassy hill to roll down.

● Serra Museum/Presidio Park

*2727 Presidio Drive (off Taylor Street). (619) 297-3258. Museum open
Tuesday–Saturday, 10 A.M.–4:30 P.M.; Sunday, noon–4:30 P.M. Adults,
$3; ages 12 and under, free.* **Ages 6 and up.**

On July 16, 1769, Father Junipero Serra, a Franciscan priest from
Majorca, Spain, founded the first of California's twenty-one missions—
and, in the process, the city of San Diego—on this hill. A walled city,

the Presidio, was built around the mission and protected by garrisoned soldiers. The city's early settlers made their homes inside the Presidio, which was all there was to San Diego until the 1820s, when people began moving off the hill into what is now Old Town. The mission remained on the hill for just five years, however, and then relocated to its present site in Mission Valley.

The Serra Museum, an impressive mission-style structure that can be seen for miles around, commemorates Father Serra and the history of San Diego. The museum's historical photos of San Diego, artifacts from Presidio excavations, and other mission and Native American artifacts are rather dry for children. The outside areas, however, should interest them. The museum portico contains displays of early mission agricultural equipment such as wine and olive oil presses.

Below the museum, in an area surrounded by low walls, children can see the ridges and hollows in the ground that are the remains of the original Presidio. The park itself is beautiful and offers picnicking and lovely views of the surrounding city.

● Marine Corps Recruit Depot Command Museum

Marine Corps Recruit Depot, San Diego. Located at Pacific Highway and Witherby Street, a quarter of a mile south of the I-5 and I-8 interchange. (619) 524-6038. Tuesday–Sunday, 10 A.M.–4 P.M. Free. **Ages 6 and up.**

The Command Museum, located in a two-story, Spanish-style building at the Marine Corps Recruit Depot, chronicles the history of the Marines from the 1840s to the present. On display are uniforms, weapons, photographs, vehicles, including a World War I ambulance and a World War II jeep, and other artifacts relating to Marine history from the Mexican War through the Gulf War. A display of the Horse Marines includes life-size horse models. Other exhibits depict Marine aviation, marksmanship, female Marines, and the modern Marine Corps. You do not need a pass to enter the Marine base to see the museum, but you do have to show your driver's license.

● The Corvette Diner

3946 Fifth Avenue, San Diego, north of Balboa Park between Washington and University streets. (619) 542-1001. Sunday–Thursday, 11 A.M.– 11 P.M.; Friday and Saturday, 11 A.M.–midnight. **All ages.**

You can not only have a hamburger at this fifties-style diner, but you can check out the red corvette parked inside. If you have to wait for a table, you can do so on a bench made from the fins of a '59 Cadillac.

Music from the forties, fifties, and sixties plays on the jukebox, and at
night a DJ broadcasts from a radio booth inside the restaurant. The decor
and the ambience here is easily a cut above the typical fifties-style diner.
You are even offered gems from the philosophy of Ralph Kramden.
The food is typical diner fare—hamburgers, soda fountain, blue-plate
specials—and kids' meals are available. The Corvette Diner is located in
the pleasant, tree-shaded neighborhood of Hillcrest.

● Mission Basilica San Diego de Alcala

*10818 Mission Road, San Diego. Take I-8 east from San Diego. Exit at
Mission Gorge Road and turn left. Turn left again on Twain Street and
follow the signs to the mission. (619) 281-8449. Daily, 9 A.M.–5 P.M.
Adults, $2; ages 12 and under, 50¢.* **Ages 8 and up.**

The first of California's twenty-one missions, Mission San Diego
moved from Presidio Hill to this site in 1774. (The mission needed a
reliable source of water, better land for farming, and to be nearer the Indian villages.) A year later, the mission was destroyed during an attack by
natives and rebuilt of adobe. Restored in 1931, the "Mother of the Missions" includes a reconstruction of the original living quarters of Father
Serra, a magnificent bell tower, an active parish church, and a small museum that includes models of Spanish galleons and artifacts from the
1846–1862 occupation of the mission by the U.S. Cavalry.

● Mission Trails Regional Park

*One Father Junipero Serra Trail, San Diego. Located eight miles northeast of
downtown San Digeo. Take I-8 to the Mission Gorge/Fairmount exit. Turn
north onto Mission Gorge Road and go four miles. The visitor center entrance
is on the left between Jackson Drive and Golfcrest Drive on Father Junipero
Serra Trail. (619) 668-3275. Park open daily, 8 A.M.–5 P.M. (until 7 P.M.
in the summer). Visitor and Interpretive Center open daily, 9 A.M.–5 P.M.
Free.* **All ages.**

Within the city limits of San Diego is a 5,700-acre park of natural
beauty. Once part of the ancestral home of the Kumeyaay Indians, Mission
Trails Regional Park preserves many of the resources used by the Kumeyaay. The park terrain includes rugged hills and vast open areas, mountains, two lakes, and a historic dam.

The focal point of the park is the stunning new Visitor and Interpretive Center. The beautiful glass and stone structure offers state-of-the-art
interactive displays on the geology, history, and plant and animal life of
the park. An observation deck provides telescopes and an awe-inspiring

view. Park personnel are on hand to answer questions and give assistance.

Outside is a trail with exhibits on native wildlife, including casts of animals indigenous to the region. There is also a model of the historic flume that carried water from the Old Mission Dam to the San Diego Mission five and a half miles below.

Hiking trails in the park range from the short and easy to the steep and difficult. From the visitors center, it is an easy 1.8-mile hike one way along the Father Junipero Serra Trail to the historic Old Mission Dam. (You can also drive there on a one-way road from the visitors center.) Telephone for information on daily guided hikes and school visits.

Chula Vista

● The Chula Vista Nature Interpretive Center

1000 Gunpowder Point Drive, Chula Vista. Located about seven miles south of downtown San Diego. From I-5, take the E Street exit in Chula Vista and go west about 200 feet. Parking and shuttle bus pick-up are clearly marked. Or take the San Diego Trolley to the Bayfront/E Street Trolley Station and Visitor Information Center. Free shuttle buses are available at either location. (619) 422-2473. Tuesday–Sunday and some Monday holidays, 10 A.M.– 5 P.M. Summers, open daily, 10 A.M.–5 P.M. Adults, $3.50; seniors, $2.50; ages 6–17, $1; under 6, free. Admission is by cash only. **All ages.**

The Chula Vista Nature Interpretive Center offers families a rare look at one of the few remaining salt marsh habitats on the Pacific Coast. The Center is located in the Sweetwater Marsh National Refuge, and private automobiles and pedestrians are not permitted. To see the reserve you must take a free trolley-style shuttle bus from the Center parking lot or from the E Street Trolley Station (see page 158).

Inside the Nature Center are aquariums containing sea life native to the coastal marsh environment and terrariums holding snakes, lizards, mice, and other shore creatures. Most of the exhibits are hands-on. For example, kids can crawl into a display and look up to see a group of flat-fish—a fish that seems to swim laying on its side. Or they can get a close-up view of the sea life in a tank by using a bioscanner—a camera and TV screen that lets them zoom in on what they want to see. Best of all for children, they can touch and feed "debarbed" stingrays, bat rays, leopard sharks, and other fish in a 4,500-gallon saltwater petting pool.

Kids can see a wide variety of migrating birds both resting and in flight from the observation desk outside the center. Bring binoculars or rent a pair at the center. Interpretive trails lead from the Nature Center through the wildlife refuge.

The Nature Center also offers special programs for children and their families, including story hours, nature craft workshops, and nature-night sleep-overs. Overnights can be arranged for scout and youth groups. The center also offers environmentally aware birthday parties.

Mission Bay Area

● Mission Bay Aquatic Park

Information Center: 2688 East Mission Bay Drive, just north of I-8 and west of I-5; reached via I-5. (619) 276-8200. Monday–Saturday, 9 A.M.– 5 P.M.; Sunday, 9:30 A.M.–4:30 P.M. Free. **All ages.**

A maze of islands, beaches, lagoons, and grass-covered coves, Mission Bay Aquatic Park is a beautiful 4,600-acre aquatic playground. Almost every type of water-sport activity is offered here, including swimming, motorboating, sailing, fishing, and water-skiing. Traffic on the bay is organized so that one water activity is separated from another. Boat rentals are available. You can fish from the beach, a small boat, or a sport-fishing boat. The swimming beaches have lifeguards during the summer. There are a number of children's playgrounds and miles of landscaped areas for picnicking. In addition to a number of hotels, campsites are available at the park. The visitors center has information on all the park's activities, as well as on activities throughout the city, and will make hotel reservations.

● Sea World

1720 South Shores Road in Mission Bay. Take the Sea World Drive exit west from the I-5. (619) 226-3901. Open daily. Hours vary by season. Telephone for current hours. Admission (includes all shows): Adults, $30.95; ages 3– 11, $22.95; under 3, free. Parking, $5. **All ages.**

Sea World is well worth a whole day's outing. It is one of the largest marine-life parks in the world: more than 200 marine mammals, 10,000 fish, and 1,600 birds inhabit its 135 acres. In addition to some very exciting shows—the most impressive being the killer whales—there are many exhibits where children can be active participants. They can pet and feed dolphins and whales, touch moray eels and bat rays, and toss fish to sea lions, seals, and walruses. Children can roll up their sleeves and explore a tide pool that duplicates California tidal life.

A fascinating exhibit for adults and children alike is Sea World's Penguin Encounter, one of the only places outside of Antarctica where you can see these charming creatures in person. The penguins live in a special enclosed compound that closely duplicates their native habitat. First from a moving sidewalk in front of the 100-foot-long observation window and then from an upper-observation deck, you'll watch the some 400 penguins as they toddle on the ice, dine on fresh fish, and swim gracefully through clear water. Less charming, but certainly fascinating, are the large sharks, displayed in a 400,000-gallon aquarium.

Shamu's Happy Harbor is a marvelous two-acre playground inside the park for children of all ages. Kids can climb, jump, crawl, explore, and get wet in all sorts of imaginative ways, including playing in a two-story fun ship, working their way through a water maze, and building their own sand castles. Since so many of the activities involve water, some parents bring a swimsuit or change of clothes for their kids.

There are a number of places to eat at Sea World. Strollers and wheel-chairs are available for rent.

● San Diego Princess Resort

1404 West Vacation Road, in Mission Bay Park at West Vacation Road and Ingraham Street. (800) 344-2626 or (619) 274-4630. **All ages.**

Across the street from Sea World, the San Diego Princess Resort sits on a forty-four-acre, tropically landscaped island in Mission Bay. This is a family resort—guests without children might even feel a little out of place here. The resort has five swimming pools, its own sandy beach, bike paths, tennis courts, and croquet and putting ranges. The airy, cottage-style rooms all have patios; some have kitchens; and there are also some cottages with up to four bedrooms. Room rates begin at $130, and there are off-season and Automobile Club–member discounts. Supervised children's activities are available during the summer.

● Belmont Park

On the beach at Mission Boulevard and West Mission Bay Drive, Mission Bay, San Diego. Take I-5 to Sea World Drive and follow the signs to West Mission Bay Drive. (619) 491-2988. Hours vary seasonally, so phone ahead. Entrance is free. Amusement prices vary. **All ages.**

Belmont Park is the home of the historic Giant Dipper Roller Coaster, originally built in 1925 as a key attraction for the Mission Beach Amusement Center. After city officials closed the amusement park in the mid-seventies, local roller coaster and history buffs successfully fought to get the coaster restored. The restorers faithfully followed the original design, while meeting the safety standards of today. The park and the Giant Dipper reopened in 1990, giving a new generation a chance to ride—and rattle—on an old-fashioned, wooden-trestled roller coaster.

In addition to the coaster, Belmont Park has a restored carousel; a small bumper-car ride; a few carnival and small-children's rides; an indoor children's playground, called Pirate's Cove, with climbing and tube-type structures; and shops and fast-food restaurants.

◼ Up the Coast

● Museum of Contemporary Art, San Diego

700 Prospect Street, La Jolla. (619) 454-3541. Downtown San Diego branch: 1001 Kettner Boulevard at Broadway, San Diego. (619) 234-1001. Both locations: Tuesday–Saturday, 10 A.M.–5 P.M.; Sunday, noon–5 P.M. The La Jolla museum is open Wednesday until 8 P.M. The San Diego museum is open Friday until 8 P.M. Adults, $4; seniors and students, $2; under 12, free. A three-day pass admits you to both museums for the price of one. Free to everyone the first Tuesday of every month. **Ages 7 and up.**

The Museum of Contemporary Art now has two locations—the stunningly renovated La Jolla museum and a small, bright space in downtown San Diego adjacent to and overlooking the trolley station. Perched on a cliff overlooking the Pacific, the La Jolla museum offers a spectacular view of the ocean, striking architecture—and, of course, changing and permanent exhibits of post-1945 art. The smaller San Diego site in the new America Plaza has changing exhibits and fun views of the trolley plaza. Both museums offer a free guide for children on the viewing of modern art.

A program called "Contemporary Kids" presents performing artists, film and video showings, and gallery workshops for children ages seven through thirteen. Check with the museum for the program schedule, which includes family activities on selected Sunday afternoons. Another program for high school students offers young people the chance to meet and talk with contemporary artists. Other programs for high schoolers include student internship and artist-in-residence workshops. School tours are also available for ages four and older.

A casual visit to the museum is best made with older children or babies (strollers are available at the desk). Some of the artwork may be frightening or inappropriate for preschool and young, school-age children. The La Jolla museum also features a pretty cafe.

● Children's Pool

Coast Boulevard, between Jenner Street and Eads Avenue, La Jolla. Open daily. Free. **All ages.**

Donated to the city by Ellen Scripps in 1931, this calm, sheltered bay is an ideal spot for children to play in the water. A breakwater wall keeps away waves, but occasionally a seal shows up. There is a lifeguard station above the bay.

● White Rabbit Children's Books

7755 Girard Avenue, La Jolla. From the northbound I-5, take the Ardath Road exit west to Torrey Pines Road. Continue on Torrey Pines until it ends, then turn right on Girard. From the southbound I-5, exit at La Jolla Village Drive, go west to Torrey Pines, then turn left and continue as instructed above. (619) 454-3518. Monday–Saturday, 9 A.M.–6 P.M.; Sunday, 11 A.M.– 5 P.M. **Infants–13 years.**

If you can't find the book you want at this well-stocked children's bookstore, they will special order it for you. If a book is out of print, they will help you find it. The store has a lovely, bright atmosphere with a fanciful train running overhead. In addition to more than six thousand titles for children from infancy through junior high, the store stocks children's records, puzzles, puppets, educational games, stationery, and stuffed animals. A half-hour story hour for children ages three and older is held every Wednesday at 10:30 A.M. in a comfortable storytelling area. The store has a monthly schedule of special events that include author signings, book celebrations, and Sunday afternoon meet-the-character storytelling events. The White Rabbit also publishes a newsletter that keeps readers up to date on new children's books and provides book reviews.

● La Jolla Cave and Shell Shop

1325 Coast Boulevard, off Prospect Street, La Jolla. (619) 454-6080. Daily, 10 A.M.–4:45 P.M. Adults, $1.50; children, 75¢. **Ages 6 and up.**

One hundred forty-five steps down a staircase inside a shell shop will lead you through an underground tunnel to the Sunny Jim Cave, a natural cave battered into La Jolla's sandstone cliffs by centuries of pounding waves. The stairs leading to the cave are steep and wet, and the passage is somewhat dark—plus, you have to climb back up the stairs. Still, given that caveat, the climb and the descent are an adventure, and the view from inside the cave to the ocean is stunning.

● Stephen Birch Aquarium-Museum

2300 Expedition Way, La Jolla. Located on a hillside above the Scripps Institution of Oceanography at the University of California, San Diego. Take the La Jolla Village Drive exit west from I-5. (619) 534-3474. Daily, 9 A.M.–5 P.M. Adults, $6.50; seniors, $5.50; ages 13–17, $4.50; ages 3–12, $3.50; under 3, free. Parking, $3. **All ages.**

On a bluff overlooking the La Jolla coastline, this beautiful facility is both an aquarium and a museum of oceanography. Replacing the old Scripps Aquarium, the Stephen Birch Aquarium-Museum is part of the Scripps Institution of Oceanography at the University of California at San Diego, one of the nation's most important centers of marine research.

The museum, to the left after you enter the building, has bright, interactive exhibits on the study of oceanography. In a mock-up of the scientific workroom of the H.M.S. *Challenger,* a late-nineteenth-century British sailing ship that investigated ocean life, kids can look under an old microscope and open drawers to see the kinds of samples the early marine scientists collected. In another hands-on exhibit, they can compare the types of instruments used on the *Challenger* with those of an oceanographer today. There are also exhibits on the differences between fresh and sea water, ocean waves, the relation of the ocean to climate, earthquakes, and much more. In an ocean supermarket, kids can use a scanner on everyday products to see how they are tied to the ocean. An eight-minute video, as you enter the museum, gives an introduction to oceanography.

The aquarium, on the right as you enter, features some thirty-three tanks of fish and marine life ranging from sardines to a giant Pacific octopus. The showpiece is a 55,000-gallon kelp forest tank that begins about two feet off the floor and keeps going up. Outside is a demonstration tide pool and a spectacular view of the ocean. The courtyard in front of the museum has picnic tables and concession carts.

● Torrey Pines State Reserve

Off North Torrey Pines Road, south of Del Mar. From I-5, take the Genesee Avenue exit and go west. Turn north on North Torrey Pines Road, follow it to the ocean and turn left into the reserve. (619) 755-2063. Daily, 8 A.M. to sunset. Visitors center open 10 A.M.–4 P.M. $4 per car. **All ages.**

Torrey Pines State Reserve protects one of the world's rarest trees, the beautiful Torrey pine. The five-needled pine, a survivor of the Ice Age, remains only two places in the world—here and on the isolated Santa Rosa Island off of Santa Barbara. The reserve is easily one of the most beautiful spots in all of Southern California. The trees, surrounded by a vivid and undisturbed sage-scrub community, grow atop wind-eroded sandstone cliffs above the Pacific. Well-marked trails lead through the preserve and down to the ocean. The trails are easy enough to be negotiated by just about anyone, including parents carrying babies, although small children need to be watched carefully on the cliffs.

Strollers and wheelchairs are permitted on the trails, but not bicycles. No dogs are allowed on the reserve, and picnicking is not permitted. The flowers, pine cones, and all of the natural elements are protected.

The visitors center, located in an old Spanish-style building, offers slide shows on the reserve and nature exhibits, such as a stuffed coyote and bobcat. Nature walks leave the visitors center at 11:30 A.M. and 1:30 P.M. on weekends.

● Quail Botanic Gardens

230 Quail Gardens Drive, Encinitas. Located 20 miles north of San Diego. Take Encinitas Boulevard east from I-5 to Quail Gardens Drive and go north about half a mile. (619) 436-3036. Daily, 9 A.M.–5 P.M. Adults, $3; ages 5–12, $1.50; under 5, free. Free the first Tuesday of every month. **All ages.**

Once the private residential property of an avid plant collector and naturalist, the Quail Botanic Gardens display plants and trees from regions of the world with climates similar to Southern California. The gardens, on thirty-one acres of canyons and sunny hillsides, are quite beautiful. Paved trails wind through the many different climate-zone displays of plants and trees ranging from cacti to exotic tropicals. Among the highlights of the gardens are a lush, tropical waterfall and an old-fashioned gazebo. There is a pond, bridges, and benches. The area is also a bird refuge and feeding station.

The namesake of the gardens, the California Quail, can still be spotted here early in the morning or late in the afternoon. Picnic tables are available outside the gardens.

● Carlsbad Children's Museum

300 Carlsbad Village Drive, Suite 103, Carlsbad, in the Village Faire Shopping Center. From I-5, take the Village Drive exit east. (619) 720-0737. Tuesday–Thursday, noon–5 P.M.; Saturday, 10 A.M.–5 P.M.; Sunday, noon–5 P.M. Phone for extended summer hours. $3.50 per person; under 2, free. **Ages 1–10.**

This small, imaginative children's museum, located in a pretty shopping complex, offers young children a variety of educational, playful exhibits. A kid-sized grocery store comes complete with cash register and conveyor belt, store apron and smocks, shopping carts, groceries, and scales. A castle-play dress-up area includes a castle, princess gowns, king's robes, and a knight's armor and chain mail. A phone system allows kids to telephone each other from different parts of the museum.

Other exhibits include computers, a puppet theater, a shadow box, a bubble tube, a fishing boat, and mirror play. There is an art area with projects that change weekly and a toddler play area. Birthday party packages are available.

● Mission San Luis Rey de Francia

4050 Mission Avenue, San Luis Rey. Four miles east of Oceanside via Highway 76. Take I-5 south from Los Angeles or north from San Diego to Highway 76. (619) 757-3651. Monday–Saturday, 10 A.M.–4 P.M.; Sunday, noon–4:30 P.M. Adults, $3; ages 12 and under, $1. **Ages 8 and up.**

One of the largest of California's missions, Mission San Luis Rey de Francia is a striking combination of Spanish, Moorish, and Mexican architecture. A self-guided tour will show you the padres' bedrooms and library, the sewing rooms, and kitchen. You'll also see the first pepper tree in California, the cloister garden, and the Native American cemetery. At the height of the mission's power, almost three thousand Native American converts lived there. Original decorations done by the Native Americans adorn the mission. Excavations are underway to unearth more of the mission's past, and you may be able to watch some work. A picnic area is in front of the mission. Kids who have seen the old *Zorro* shows on the Disney Channel may be interested to know that part of the mission was used as background for them.

■ Inland

● San Diego Railway Museum

Campo Train Operations and Museum: 916 Sheridan Road, Campo. Campo is located 45 miles east of San Diego. Take the Buckman Springs exit from I-8 and go south to Highway 94, then west one mile to Campo; follow signs to the museum. (619) 697-7762 (taped information); (619) 595-3030 (business office); (619) 478-9937 (Campo Depot, weekends). Weekends, 9 A.M.–5 P.M. Trains depart at 12:01 P.M. and 2:30 P.M. Adults, $10; seniors, $8; ages 6–12, $3; under 6, free. La Mesa Depot: La Mesa and Spring streets, La Mesa. Weekends, 1–4 P.M., or by appointment. Free. **All ages.**

The San Diego Railroad Museum is a volunteer organization dedicated to preserving the nation's railroad heritage. The museum maintains an extensive collection of historic locomotives, freight cars, and passenger cars at its Campo Museum and Train Operation Center. Among them are a pair of plush private cars used by Franklin D. Roosevelt when he was campaigning for his second term. You can tour the cars and watch the members at work restoring the trains. But best of all, you can take a train ride. Trains leave Campo at 12:01 and 2:30 P.M. on weekends (you should be there at least an hour before) for an hour-and-a-half round-trip scenic ride through the hills of the San Diego backcountry. The trains run over the old San Diego & Arizona Railway, originally built through Campo in

1915. The excursions are geared for families and are a lot of fun. Before or after the train ride, you can take a guided tour of the Campo facility. You may be able to watch some of the restoration work, and you will get a close-up look at their extensive collection of freight and passenger cars. A small store sells railroad souvenirs, soft drinks, and packaged sandwiches and snacks. There are shaded picnic grounds, and you can take food on the train. Longer rail excursions to Jacumba (California), Tecate (Mexico), and elsewhere also take place throughout the year.

The museum also maintains the 1894 **La Mesa Depot,** which members restored, in downtown La Mesa. The depot, open weekends, is furnished with authentic turn-of-the-century equipment and artifacts. Outside you'll see a freight train with a steam locomotive.

● Antique Gas and Steam Engine Museum

2040 North Santa Fe Drive, Vista. Exit the I-5 on Highway 76 in Oceanside. Take Highway 76 east seven miles to North Santa Fe Street. Turn south and go two miles to entrance. (619) 941-1791. Daily, 10 A.M.–4 P.M. Free, however admission is charged for the semiannual shows. **All ages.**

Located on forty acres of rolling farmland that is leased from the county, the Antique Gas and Steam Engine Museum preserves and restores farm equipment and machinery powered by steam and gas engines. The big events of the year here are the semiannual shows held the third and fourth weekends in June and October. There are farming demonstrations, a threshing bee, tractor and antique equipment parades, train rides, hayrides, fiddlers and square dancing, and an old-fashioned barbecue. You'll also see a blacksmith shop in operation, farmhouse exhibits, a steam-operated sawmill, horse-drawn equipment, and more.

If you come at a time other than a show event, the museum is very quiet, but still enjoyable. You can roam around the grounds and see the old equipment. Most days, you'll be able to see someone working on the machinery. There is a small park with a couple of swings and a museum with a jumble of antique equipment.

● San Diego Wild Animal Park

Located 30 miles north of downtown San Diego via I-15/Highway 163. From Los Angeles, take the I-5 south to Highway 78 at Oceanside; take Highway 78 east to the I-15 at Escondido; take the I-15 south to Via Rancho Parkway and follow signs to the park. (619) 234-6541. Open daily at 9 A.M.; closing hours vary by season. Ticket package includes admission, monorail, and all shows: Adults, $18.95; ages 3–11, $11.95; under 3, free. Parking, $3. **All ages.**

Within the city limits of San Diego is an 1,800-acre wildlife preserve where exotic animals roam freely in a setting similar to their native homelands. You won't get as close a look at the animals as at the San Diego Zoo, the Wild Animal Park's parent institution. However, you will get to see how animals such as lions, Bengal tigers, elephants, rhinos, and giraffes behave in the wild, in African and Asian settings.

You enter the park through Nairobi Village, a recreated African village. Children will enjoy the petting *kraal,* where they can pet deer, sheep, and other gentle animals, and the Hidden Jungle, where they are surrounded by butterflies, hummingbirds, orchids, and other tropical plants and birds. They will also enjoy the Animal Care Center, where they can look through the windows to see the baby animals being cared for and fed. In Mombasa Lagoon, kids can put on a pair of fox ears to experience the acute hearing of a bat-eared fox, crawl into a large turtle shell, and explore other interactive exhibits. There are also a number of animal shows and exhibits in Nairobi Village.

To see the rhinoceroses, zebras, cheetahs, and other wild animals, you take a five-mile, fifty- to sixty-minute ride on a monorail from Nairobi Village. The train makes ample stops for observation, and the driver-guides identify the animals. The monorail ride is best taken in the early morning or late afternoon, because the animals often sleep in the midday heat. (The monorail ride can be very difficult with small children, however. You can't get off once the monorail starts, and sixty minutes can be a very long time on a crowded tram with a restless two-year-old.)

You can also see some of the animals from a safe distance on the 1.75-mile Kilimanjaro Hiking Trail that leads out of the Nairobi Village. There is a picnic place along the trail. The park also includes other picnic areas and a variety of restaurants and snack bars.

A new Roar and Snore camping safari lets families camp in a tent overnight in the park. Nature hikes, a campfire, and encounters with the animals are part of the adventure. (For more information on the program, phone 619-738-5049.)

● San Pasqual Battlefield State Historic Park

State Highway 78, just east of the San Diego Wild Animal Park. (619) 220-5430. Saturday and Sunday, 10 A.M.–5 P.M. Telephone about school group tours. Free. **Ages 6 and up.**

One of the bloodier battles of the Mexican-American War was fought between American and native Californian troops in this quiet valley. The battle is commemorated by this state historic park. A visitors center has displays (with text in both English and Spanish) on the battle and on the

Native Americans of the valley. A ten-minute video on the Mexican-American War is also shown. The park has a nature trail, and picnicking is permitted.

● Lake Wohlford

Northeast of Escondido. From Escondido, take S-6 (Valley Parkway, then Valley Center Road) to Lake Wohlford road. Turn right and go about two miles to lake. (619) 738-4346. Daily, 6 A.M.–7:30 P.M. **All ages.**

There is a fine picnic area on the shores of this pleasant lake set in rugged hills. The lake offers boating and excellent fishing (a license is required), but no swimming. Lake Wohlford Resort (phone: 619-749-2755) has boat rentals, bait, and tackle. The cafe also serves a really good catfish and hush puppy dinner. Cafe hours are Monday through Thursday, 5 A.M.–2 P.M.; Friday and Saturday, 5 A.M.–8 P.M.

● Bates Brothers Nut Farm

15954 Woods Valley Road, Valley Center. Take the S-6 north from Escondido to Valley Center. (619) 749-3333. Daily, 9 A.M.–5 P.M. Free. **All ages.**

This farm is a pleasure, offering visitors spacious green picnic grounds in a pretty country setting. Ducks, goats, sheep, and other farm animals reside behind fences and can be petted. A country store sells the farm's products and bags of feed for the animals. Although you can tour the nut processing facilities by request on weekdays, the attraction of this place for children are the animals and the green open spaces in which to run and play.

● Palomar Observatory

From Oceanside, take Highway 76 past Pala and five miles beyond Rincon Springs; turn left on S-6 and continue up the mountain. (619) 742-2119. Daily, 9 A.M.–4 P.M. Free. **All ages.**

High on Palomar Mountain is the giant Hale telescope, whose 200-inch-diameter mirror gathers light beams from distant galaxies and focuses them on photographic plates to produce pictures of those galaxies. The massive telescope can be viewed from a glassed-in balcony viewing room. (Wear sweaters; it's cool inside.) Nearby is a small museum containing a model of Hale's mirror and illuminated color photographs of the planets, some of the galaxies, and star clusters.

There are a number of nice spots for picnics and outdoor activities in the area. One picnic ground is close to the observatory near the Palomar Mountain Forest Station. Heading down the road from Palomar Observatory, you can go west at Summit Junction for about three miles on S-7 to **Palomar Mountain State Park,** nearly two thousand acres of parkland in a lush, densely wooded mountain region with magnificent views. The park has complete facilities for camping, good picnic areas, and plenty of hiking trails.

A short distance east of Summit Junction is **Palomar Mountain County Park,** a small but beautiful forested mountain park with picnic tables, fireplaces, and restrooms.

You could also return to Highway 76 and travel east to the **San Luis Rey Picnic Area,** a lovely spot with a rushing stream, shade trees, and picnic facilities. If you go a little farther east on Highway 76, you can picnic at Lake Henshaw (which can also be reached by going east on S-7 from Summit Junction).

● Julian

Sixty miles northeast of San Diego at the junction of Highways 78 and 79. From Los Angeles, take I-5 south, then go east on 78. From San Diego, take I-8 east, then go north on 79. **All ages.**

In the late 1860s, prospectors struck gold in the mountains near the settlement of Julian. False-front stores, gaudy hotels, saloons, and dance halls sprang up to serve the prosperous miners. When the boon ended, the town settled into being a sleepy little agricultural community.

Today Julian still has its original false-front stores, wooden sidewalks, old homes, and elegant old hotel. You can sip a soda at an old-fashioned marble counter in the drugstore. Less than a block away is an old one-room school, now used as a library but still retaining its old-fashioned school desks.

A small museum is housed in an old masonry building that was once a brewery and a blacksmith shop. The **Julian Museum,** located at 2811 Washington Street (phone: 619-765-0227), is open November–May, Tuesday–Sunday, 10 A.M.–4 P.M., and on weekends, 10 A.M. to 4 P.M., the rest of the year. Among the exhibits are turn-of-the-century clothing, household equipment, dolls, a foot-treadle printing press, and a mail pouch with a parachute that was dropped in 1938 on Julian's first airmail delivery.

Kids will enjoy a tour of the **Eagle Mine** at the end of C Street (open 10 A.M.–2 P.M., daily; phone: 619-765-0036). At the end of the tour, kids can pan for gold. There are a number of home-style restaurants in the town. Julian can get very crowded on holiday and summer weekends; you might wish to schedule your trip to avoid these times.

● Cuyamaca Rancho State Park

Highway 79 between Julian to the north and Descanso Junction to the south. Take I-8 east from San Diego and go north on Highway 79. (619) 765-0755. Open daily. Day use: $5 per vehicle. Campsites: weekdays, $15; weekends, $16. (Reservations should be made at least ten days in advance by phoning DESTINET at 800-444-7275). Park headquarters is seven miles south of Cuyamaca Lake, a half-mile east of Highway 79. Open Monday–Friday, 8:30 A.M.–4:30 P.M.; Saturday and Sunday, 10 A.M.–2 P.M. **Ages 6 and up.**

Located about forty miles east of San Diego on the western slopes of the Laguna Range, this popular state park stretches over some 21,000 acres. The terrain includes high mountain peaks; dense forests; many open meadows; and a wide range of flowering plants, streams, and springs. The varied bird and animal population includes deer, raccoons, squirrels, badgers, skunks, and bobcats. There also have been mountain lion sightings in the area, so keep a close eye on children. There are more than one hundred miles of hiking and riding trails, and the park generally has snow in the winter. Cuyamaca Lake is stocked with trout each year. Overnight camping is available in two campgrounds. The park gets heavy use on weekends.

The park's visitor center, located in the historic, native-stone and oak Dyar house, is a good source for park maps and information. The headquarters includes a small museum that interprets the Native American era of Cuyamaca.

● Laguna Recreation Area

About 12.5 miles north of the junction of I-8 and S-1. Take I-8 east from San Diego past the towns of Alpine and Pine Valley. Go north on S-1 about 12.5 miles to recreation area. Descanso Ranger District phone: (619) 445-6235. Open daily. Free. Laguna Visitors Information Center is located at Sunrise Highway and Shriner's Road, across from Laguna Lodge. Phone: (619) 473-8547. Saturday and Sunday, 9 A.M.–4 P.M. (May close at lunch.) From Memorial Day to Labor Day also open Friday, 2–6 P.M. **All ages.**

In the heart of the Cleveland National Forest, the Laguna Recreation Area is in a lovely setting of pine and oak trees. Most of the area is about six thousand feet in elevation, sunny and warm in the summer with cool nights, and cold with some snow during the winter. The area is beautiful, with high peaks, two small lakes, views of the desert below, vast stands of oak, sycamore, pine, big-cone spruce, fir and incense cedar, wildflowers in the spring, and a variety of bird and animal life. Desert View, a quarter of a mile north of Mount Laguna, offers the best picnic facilities in the area, plus a great view of the desert.

Stop in at the Mount Laguna Visitors Center (open weekends) for detailed information on hiking trails, self-guided nature trails, and on weekends during the summer, naturalist-led nature walks.

● Anza-Borrego Desert State Park

From Los Angeles and Orange County, take I-5 south to Highway 76 at Oceanside. Travel east on Highway 76 for 69 miles. At the end of Highway 76, turn left onto Highway 79 and go five miles to S-2. Turn right on S-2 and go 5 miles to Highway S-22. Turn left on Highway S-22 through the town of Ranchita and down a twelve-mile, eight percent grade. At stop sign, turn left for Visitors Center. From San Diego, take I-8 east to the Highway 67 off-ramp north to Romona. Go through Romona to Santa Ysabel. Turn left on Highway 79. Go about ten miles to Highway S-2, turn right on S-2, and follow directions above. Park headquarters is in Borrego Palm Canyon, three miles northwest of Borrego Springs. (619) 767-5311. For a list of lodgings, contact the Chamber of Commerce, Borrego Springs, CA 92004. Phone: (619) 767-5555. **All ages.**

Extending almost the entire length of San Diego County's eastern border region, from Riverside County to the Mexican border, is Anza-Borrego Desert State Park. The nation's largest state park, it comprises more than a half-million acres. Although much of the land is a raw desert wilderness that should be explored only by experienced desert hands, the park still has a great deal to offer casual visitors and families. Along accessible trails are oases of fan palms, wild plum trees, elephant trees, tamarisks, oaks, cottonwoods, creek beds with lush vegetation, and surrealistic sandstone canyons sculpted by millions of years of wind and rain.

Borrego Palm Canyon, the site of the park headquarters, is probably the best spot for families. The main campground includes sun shelters, gas stoves, showers, and RV hookups. In this area are date groves, a viewpoint overlooking the spectacularly eroded Borrego Badlands, and a self-guided nature trail leading up to a canyon of palms. Nature programs, tours, and campfire programs are given by park rangers on the weekends from November through May. The park headquarters will provide you with maps and all sorts of other information, including places to take younger children in the park.

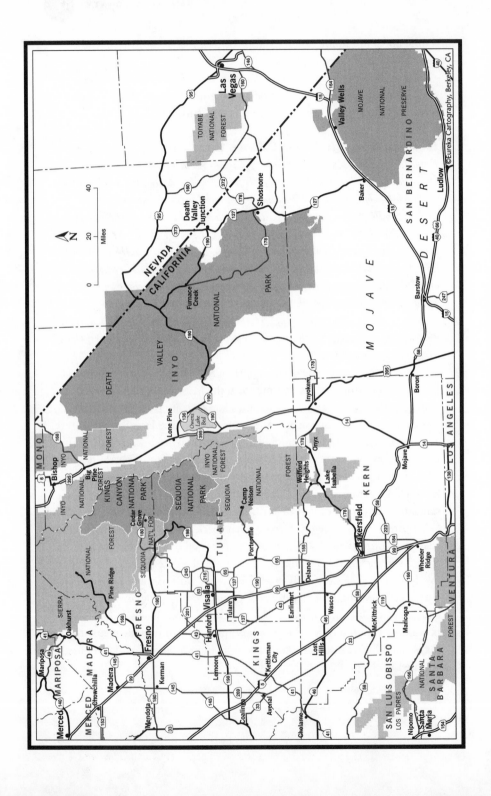

Inyo, Kern, and Tulare Counties

THE HEART OF California's agricultural production, scenic forests, and a vast and fascinating desert are all part of the landscape of these counties. Many of the things to do with children in this region are nature activities, from an exploration of Death Valley to a visit to see one of the last remaining herds of dwarf elk, or a trip to look at the world's oldest trees.

In addition to natural wonders, these counties also offer children some of the state's most exciting historical attractions. At the Kern County Museum in Bakersfield, kids can explore the creation of an entire frontier town. At the town of Laws, near Bishop, they can play in an eleven-acre restoration of a nineteenth-century railroad community complete with trains. And on selected Sundays during the year, families can see a mock Civil War battle in a historic fort that once housed the country's only camel cavalry.

Although these counties cover a huge area, the places suggested in this chapter can be reached easily from either Bakersfield, Bishop, or Death Valley.

In and Around Bakersfield

● Kern County Museum and Lori Brock Children's Discovery Center

3801 Chester Avenue, Bakersfield. (805) 861-2132. Monday–Friday, 8 A.M.–5 P.M. Saturday and holidays, 10 A.M.–5 P.M.; Sunday, noon– 5 P.M. (Tickets sold until 3:30 P.M., daily.) Adults, $5; seniors, $4; children ages 3–12, $3; under 3, free. **All ages.**

A museum building, a sixteen-acre outdoor village of historic structures, and a children's discovery center are all part of the Kern County Museum. The outdoor village is set up like a nineteenth-century town, with tree-shaded streets and large grassy areas. The fifty-some original and reconstructed structures range from a completely furnished Victorian mansion to a log cabin. Kids can peer through glass partitions to see the interiors of the buildings, which are furnished in a rich historical detail that often includes mannequins in period costumes. There's a general store from 1889, stocked the way it would have been; a railroad station with a shoeshine stand that advertises shines for ten cents; a one-room school-house; and authentically furnished doctor's, dentist's, and newspaper offices. Other buildings include an undertaker's shop, a bank, dressmaker and watchmaker shops, a courthouse, jail, and so on—in other words, a complete town. The village is laid out with lots of green space between the buildings, and there are plenty of shady places to rest, play, or have a picnic.

The museum building, a large Spanish-style structure adjacent to the museum, contains exhibits on the human and natural history of the area. Among the displays in the two-story, older building are Native American artifacts, stuffed wildlife, old rifles, and antique cars and carriages.

The Lori Brock Children's Discovery Center, a small, hands-on museum for kids, is also part of the Kern County Museum. Workshops and other activities are held at the Discovery Center throughout the year, and there is a program of summer classes. The Kern County Museum also has a number of special events geared toward kids and families throughout the year.

● Bakersfield Museum of Art

1930 R Street, central Bakersfield. Monday–Saturday, 9 A.M.–4 P.M. Gates locked at 4 P.M. Adults, $3; children, free. **Ages 8 and up.**

Bakersfield has a small, pleasant museum of art that features a permanent collection of California regional art and changing exhibits. Some of the changing exhibits, in particular, may interest kids, such as a past one on aviation art. The museum also has exhibits of student art and offers art classes for children.

● California Living Museum

14000 Alfred Harrell Highway, Bakersfield. Northeast of central Bakersfield about thirteen miles via Alfred Harrell Highway (178). Located on frontage road near Lake Ming. (805) 872-2256. Wednesday–Sunday, 9 A.M.–4 P.M. No tickets sold after 3 P.M. Adults, $3.50; seniors, $2.50; ages 3–12, $2; under 3, free. **All ages.**

The California Living Museum is a combination zoo, botanical garden, and natural history museum devoted to California wildlife. You'll get a close-up look at coyotes, bobcats, kit foxes, a pair of mountain lions, a porcupine, and other animals native to California. Most of the animals displayed are unreleasable into the wild because of injuries or other reasons. The museum's birds of prey collection includes native hawks, owls, and eagles—all disabled and unable to survive in the wild. Other exhibits include an earth-covered reptile house, a walk-in bird aviary, a tortoise enclosure, and a pleasant waterfowl lagoon. A nature trail follows a simulated Kern River, and a children's park allows kids to get up close to a variety of tame animals. All exhibits can be reached by wheelchair, and strollers are available. There are shaded picnic areas on the museum grounds. The grounds are dusty, so dress accordingly. Also, it can get very hot in the desert sun, so you probably will want to avoid a midday visit in the summer.

● Hart Memorial Park

Northeast of Bakersfield thirteen miles on Alfred Harrell Highway (178). (805) 872-5149. Daily, 6 A.M.–10 P.M. Free. **All ages.**

This eighty-acre park along the Kern River includes a safe place to play in the water, a casting pond, shady picnic grounds, and children's playgrounds. You can also rent boats, canoes, aqua cycles, and pedal cruises at the snack bar.

● Rankin Guest Ranch

Box 36, Caliente 93518. From Bakersfield, take Highway 58 east; turn onto the Caliente cutoff road and proceed thirteen miles. (805) 867-2511. Reservations required. Guest season: about April 1–October 1. **All ages.**

In the hands of the same family since 1863, The Rankin Ranch is a 31,000-acre working cattle ranch that—luckily for us—has also been hosting guests for the past thirty or so years. Guests stay in rustic but very comfortable cabin rooms, spread out on the wooded grounds for privacy. Each cabin has two spacious, separate rooms that can be connected for families. (Two kids can also sleep comfortably in the room with you.) Families join the other guests, ranch hands, and members of the Rankin family for three hearty meals a day served either outdoors or in a homey dining room.

The ranch is located in a beautiful setting in the Tehachapi Mountains. There's a shaded swimming pool, an oak-paneled lodge with a fireplace, comfortable chairs, board games, and a pool table for the twelve-and-older set. Horseback rides take guests through mountain-and-meadow country. Other activities include hayrides and barbecues, fishing in a small lake and in Walker's Basin Creek, hiking on quiet country roads, tennis, archery, horseshoes, and all sorts of enjoyable family evening entertainment. (Best of all, there is no television.)

During the summer and school vacations, the ranch has a children's counselor on staff who supervises special programs for children from ages four to twelve, including picnics, crafts, horseback riding instruction and horseback rides.

All activities—including the children's programs, fishing, and horseback riding—and all meals are included in the price. The daily rate for two adults sharing a cabin is $135 each. For each child ages six through eleven in the same room with an adult, the rate is $85. Two or more children in a separate adjoining room from the parents are $120 each. Four- and five-year-olds in the same room with parents are $60 each; children under four years are $30; and children under two years are free. Cribs and high chairs are available. Weekly and off-season rates are less. The top guest capacity is about thirty-five people at a time.

A stay at the Rankin Guest Ranch is an out-of-the-ordinary vacation experience, and it cannot be recommended too highly.

● Tehachapi Mountain Park/Tehachapi Train Loop

Seven miles southwest of Tehachapi; forty miles east of Bakersfield on Highway 58. (805) 822-4632. Free. **All ages.**

At an altitude ranging from five thousand to seven thousand feet, this pleasant mountain park offers hiking during the summer months and sledding and tobogganing during the winter. The pine-shaded, 570-acre park is full of birds, squirrels, and, occasionally, deer.

About ten miles north of the park is the famous Tehachapi (Walong) Loop, built in 1876 to get trains through the rugged mountain pass. The rails here appear to be making two circles, winding around themselves in a knot. From a viewpoint on a dirt road beside the tracks (off Highway 58 near Keene, just west of the historical marker), you can watch trains of more than eighty-five cars loop over themselves, with the engine passing just eleven feet above the cars still entering the tunnel below. The trains pass through fairly frequently, and it is worth a wait to see such an unusual sight.

● Lake Isabella

South of Kernville. From Bakersfield, take Highway 178 east. (619) 379-5646. Open daily, year-round. Free. **Ages 6 and up.**

Lake Isabella is the largest freshwater lake in Southern California. Nine miles across at its widest point, the lake has thirty-eight miles of shoreline. It is ranked as the top lake for catching bass in California. Rainbow trout, blue gill, and catfish also make their home here. Boat rentals are available. There are numerous camping and picnicking areas around the lake. The lake is at the base of the Sequoia National Forest. For information about camping and other activities in Sequoia, stop by or contact the U.S. Forest Service's new visitors center off Highway 155, just south of the lake's main dam at 4875 Ponderosa Road. The mailing address is: P.O. Box 3810, Lake Isabella, CA 93240-3810.

● Buena Vista Aquatic Recreation Area

Near Taft via Highway 119. Located about twenty-five miles west of Bakersfield. From Bakersfield, take Highway 99 south to Highway 119; go west on 119 to Enos Lane (Highway 43) and turn left. (805) 763-1526. Open daily, 5 A.M.–10 P.M. Day use: $5 per vehicle (up to 10 people). Dogs, $3; boats, $7. **All ages.**

This Kern County–operated, 980-acre recreation area includes an 86-acre fishing lake and an 873-acre boating lake with areas designated for watercycles. There are two swimming lagoons, as well as a bike path and playgrounds. Picnic areas are located throughout the park, but you should come early for a spot in the shade. Overnight camping is available in developed sites. Buena Vista gets very crowded on summer weekends, so be prepared for a wait to enter.

● Tule Elk State Reserve

Located 20 miles west of Bakersfield near Tupman. From Bakersfield, take Stockdale Highway west twenty miles, then turn south on Morris Road to Station Road. The reserve is located about a quarter mile west on Station Road. From the I-5, take the Stockdale Highway exit west three miles. (805) 765-5004. Open daily, 8 A.M. until sunset. Parking, $3. **All ages.**

One of the last herds of rare California tule elk resides in a 946-acre park created especially for their preservation. The animals are about two-thirds the size of other species of elk and are much lighter in color. The herd roams freely through the reserve. Perhaps the most certain time to see them is in the morning, although if you plan to stay a couple of hours at the reserve, you almost always will get a chance to see them. Park personnel are happy to answer questions about the animals. A small visitors center is open every Sunday from 1 to 5 P.M.

The reserve has a covered viewing platform with a telescope, but you should remember to bring binoculars. There are shady picnic tables, barbecue pits, running water, and restrooms in the grassy viewing area. You may want to come here for a picnic or in combination with a visit to the nearby Buena Vista Aquatic Recreation Center, just in case the elk don't show.

Calves are born during April and May, and you can take a special tour to see the calves every Saturday from mid-April through May. The tours begin at 8:30 A.M. and last about an hour and a half. The reserve also has a junior ranger program for children ages seven to twelve that is usually scheduled at 11 A.M. on the same day as the tours. Call the reserve for more information on both programs.

● Fort Tejon State Historic Park

Fort Tejon exit off I-5, 3.5 miles north of Lebec (thirty-six miles south of Bakersfield). (805) 248-6692. Park open daily, 8 A.M.–4 P.M. Adults, $2; ages 6–12, $1; under 6, free. Battle and Living History Days admission: Adults, $3; ages 6–12, $2. **All ages.**

Fort Tejon was established by the U.S. Army in 1854 to protect and control the Native Americans living on the Sebastian Reservation in the southern San Joaquin Valley, and to protect government property at the reservation. In addition, the troopers guarded miners, chased bandits, and generally offered protection to the southern part of the state. The fort also had the only camel cavalry in the United States. On the orders of then-secretary of war Jefferson Davis, who was later to be president of the Confederacy, camels were imported to the post for carrying supplies to isolated desert posts. The camels worked out splendidly, but the experiment was abandoned at the outbreak of the Civil War. The fort itself was abandoned in 1864.

Fort Tejon is now restored as a state historic park. A map, available at the headquarters museum, leads you in a half-mile loop around the historic area of the old fort grounds. (This area is only half of the original army post; the rest stood where the freeway and the Tejon Ranch presently are.) You'll see the reconstructed barracks building, with officers and enlisted men's rooms; the first sergeant's rooms, with uniforms and equipment; and the commander's house. All are furnished as they would have been in the 1850s. Also on the trail is the guardhouse, jail, and the original, unrestored officer's quarters. A path through the meadow leads to the fort cemetery. Next to Grapevine Creek, near the park entrance, is a grassy picnic area under big shade trees.

On the third Sunday of every month from May through October, a mock Civil War battle takes place in the park, complete with blue- and grey-uniformed soldiers, old guns, and cannons. (Bring your own folding chairs or blankets, as no seating is provided.) The park also has a program of Living History Days with volunteers dressed in period attire and activities for children. Phone for the schedule.

● Colonel Allensworth State Historic Park

Twenty miles north of Wasco on Highway 43. Take Highway 46 east from I-5 or west from Highway 99, then go north on Highway 43. (805) 849-3433. Open daily. Day use: $3 per car. Campsites: $8. **All ages.**

The town of Allensworth was founded in 1908 by Colonel Allen Allensworth as a self-governing and completely self-sufficient community for African Americans—a place where they could live and work in peace. An escaped slave who served with the Union forces during the Civil War, Allensworth was also a successful restaurateur, a minister, an army chaplain, and the highest-ranking African American military officer of his time. The town he founded prospered—there was a school, church, library, post office, hotel, and shops—until its water supply eventually failed. Allensworth was slowly abandoned, its buildings left to decay.

In 1974 the town became a state historic park, and the town's appearance is slowly being restored. The visitors center, open daily from 10 A.M. to 4 P.M., has displays and shows a thirty-minute film on Colonel Allensworth and the town. Nearby is the restored school and the reconstructed home of Colonel Allensworth. Both buildings are open on request. This area includes green lawns and shaded picnic grounds. Five other buildings have been restored—you can look through their windows. The rest of the town awaits restoration and is rather desolate.

The park has a semi-improved campground (no hookups). Special events take place in the park throughout the year, including an old-time jubilee and celebrations of African American History Month.

The Bishop Area

● Bishop City Park and Visitors Center

690 North Main Street, corner of Main (Highway 395) and Park Avenue, Bishop. Free. Visitors Center: (619) 873-8405. Hours: Monday–Friday, 9 A.M.–5 P.M.; Saturday and Sunday, 10 A.M.–4 P.M. **All ages.**

Children will enjoy feeding the ducks who make their home on the lake in this scenic city park. In addition to a beautiful setting, this large park includes a stream where you can fish for trout, a swimming pool with a water slide and showers, well-equipped children's playgrounds, a gazebo, picnic facilities—including a pavilion for sheltered eating—ball fields, and tennis courts. It has a friendly, relaxed atmosphere. On Monday evenings in the summer from 8 to 9 P.M., the Bishop Community Band plays to an audience stretched out on blankets and lawn chairs.

The Visitors Center adjacent to the park offers tourist information for the region and a most helpful staff.

● Laws Railroad Museum and Historical Site

Laws. From Bishop, take U.S. 6 northeast five miles, then go east half a mile on Silver Canyon Road. (619) 873-5950. March–mid-November: Daily, 10 A.M.–4 P.M. The rest of the year: weekends only, weather permitting.

Closed New Year's, Thanksgiving, and Christmas Day. Free, but donations appreciated. **All ages.**

The Laws Railroad Museum and Historical Site is an eleven-acre restoration of the once-active railroad community of Laws. You'll see the 1883 depot—with its displays of railroad artifacts, western items, and a working model railroad—and the old stationmaster's house, restored and furnished with turn-of-the-century items. Other buildings include the Laws post office, with old-fashioned equipment, and the Wells Fargo Building, with gold-weighing scales and displays of Native American artifacts. There are loading bunkers, a water tower, an oil tank, a hand-operated turntable, a boxcar town, a farm-wagon display, mining equipment left over from the Nevada gold rush, and more. Best of all is the Slim Princess, a narrow-gauge locomotive that is just waiting for kids to climb aboard and ring the old cattle-warning bell in its cab.

● Ancient Bristlecone Pine Forest

East of Big Pine. From Big Pine, south of Bishop, go east on Highway 168 to Westgard Pass; turn north on White Mountain Road. Daily, June–October, weather and road conditions permitting. Free. For more information, contact White Mountain District Visitors Center, 798 North Main Street, Bishop. (619) 873-2500. **All ages.**

The oldest-known living things on earth can be examined in the Bristlecone Pine Forest, a part of the Inyo National Forest. The bristlecone pines here in the White Mountains have survived more than 4,000 years, exceeding the age of the oldest giant sequoia by 1,500 years. A paved road leads to Schulman Grove, where the gnarled trees have been sculpted into astonishingly beautiful shapes and forms by the elements of centuries. An information center details some of the things scientists have learned from studying the trees. There are two self-guided nature trails. One leads to Pine Alpha, the first tree to be dated in age at more than 4,000 years. The other trail leads past the oldest of the trees, including the 4,700-year-old Methuselah tree. There are chemical toilets and a picnic area at Schulman Grove, but no water is available.

Eleven miles farther up the mountain, by way of a dirt road with spectacular views, Patriarch Grove is set within a large, open bowl, exposed to wind and weather. The trees here have been sculpted by the elements into almost abstract shapes. A self-guided trail leads past the Patriarch Tree, the largest bristlecone pine in the world. There are picnic tables, an outdoor display cases, and toilets at the grove.

Dress warmly when you visit the forest. Bring an adequate supply of water, and be sure to have a full tank of gas.

● Eastern California Museum

Corner of Grant and Center streets, Independence. Independence is south of Bishop and Big Pine on Highway 395. From Highway 395, exit at Center Street. (619) 878-0258. Wednesday–Monday, 10 A.M.–4 P.M. Free. **Ages 6 and up.**

Perhaps this museum's most interesting feature for children is its Little Pine Village, a group of old buildings furnished with original items. The buildings include a general store, blacksmith shop, livery stable, millinery shop, and barber/beauty shop. The five-acre museum grounds also have displays of Native American dwellings and antique wagons. The museum building houses Native American and pioneer artifacts, historical photographs, and natural history displays relating to this eastern Sierra region.

The Eastern California Museum also administers the **Commander's House,** a restored and furnished eleven-room Victorian that is the only structure remaining of Camp Independence, established in 1862 to protect early Owens Valley residents from Indian attacks. You can take a free guided tour of the house, which is located one block north of Center Street on Highway 395, on weekends, May through Labor Day, 2–4 P.M.

● Mount Whitney Fish Hatchery

Located a mile west of Highway 395, two miles north of Independence. Follow the signs from Highway 395. (619) 878-2272. Daily, 8 A.M.–5 P.M. Free. **All ages.**

The Mount Whitney Fish Hatchery is one of the sources for the fish that are planted in Southern California streams. There are no tours, but you are welcome to walk around on the grounds. In order to protect the fingerlings and hatching eggs, visitors are not usually admitted into the hatchery itself. But you can see larger trout swimming in the concrete raceways just north of the building. The hatchery, built of native stone in 1917, is a very attractive place, and its tree-shaded grounds include an inviting area for picnicking.

● Devil's Postpile National Monument

The monument is reached via Highway 203, which leads west from Highway 395 and the Mammoth Visitors Center. (619) 934-2289. Open daily, mid-June to mid-October. Free. Except for vehicles with camping permits, private vehicles are not allowed beyond Minaret Summit between 7:30 A.M. and 5:30 P.M., July 1–Labor Day. A shuttle bus service stops a half-mile from the Postpile. Tickets and schedule information are available at the Mammoth Mountain Ski Area. Fee: $7 per person. **Ages 6 and up.**

When nature appears to be an imitation of man-made things, it causes us to stop and wonder. The Devil's Postpile is just such a place. At this remote national monument up in the Sierra Nevada near the Mammoth ski area, thousands of symmetrical gray granite columns rise to a height of more than sixty feet. Caused by volcanic upheaval in the distant past, the formation presents a striking example of the wonders of nature. Pieces of granite have broken off and created a large pile at the base of the formation, which you can walk up and touch. As easy trail leads to the top of the columns, where glaciers have polished the surface to resemble tile inlays.

Death Valley

● Death Valley Monument

Park headquarters is located at Furnace Creek. Take Highway 190 east from Highway 395 one mile south of Lone Pine, or take Highway 127 north from I-15 at Baker. (619) 786-2331. Visitor season is October–May 15. Limited service offered during the summer months when the valley gets intensely hot. Admission: $5 per vehicle. **Ages 6 and up.**

This enormous desert valley is a place of great extremes. During the summer months, temperatures frequently reach 120 degrees, and they've been known to go as high as 134 degrees. The area contains the lowest point in the United States, Badwater, which is 282 feet below sea level. Nearby is Telescope Peak at 11,049 feet above sea level. Despite the desolate environment, plant and animal life are found everywhere. Some plants—such as Death Valley sage, rattleweed, and the panamint daisy—can be found only in this area.

You should begin your visit at the Monument Headquarters and Visitors Center in Furnace Creek. Maps and all sorts of general information, including a leaflet giving hints on safe driving in the desert, are available, and park personnel are on hand to answer questions. You will get suggestions on what to see in the amount of time you have to spend, including the driving time from the visitors center. Orientation programs are presented every half-hour, and there are frequent ranger-led hikes. A small museum at the visitors center acquaints you with the area's geology and plant and animal life. Two miles north of the visitors center, you can see the famous twenty-mule-team wagon at the site of the Harmony Borax Works.

The tourist season begins in October and last untils mid-May. There are campgrounds at Furnace Creek and elsewhere in the Monument. For reservations, phone 800-365-CAMP. Motel and resort accommodations are available in Furnace Creek and at Stovepipe Well Village. Death Valley roads and campgrounds get extremely crowded during winter three-day weekends, Thanksgiving weekend, Christmas–New Year's week, Easter week, and during the annual Death Valley Forty-Niners encampment on the first or second week of November. Make sure that you have plenty of gas and oil and that your car is in good condition when traveling in this area. Carry water both for your family and your car. Do not venture off the paved roads, and never leave your car if you have car trouble.

● Scotty's Castle

North end of Death Valley, fifty-three miles north of the Furnace Creek Visitors Center. (619) 786-2392. Open daily, 9 A.M.–5 P.M. Adults, $8; ages 6–11, $4; under 6, free. **Ages 8 and up.**

In the middle of this lonely desert area is a Spanish-Moorish mansion constructed years ago by two thousand workers at a cost of $2.5 million. The mansion was built at the whim of Walter Scott—Death Valley Scotty—an eccentric millionaire who loved the valley. The Death Valley Park Service offers tours through the castle, which is furnished with luxurious rugs, tapestries, rare art treasures, and elaborate furniture. The castle is quite a contrast to the starkness of many of the local desert towns.

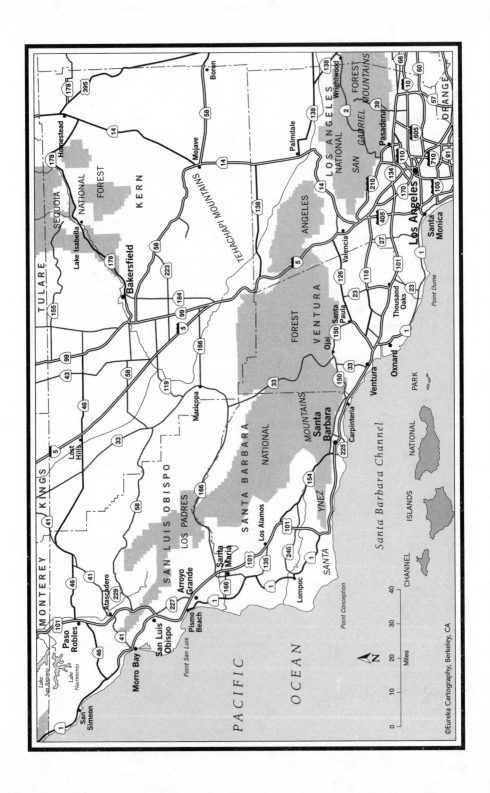

©Eureka Cartography, Berkeley, CA

Santa Barbara, Ventura, and San Luis Obispo Counties

THERE MAY BE an ugly spot between Morro Bay and Ventura, but I haven't seen it. Santa Barbara, with its Mediterranean setting and architecture, is one of California's most beautiful cities. The year-round good weather and slower-paced lifestyle here make outdoor activities—from boating to horseback riding to walking—a pleasure for families. The city has worked to preserve its history. The lovely Mission Santa Barbara is among the many places where kids can get a sense of Santa Barbara's colorful past. The Santa Barbara Visitors Information Office at One Santa Barbara Street (phone: 805-965-3021) provides visitors with accommodation information, maps, a calendar of current events, and other helpful information.

North of Santa Barbara, the Santa Ynez Valley offers some wonderful small towns to explore. South and east of Santa Barbara in Ventura, Ojai, and the Santa Clara Valley, the variety of places to go with children includes uninhabited islands in the Pacific.

Up the coast, San Luis Obispo is a city that has preserved its history as well as its small-town charm. The San Luis Obispo Chamber of Commerce, at 1039 Chorro Street (phone: 805-543-1323), offers a variety of literature for visitors. A few miles away, the once-quiet fishing village of Morro Bay offers families a wide choice of waterfront activities, including the opportunity to visit what may be Southern California's most beautiful state park.

 In and Around Santa Barbara

● Santa Barbara Zoological Gardens
500 Niños Drive, Santa Barbara. From Highway 101, take either the Milpas Street exit south or the Hot Springs Road/Cabrillo Boulevard exit to Cabrillo Boulevard. Turn toward the mountains at Niños Drive. (805)

962-6310 (tape) or (805) 962-5339. Daily, 10 A.M.–5 P.M. Tickets sold until 4 P.M. Adults, $5; ages 2–12 and seniors, $3; under 2, free. **All ages.**

This small zoo is a delight. Situated on a beautiful eighty-one-acre hilltop overlooking the Pacific, the zoo houses some five hundred animals, including lions, tigers, red pandas, gibbons, lemurs, sea lions, elephants, giraffes, and llamas. A recent addition is Max, a lowland gorilla. The animals reside in habitats that resemble their natural homes. The zoo's small size makes it easy for children to see everything, and the exhibits are designed so that small children can see without having to be lifted. The zoo, which was once the site of a palatial estate, includes beautiful gardens and rolling green lawns.

A Children's Discovery Area features a barn where kids can watch chicks hatching. The zoo also has a pleasant playground and a small carousel. Above the playground is a large, grassy picnic area with a spectacular view of Santa Barbara Harbor. (The zoo is so manageable that you can walk back to the car to get the picnic lunch when you're ready to eat.) A miniature train that adults as well as children can ride circles the park about every fifteen minutes. The zoo has a new restaurant overlooking Swan Lake, and there are snack vendors. Strollers and red wagons are available to rent. During the summer, a Zoo Camp is offered for children between age three and grade six. Workshops during the year are offered for all ages, and a birthday party package is also available.

● Andree Clark Bird Refuge

1400 East Cabrillo Boulevard, just west of the Cabrillo Boulevard exit from Highway 101, south of downtown Santa Barbara. Open daily during daylight hours. Parking is on the north side of the lagoon, near the intersection of Cabrillo Boulevard and Highway 101. Free. **All ages.**

Next to the Santa Barbara Zoological Gardens is a lovely lagoon in a garden setting that serves as a refuge for a wide variety of freshwater birds. Kids can bring bread crumbs to feed the birds. (The best location to feed them from is the clear area on the eastern shore.) A footpath and a bikeway skirt the lagoon.

● Art Show on the Boulevard

Cabrillo Boulevard, along a one-mile stretch from Sterns Wharf toward East Beach, Santa Barbara. From Highway 101, take either Cabrillo Boulevard or State Street exit. Sunday, 10 A.M. to sunset. Free. **Ages 10 and up.**

Every Sunday, local painters, sculptors, leather workers, potters, toy makers, and other craftspeople display their wares on the grass between the beach and Cabrillo Boulevard. It's a colorful display that stretches a mile. The variety is pleasing and the atmosphere can be fun for older children.

● Sea Center

211 Sterns Wharf, Santa Barbara. (805) 962-0885. Take the Cabrillo Boulevard exit off Highway 101 and follow Cabrillo north. Sterns Wharf is at the foot of State Street. Monday–Friday, noon–5 P.M.; Saturday and Sunday, 10 A.M.–5 P.M. Summer hours: Daily, 10 A.M.–5 P.M. Touch tank open daily, noon–4 P.M. Adults, $2; seniors and teens, $1.50; ages 3–12, $1; under 2, free. There is pay parking on the wharf. **All ages.**

The Sea Center is a small, bright museum on Sterns Wharf, operated by the Santa Barbara Museum of Natural History. The focus of the center is the marine environment of the Santa Barbara Channel. Life-size models of a grey whale and a bottle-nosed dolphin are suspended from the ceiling, and the open upstairs gallery lets you see them up close. There are a number of aquariums and some interactive exhibits. Chumash artifacts and some sunken ship remains are also displayed. The most enjoyable part of the center for children is the touch tank located outside. During the summer, the Sea Center adds a daily schedule of interactive programs for kids.

Next door to the Sea Center, the visitors center of the **Nature Conservancy** has nature exhibits and information on the organization's activities. Elsewhere along the wooden wharf are restaurants, snack food, a bait and tackle supply, and a chance to watch the fishermen (and the pelicans and other sea birds) at the pier's end.

● Yacht Harbor and Breakwater

West Cabrillo Boulevard, Santa Barbara. From Highway 101, take either the State Street or Castillo Street exit, go south to Cabrillo and then west to the harbor and breakwater. Open daily. The walkway is lighted at night. **All ages.**

A paved walkway on top of the breakwater protecting the Santa Barbara Yacht Harbor provides a captivating half-mile walking tour of the harbor. In addition to seeing hundreds of pleasure craft, kids will get a close-up view of the local fishing boats. If you want to get out on the water yourself, you can rent one of a variety of various-sized motorboats, sailboats, and rowboats from **Santa Barbara Boat Rentals** (phone: 805-962-2826) at the breakwater.

Sealanding Sportfishing (phone: 805-963-3564) sells bait, rents tackle, and runs daily sportfishing boats. Half-day boats usually leave at 7 A.M. and 12:30 P.M. on weekends and 10 A.M. on weekdays. The cost is

$25 for adults and $20 for children ages 14 and younger. Longer trips are also available. Rates include bait, and all boats have a galley. They also offer whale-watching cruises in the winter.

● Carriage Museum

129 Castillo Street, Santa Barbara. From Highway 101, take the Castillo Street exit south. (805) 962-2353. Sunday, 1–4 P.M. (docent present). Also usually open daily, 9 A.M.–3 P.M., to look around. Free, but donation requested. **Ages 6 and up.**

The horse-drawn carts and carriages in this museum were used by pioneer Santa Barbara residents and donated by their descendants. Among the displays are stagecoaches, buggies, army wagons, a bright red steam pumper for fire fighting, and a black hearse complete with coffin. During Santa Barbara's annual Old Spanish Days parade in August, the carriages leave the museum to ride down the streets of Santa Barbara again. Volunteers are usually working to restore the carriages every day, and kids can watch. A docent is on hand Sunday afternoons.

● Fernald House and Trussel-Winchester Adobe

414 West Montecito Street, Santa Barbara. (805) 966-1601 (Santa Barbara Historical Society). Open Sunday only, 2–4 P.M. Free. **Ages 8 and up.**

These two restored nineteenth-century houses sit next door to each other. The gabled Fernald House is a fourteen-room Victorian mansion. Its hand-carved stairway and handsome furnishings give children a glimpse of what life was like for affluent families in that period. The adobe house next door was built in 1854, partially with timbers from the wrecked ship *Winfield Scott*. Authentically furnished, the adobe is typical of the Santa Barbara architecture of the period. The houses, which are fun to see, are only open for tours two hours on Sunday afternoon.

● El Presidio de Santa Barbara State Historic Park

123 East Canon Perdido Street (one block south of Carrillo Street, two blocks east of State Street), downtown Santa Barbara. (805) 966-9719. Daily, 10:30 A.M.–4:30 P.M. Free. **Ages 6 and up.**

Founded in 1782, the Royal Presidio of Santa Barbara was the last in a chain of four military posts established in California by imperial Spain. Serving as the military headquarters and the site of civil government for an area extending from Los Angeles to just south of San Luis Obispo, the Santa Barbara Presidio was located in what is today a four-city-block area of downtown Santa Barbara.

An extensive archaeological excavation and historic reconstruction of the Presidio has been under way since the mid-sixties. (By that time only two of the original Presidio structures remained.) You can watch the excavation from behind a chain-link fence and visit the structures that already have been rebuilt. You'll see the adobe bricks used for the reconstruction stacked in the yard, and you may be able to see the bricks being made. The park headquarters is located in the restored Cañedo Adobe, which once housed Presidio soldiers and their families. Inside are displays, including a model of the Presidio as it appeared in the 1790s. The Presidio chapel has been beautifully and painstakingly reconstructed on its original foundations—many of Santa Barbara's earliest settlers lie buried beneath the tile floor. Between the chapel and the park headquarters are the reconstructed Padre's Quarters, complete with rawhide bed. On the other side of the chapel is the reconstructed Comandancia, including a recreated office and living room that look the way they might have when the original Presidio commandant used them. Outside, children will enjoy seeing a model of a carreta, an ox-drawn cart, complete with life-size oxen. Across the street is one of the oldest surviving structures in California, El Cuartel, originally one in a row of buildings that housed soldiers and their families. (The interior is closed for restoration.)

● Santa Barbara Historical Museum

136 East de la Guerra Street, two blocks south of Carrillo Street and two blocks east of State Street, downtown Santa Barbara. (805) 966-1601. Tuesday–Saturday, 10 A.M.–5 P.M.; Sunday, noon–5 P.M. Guided tours Wednesday, Saturday, and Sunday at 1:30 P.M. Free. **Ages 8 and up.**

Housed in a lovely mission-like adobe building (the bricks used to construct the museum were made from soil on the site), the Santa Barbara Historical Museum presents permanent and changing exhibits on the city's rich multicultural past. The exhibits are organized around the distinct eras and cultures of Santa Barbara's history from the native Chumash and the European explorers through the Spanish, Mexican, and Yankee eras and the city's Chinese culture. The museum's collection includes paintings, photographs, period costumes and household items, guns and saddles, antique dolls and toys, carriages—including a rickshaw—musical instruments, models of sailing ships, and much more. Exhibits may range from the European discovery of the Santa Barbara Channel to cowboy life to Santa Barbara in the movies. The museum is pretty much of a "no-touch" experience, but well worth a visit. In back is a lovely, tree-shaded courtyard with a fountain. At the rear of the courtyard, children can see an old stamp mill once used for grinding gold ore.

● Lobero Theatre

33 East Canon Perdido Street, Santa Barbara. (805) 963-0761. Box office open Monday–Saturday, 11 A.M.–5:30 P.M., plus two hours before performances. **Ages 6 and up.**

The historic Lobero Theatre is one of the oldest legitimate theaters continuously operating in California. Home to a number of Santa Barbara theater, dance, and music companies, the Lobero presents a year-round program of plays, musicals, and other entertainment ranging from chamber music and ballet to children's theater and films.

● Santa Barbara Public Library

40 East Anapamu Street (one block east of State Street, two blocks north of Carrillo Street), downtown Santa Barbara. (805) 962-7653. Monday–Friday, 10 A.M.–9 P.M.; Friday and Saturday, 10 A.M.–5:30 P.M.; Sunday, 1–5 P.M. Free. **All ages.**

Santa Barbara has an attractive and very inviting central library. The original building opened in 1917 with wings added in 1930 and 1979. Murals illustrating the adventures of Don Quixote adorn the main lobby. To the right as you enter, the Faulkner Galleries display works by local artists.

The children's library is to the right after you enter the main library. Preschool story times are offered every Tuesday and Thursday morning at 10:30. Puppet plays put on by the Library Players and other special activities for kids take place throughout the year. You can pick up a printed schedule at the library.

● Santa Barbara Museum of Art

1130 State Street at Anapamu Street, downtown Santa Barbara. (805) 963-4364. Tuesday, Wednesday, Friday, and Saturday, 11 A.M.–5 P.M.; Thursday, 11 A.M.–9 P.M.; Sunday, noon–5 P.M. Adults, $4; seniors, $3; ages 6–17, $1.50; under 6, free. Free every Thursday and on the first Sunday of the month. **Ages 6 and up.**

Santa Barbara has one of the finest regional art museums in the country. Housed in bright, airy galleries, the collection ranges from ancient Egyptian to contemporary art. The works include Greek and Roman sculpture; Egyptian antiquities; Asian art, including an impressive display of nineteenth-century Japanese armor; old masters; American art; European art, including paintings by Monet and other Impressionists; and photographs. The museum's small size, as well as the scope of its collection, gives children a good opportunity to find works that interest them.

In addition to its permanent displays, the museum offers changing exhibits from its own collections and from traveling shows. The museum has a large collection of dolls and toys that it sometimes displays in a changing exhibit. Classes, summer holiday camps, and workshops for children and families are offered at the museum's **Ridley-Tree Education Center,** located at 1600 Santa Barbara Street, a short walk away. Museum tours and programs for schoolchildren are available throughout the year. The museum also holds special family-day celebrations.

● Kid's World
Corner of Micheltorena and Garden streets in Alameda Park, three blocks east of State Street and three blocks north of Anapamu Street, downtown Santa Barbara. Free. **Ages 1–12.**

Designed by an architect working with input from Santa Barbara schoolchildren, this playground is a kid's dream. The architect, Bob Leathers of New York, met with a large group of elementary schoolchildren who told him what they would like in a playground. Later, he worked with a smaller group of children to refine the blueprints. Paid for in part by donations from kids, the playground was built by some four thousand volunteers in five days—and what a playground it is! Built with a fanciful castle motif, the large playground includes lookout towers, wooden suspension bridges, climbing ropes, steering wheels, tire steps, cubbies for hiding, and about a zillion places to climb and run. There are balance beams, tire swings, a glider, rings, a "bouncy" bridge, a circular slide, and even a play shark and whale. The kid designers asked for and got a finger maze (that's one kids follow with their fingers), as well as a large, built-in tic-tac-toe board. Toddlers and preschoolers each have their own play area, and seating for adults has been incorporated into the structure. All kids should be lucky enough to have a playground like this in their town.

● Mission Santa Barbara
Upper end of Laguna Street, Santa Barbara. From Highway 101, take the Mission Street exit and turn left at Laguna Street. (805) 682-4713. Daily, 9 A.M.–4 P.M. Adults, $3; under 16, free. **Ages 8 and up.**

On a hill overlooking the city is the beautiful Mission Santa Barbara. Established in 1786, the mission is still used as a parish church. It is the only one of the California missions that has remained continuously in the hands of the Franciscans; the altar light has burned constantly since the mission was built.

On a self-guided tour through the mission, you'll see a typical padre's bedroom, the kitchen, eighteenth- and nineteenth-century furniture and kitchen utensils, examples of mission crafts and tools, and a Chumash Indian room. Displays include a history of the mission site, an exhibit on the mission's construction, and a collection of early photographs. The tour also passes through the flower-filled courtyard, the sanctuary, and the cemetery, whose crypts reflect the various degrees of wealth of the parishioners. In front of the church, a Moorish fountain flows into an ancient laundry trough. The mission faces a spacious and lovely grassy park where you can relax in the sun.

● Museum of Natural History

2559 Puesta de Sol Road (two blocks north of the mission; follow signs), Santa Barbara. (805) 682-4711. Monday–Saturday, 9 A.M.–5 P.M.; Sunday, 10 A.M.–5 P.M. Adults, $5; seniors and ages 13–17, $4; under 13, $3. Free on the first Sunday of every month. **Ages 3 and up.**

Surrounded by eleven acres of wooded ground, this museum focuses on the natural history and anthropology of the Pacific Coast. Each of the exhibit halls houses a different permanent collection, such as fossils or Native American artifacts. The Bird Hall includes two giant California condors, one hanging from the ceiling with its great wings outstretched. The Insect and Plant Interactions Hall uses live specimens, activity drawers, videos, and interactive computer displays to explore local plant and insect life. The new Reptile and Amphibian Hall, Lizard Lounge, features all kinds of live, cold-blooded creatures, as well as interactive exhibits. The Chumash Indian Hall has the largest collection of Chumash artifacts in the West, including a full-size replica of a Chumash canoe. Other highlights include a full-size model of a thirty-three-foot giant squid hanging from the ceiling in the Marine Hall, a cast of a pygmy mammoth skeleton recently uncovered on Santa Rosa Island, and the complete skeleton of a giant grey whale that is in front of the museum as you enter. You can also stroll the museum grounds, which are quite beautiful. The museum cafe serves sandwiches, cold drinks, and other items beside Mission Creek.

The museum **planetarium** presents thirty-minute shows for children ages six and up on Wednesday, Saturday, and Sunday afternoons, and every afternoon during the summer (telephone 805-682-3224 for information on planetarium shows). In addition to the planetarium, the Astronomy Center at the museum includes a **Space Lab** with state-of-the-art interactive computer exhibits. The Space Lab is open from noon to 4 P.M., daily. The museum also sponsors winter whale-watching trips and offers summer science classes for children and families.

● Santa Barbara Botanic Garden

1212 Mission Canyon Road (1.5 miles north of the mission), Santa Barbara. (805) 682-4726. November–February, weekdays, 9 A.M.–4 P.M.; Saturday and Sunday, 9 A.M.–5 P.M. Rest of year, weekdays, 9 A.M.–5 P.M.; Saturday and Sunday, 9 A.M.–6 P.M. Adults, $3; seniors and teenagers, $2; ages 5– 12, $1; under 5, free. **All ages.**

In the foothills above Santa Barbara, up the canyon from the mission, is a beautiful sixty-five-acre garden of native California plant life. Five and a half miles of scenic, easy trails meander through a meadow of wild-flowers, a grove of redwood trees, oak woodlands, an area of desert plants, mountain chaparral, and a growth of manzanita. The trails lead up and down the canyon, along a stream, and to the historic Mission Dam built by Native Americans at the beginning of the nineteenth century—it supplied water to the mission. Redwood benches are placed all along the trails, and there is a small picnic area.

The gravel-covered trails are accessible by strollers. The admission counter has trail maps and a schedule of activities. The Botanic Garden also has an extensive education program that includes activities for children.

● Santa Barbara by Bike

Directions to the bike paths and a path map are available from the San Barbara Visitors Information Service, 1 Santa Barbara Street, Santa Barbara. (805) 965-3021. **Ages 8 and up.**

Santa Barbara is a marvelous place for bicycling. The area is both scenic and relatively flat, and the weather is nearly always comfortable. A four-mile bikeway runs along the beachfront from the bird refuge to the mesa on the west. Branches of the bikeway also extend through the city, and a path runs from Goleta through the University of California campus. There are also plenty of bicycle racks throughout downtown and along the traveled routes. If you wish to rent bikes, **Beach Rentals** at 22 State Street, across from Stearns Wharf, has a good selection (phone: 805-966-6733). Rates start at about $5 an hour. They are open daily. For a differ-ent kind of biking experience, **Cycles Four Rent** (corner of State and Mason streets, and at the Red Lion and Sheraton hotels) rents a four-wheeled buggy-like bike that can carry up to four grown-ups (phone: 805-966-3804).

● Stow House

304 Los Carneros Road, Goleta. From Highway 101 just north of Santa Barbara, take the Los Carneros Road exit north. (805) 964-4407. Saturday and Sunday, 2–4 P.M. $1 per person. **All ages.**

The oldest frame house in Goleta Valley (dating from 1872) has been completely restored and furnished with Victorian trappings, including period clothing and toys. The tree-shaded grounds include a bunkhouse, a small museum, and a blacksmith's barn complete with tools from the 1800s. Every October the **Goleta Lemon Festival** is held here with lemonade, pies, entertainment, and children's activities. Other special events take place on the Fourth of July and during the Christmas season.

● South Coast Railroad Museum

300 North Los Carneros Road, Goleta. (805) 964-3540. Wednesday–Sunday, 1–4 P.M. Free, but donation requested. **All ages.**

Also on the grounds of the Stow House is Goleta's relocated 1901 Southern Pacific Depot. The depot has been authentically restored to look the way it did in the early part of the twentieth century. Photographs, railroad memorabilia, and some hands-on exhibits are located in the railroad agent's office and passenger waiting room. A three-hundred-square-foot model railroad is also on display. Miniature train rides are offered most days.

● Stow Grove County Park

La Patera Lane, Goleta. From Highway 101, take the Los Carneros Road exit north, turn right on Cathedral Oaks Road, and proceed to the park. Open daily. Free. **All ages.**

Near the Stow House is the pretty Stow Grove Park, where you can picnic in a grove of redwood trees. The thirteen-acre park was formerly a part of Stow Ranch. There are picnic tables and barbecues.

● Miramar Hotel

Box 429, Santa Barbara, CA 93102. Located three miles south of Santa Barbara on Highway 101 at the San Ysidro exit. (805) 969-2203 or (800) 322-6983. **All ages.**

Not only is the white- and blue-trimmed Miramar the only hotel in Santa Barbara with rooms right on the beach, but it is one of the most reasonably priced. The accommodations are plain but comfortable, and the hotel is a bit funky, but it is a great place for families. Rooms start at $75 and go up to $155 for an oceanfront. The grounds are spacious, with a lot of lawn space for playing. There is playground equipment, shuffleboard, paddle tennis, two heated pools, and, of course, the ocean. Kids, in particular, will enjoy the Santa Fe–Amtrak Railroad dining-car diner that is open daily for hot and cold snacks.

● The Big Yellow House Restaurant

*108 Pierpont Avenue, Summerland, five miles south of Santa Barbara.
(805) 969-4140. Sunday–Thursday, 8 A.M.–9 P.M.; Friday and Saturday,
8 A.M.–10 P.M.* **All ages.**

The Big Yellow House Restaurant is easy to spot from Highway 101.
The name is apt—it's a big yellow house overlooking the highway. If you
are traveling with children to Santa Barbara from a southern location, you
might want to use the restaurant as a landmark—something for the kids
to spot on the way there and a place to eat on the way back.

There are six dining rooms in the refurbished nineteenth-century
house, and the interior style is Victorian. This is a family restaurant.
Breakfast, lunch, and dinner are served daily. Dinner starts at $6.95 for
adults, and there are children's meals. It's a good idea to phone ahead for
reservations.

● Santa Barbara Polo Club

*Highway 101 at Nidever Road, Carpinteria, south of Santa Barbara.
Coming southbound on Highway 101, exit at Padaro Lane. Go north to Via
Real and turn right to entrance. Coming northbound, exit Highway 101 at
Santa Claus Lane. Go north on Via Real to Nidever Road and turn left to
entrance. (805) 684-8667. Every Sunday, April–October, 1 and 3 P.M.
Adults, $5; children under 12, free.* **Ages 6 and up.**

For a change of pace in the world of spectator sports, you might
want to take your children to see a polo game. One of the country's better-
known fields is just south of Santa Barbara in the city of Carpinteria.
Matches are played every Sunday from April through October at 1 P.M.
and 3 P.M. The club has a snackbar, or—better yet—you can bring a
picnic lunch.

● Santa Claus Lane

*Off Highway 101, a half-mile west of Carpinteria, eight miles south of Santa
Barbara. Open daily.* **All ages.**

This short side street between Summerland and Carpinteria is a year-
round tourist village with a Christmas theme. The Toyland shop has a
wide range of toys and games. A bakery features Christmas cookies; as you
walk in, all the traditional scents of Christmas hit you. Several other
places to eat serve food that is not tied to December 25. Mail can be post-
marked from here with a Santa Claus postmark. Santa Clause Lane does
not merit a special visit on its own, but it makes a pleasant stop if you are
traveling past.

● **Carpinteria Valley Museum of History**

956 Maple Avenue, Carpinteria. (805) 684-3112. Tuesday–Friday, 1:30–4 P.M.; Saturday, 10 A.M.–4 P.M.; Sunday, 1:30–4 P.M. Free. **Ages 6 and up.**

The exhibits in this museum depict the lives of the area's pioneer families. Of particular interest to kids is the turn-of-the-century schoolroom. Chumash Indian ornaments, utensils, and other artifacts are also displayed. A new wing has exhibits on agriculture and the oil boom.

Ventura, Oxnard, Thousand Oaks Area, and the Santa Clara Valley

● **Ventura County Museum of History & Art**

100 East Main Street, Ventura. Take California Street exit from Highway 101 and turn left on Main Street. (805) 653-0323. Tuesday–Sunday, 10 A.M.–5 P.M. Adults, $3; ages 16 and under, free. **Ages 6 and up.**

Ventura has both a rich history and an attractive downtown historic district. Colorful exhibits on the history of the county from the Chumash Indian days through the early part of this century are displayed in the Ventura County Museum of History & Art. Housed in a bright, appealing, adobe-style building, the museum rotates a fine historical collection in three galleries, each representing a major period of Ventura history. Among the exhibits you may see are an authentic reproduction of Chumash rock paintings; a Spanish breastplate excavated on the Ventura beach in the 1870s; rancho and Victorian costumes; a silver cowboy saddle; a model of the Yankee clipper *Richard Robinson;* and the exact scale replica of the San Buenaventura Mission and early Ventura business section as it stood 1880.

Doll-sized historical figures are displayed in another gallery that should interest children. Crafted by artist and historian George Stuart, the authentically rendered figures are one-quarter life-size and dressed in detailed costumes. A final museum gallery features rotating art exhibits ranging from folk to fine art and photography. Outside is an extensive and fascinating collection of early farm equipment, displays of the early oil-drilling process, and an old oil pump. Surrounding the museum is a grassy park with picnic tables. The mission and the Albinger Archaeological Museum are just across the street.

● **Albinger Archaeological Museum**

113 East Main Street, Ventura. (805) 648-5823. Wednesday–Friday, 10 A.M.–2 P.M.; Saturday and Sunday, 10 A.M.–4 P.M. June–August open: Wednesday–Sunday, 10 A.M.–4 P.M. Free. **Ages 6 and up.**

When the buildings that stood next to the mission were demolished in 1973, archaeologists found evidence of what would prove to be a rich archeological site. Since then, excavations have uncovered more than 30,000 artifacts dating through some 3,500 years of history. Many of the artifacts are on display in the museum, including milling stones that once belonged to the prehistoric residents of this site. Other artifacts include Chumash arrowheads and bone whistles, Spanish crucifixes, an early 1800s pistol barrel, coins and medicine bottles belonging to early twentieth-century Chinese immigrants, and even some old bottles tossed from a saloon that operated during the 1870s. Other exhibits explain what archaeology is and what archaeologists do. If you ask, the curator will be happy to show you a ten-minute slide show on the area's history.

Outside, you can take a close-up look at the digs. In addition, you'll see the remains of an ancient earth oven, the foundations of the original mission church, the remains of an adobe brick factory, and a replica of a Chumash canoe.

● Mission San Buenaventura
211 East Main Street, Ventura. From Highway 101, take the California Street exit and turn left on Main Street. (805) 643-4318. Daily, 10 A.M.– 5 P.M. Adults, $1; children, 50¢. **Ages 8 and up.**

Founded in 1782 by Father Junipero Serra, this was the ninth California mission. The stone and adobe church building, which has been beautifully restored, was completed in 1809. The church is still in daily use. A small museum contains Chumash Indian artifacts and items from the early days of the mission. Children may be most interested in the garden, which contains an olive press and an old water pump.

● Adventures for Kids
3457 Telegraph Road, at Mills Road, Ventura. (805) 650-9688. Monday– Saturday, 10 A.M.–5 P.M. Open on Sunday, seasonally. **All ages.**

Kids can climb into a wooden boat to look at books in this charming children's bookstore. There is also plenty of room to sprawl in the recently expanded store. The owner, Jody Fickes Shapiro, is a former librarian, and she has arranged her store like a library: the books are organized by subject matter. The selection ranges in age appeal from a baby's first books to a substantial collection of young adult books. There's a large section of young children's books, and an impressive collection of books on children for parents and teachers. The store includes a gallery of art from children's books.

If the store does not have a book in stock, they will special order it for you, and they offer free gift wrapping. There is a story time every Tuesday at 10:30 A.M. and Saturday at 3 P.M., year-round; these are open to all ages, although groups are requested to call ahead. The store's extremely knowledgeable staff includes former teachers and a grandmother. The bookstore sells and rents children's and family videos. They also sell children's CDs and audiocassettes, rhythm instruments, puzzles, puppets, rubber stamps, and stickers. Adventures for Kids publishes an excellent newsletter three times a year that reviews children's books and lists upcoming special events and appearances by authors and illustrators.

● Ventura Harbor Village

1559 Spinnaker Drive, Ventura. Exit Ventura Freeway at Seaward, turn left at Harbor and right on Spinnaker Drive. (805) 644-0169. Open daily.
All ages.

Ventura Harbor Village is an attractive shopping/dining/entertainment complex on the harbor in Ventura. It's a nice place to stroll and look at the boats. There are a number of restaurants and snack bars where you can get a harborside table or eat outside. A merry-go-round operates daily in the carousel marketplace. Kids may want to stop at the **Harbor Kite & Toy Store** (phone: 805-654-0900), which has a good selection of kites and toys. The *Bay Queen* (phone: 805-642-7753) offers forty-minute narrated harbor cruises that leave from the village. They also rent paddleboats.

● Channel Islands National Park/Island Packer Cruises

1867 Spinnaker Drive, Ventura. (805) 642-1393 (reservations); (805) 642-7688 (recorded information). Reservations required. **Ages 8 and up.**

Eight islands extending over a range of 150 miles make up this chain off the Southern California coast. Five of these islands have been set aside by the government as Channel Islands National Park. You can reach the five islands on boat trips offered by Island Packers.

Anacapa, the closest island, some fourteen miles off the shore of Ventura, is reached by a three-hour round-trip boat ride. (Daily excursions are offered year-round. The boat leaves Ventura dock beginning at 9 A.M. and returns six to eight hours later.) It's quite an adventure for kids. Seals and sea lions are pointed out along the way, and you may even see migrating whales. An eighteen-foot skiff takes five people at a time from the boat to the island. Anacapa, actually a chain of three small adjacent islets, is undeveloped and has wild areas, trails, and tide pools. Adults should be in good physical condition and children should have the stamina for a rugged outdoor day. (You must climb 153 steps to get from the landing cove to the island top, for a start.) There are no facilities on the island, except latrines, so bring your own food and water. A somewhat shorter version of this trip, spending only two hours on the island, is also available. Special weekend and weekday trips are also made to Frenchy's Cove on West Anacapa. There is a beautiful beach here with clear water where you can swim, picnic, and explore the tide pools. The cost for the Anacapa trip is $37 for adults and $20 for children twelve and under. Half-day, nonlanding excursions to Anacapa that include a narrated cruise along the island's rugged north shore are available from April through November (adults, $21; children, $14).

Santa Barbara Island, forty-six miles offshore from Ventura, is home to the huge northern elephant seal. Reached by a three-hour trip each way, this island offers the opportunity to observe the elephant seals and other wildlife. The fare is $49 for adults and $35 for children. Trips are made from late March through October.

Other one- and two-day excursions are available to San Miguel Island and to Santa Rosa Island, home of the rare Torrey Pine. The crossings to both islands, however, can be long and rough. Trips are also available to the Santa Cruz Island Preserve. These are rugged nature trips; participants must be in good physical condition, and children must be at least nine years old. Camping and whale-watching trips are also available. Reservations should be made at least a month in advance for any weekend trip.

● Channel Islands National Park Visitors Center

1901 Spinnaker Drive, Ventura. At the west end of Spinnaker Drive. (805) 658-5730. Daily, 8 A.M.–5 P.M. Free. **All ages.**

A good place to prepare for your visit to the Channel Islands—or as a stop in itself—is the Channel Islands National Park Visitors Center in the Ventura harbor. Exhibits include photo displays, Chumash Indian artifacts, a simulated caliche ghost forest, native plant and animal displays, and an indoor tide pool. A twenty-five-minute film on the Channel Islands is shown, and ranger programs take place on weekend afternoons at 2 and 3 P.M. On a clear day you can see the nearest islands from an observation tower atop the visitors center.

● Olivas Adobe

4200 Olivas Park Drive, Ventura. Take the Victoria Avenue exit from Highway 101 and follow the signs. (805) 644-4346. Grounds open daily, 10 A.M.–4 P.M. House open weekends, noon–4 P.M. Free. **Ages 6 and up.**

In 1841 Raimundo Olivas and Felipe Lorenzana were awarded a grant of land near the mouth of the Santa Clara River as payment for their service in the Mexican army. Calling their land Rancho San Miguel, they planted grain, fruit trees, and grapevines and raised cattle. When the gold rush of 1848 brought hordes of gold seekers to California, rancho owners like Olivas became rich by driving their cattle north to meet the miners' demands for food.

The large, two-story adobe you see today was begun in 1847 to accommodate Olivas's growing family. It was the first two-story adobe in the area. (The family's original one-room adobe is still standing in the southwest corner of the courtyard.) The adobe was inhabited by a succession of owners almost continually until it was donated to the city.

On a tour of the nicely restored adobe, you can see the upstairs bedrooms, with rancho-style hats hanging on the bedposts. Downstairs are the furnished living room, dining room, kitchen, and chapel. Kids will be impressed by the short doorways and the old newspaper—once used as insulating material—exposed in a wall section. Some old farm equipment is in the yard, and a Chumash Indian thatched hut is among the displays at the visitors center. The adobe is surrounded by a lovely six-and-half-acre park.

● Ventura County Maritime Museum

2731 South Victoria Avenue (in Fisherman's Wharf at Channel Islands Harbor), Oxnard. From Los Angeles, take the Ventura Freeway (101) west to Victoria Avenue exit in Oxnard. Drive southwest about seven miles to Channel Islands Boulevard. Turn right into the parking lot on Channel Islands Boulevard just past the intersection of Victoria Avenue. (805) 984-6260. Thursday–Monday, 11 A.M.–5 P.M. Open daily in the summer. Adults, $3; ages 5–12, $1; under 5, free. **Ages 8 and up.**

The highlight of the new Ventura County Maritime Museum is the nine ship models built by Edward Marple, a local model shipbuilder, over the course of twenty-five years of his life. These elaborate models under glass include the 1794 *Mars*, Sir Admiral Hood's ship; the 1637 *Sovereign of the Stars*, which was the most ornate ship ever built; and the Mississippi riverboat, the *Robert E. Lee.* A docent is on hand to point out to kids such features on the model ships as the real gold leafing and the tiny unicorn on the *Sovereign of the Stars* and the miniature steam calliope atop the *Robert E. Lee.* Another exhibit has models of sailing ships ranging from a 2000 B.C. balsa canoe to a 1950s Chinese junk. Marine art and ship prototypes are also displayed.

The museum is located in Fisherman's Wharf, a shopping/eating complex built in the style of a New England fishing village, in the Channel Islands Harbor. Kids may enjoy seeing the statue of the yellow-slickered fisherman by the dock and the old fire department hose nearby.

The **Harbor Hopper Ferry** operates like a taxi through the Channel Islands Harbor. You can hail the water taxi from the dock, travel one or more stops through the harbor, get off and explore, then hail the taxi back. You can also call for the taxi by phoning 985-HOPP.

● Gull Wings

418 West Fourth Street, downtown Oxnard. (805) 483-3005. Wednesday–Friday, 1–5 P.M.; Saturday, 10 A.M.–5 P.M.; Sunday, 1–5 P.M. Open Tuesday–Friday mornings for groups by appointment. Adults, $3; children, $2; ages 2 and under, free. Discounts for groups. **Ages 1–10.**

A fully equipped medical room with an operating table, wheelchair, casts, and medical uniforms is one of the highlights of this small hands-on museum for children. Children can try on firefighter and other uniforms stored in "Me Cabinets," or they can sort bins of vegetables in their own farmers' market. A tot area for small children is set up like a camping trip with tent, fishing poles, and campfire. In other exhibits, kids can handle fossils and gems, experiment making bubbles, perform science experiments, or try out a computer that has four different games. Special events and family workshops take place throughout the year. You can arrange to have your child's birthday party at the museum, and family memberships are available.

● CEA/Seabee Museum

U.S. Naval Construction Battalion Center, Gate A (Channel Islands and Ventura Road, southwest of Highway 101), Port Hueneme. (805) 982-5163. Monday–Friday, 8 A.M.–4:30 P.M.; Saturday, 9 A.M.–4:30 P.M.; Sunday, 12:30–4:30 P.M. Free. **Ages 6 and up.**

Seabees fought in the U.S. Navy with bulldozers and shovels rather than with ships and guns. Their equipment is on display here along with some of their history. Exhibits include uniforms, an underwater diving display, outrigger canoes, World War II dioramas, weapons, flags, and tools. The museum is located on an operating naval base.

● Stagecoach Inn Museum

51 South Ventu Park Road, Newberry Park. From Los Angeles, take the Ventura Freeway (101) past Thousand Oaks, exit at Ventu Park Road. (805) 498-9441. Wednesday–Sunday, 1–4 P.M. School tours are given on Wednesday mornings. Adults, $2; seniors and ages 5–12, $1; under 5, free. **Ages 6 and up.**

The Stagecoach Inn opened in 1876 as a stopover for weary travelers journeying between Los Angeles and Santa Barbara by stagecoach. The inn, which was originally located where the freeway meets Ventu Park

Road, has been recreated with detailed authenticity. The docent-led tour begins in the hotel's parlor and dining room, which is furnished exactly as it might have been when the stage travelers relaxed there. The kitchen has a coal-burning stove, wooden sink, water pump, and old-time utensils. There is an authentic 1850s Wells Fargo safe in the hotel office. Among the rooms you'll see upstairs is a furnished guest room said to be inhabited by a ghost.

Outside, you can see a real stagecoach. Also on the museum grounds is a village complex—made of replicas of a Spanish/Mexican adobe of the early 1800s, a wooden pioneer cabin, and a Chumash thatched hut—representing the historic eras of the area. A carriage house with coaches, horse tack, and tools is also on the grounds. (The village, carriage house, and other outside structures are only open on weekends.) A nature trail winds through the complex. There's also a park with picnicking and a children's playground adjacent to the museum.

● Moorpark College Exotic Animal Compound

7975 Campus Drive, Moorpark. Located at the west end of California 118 between the cities of Simi Valley and Moorpark. (805) 378-1441. Saturday and Sunday, 11 A.M.–5 P.M. Adults, $4; seniors, $3; ages 2–12, $2. **All ages.**

Moorpark College offers a unique program in the training and management of exotic animals for students interested in becoming zookeepers or animal trainers. On weekends, every hour on the hour from noon to 4 P.M., the students demonstrate what they are learning in a fifteen- to twenty-minute show for the public. Each show is different and you can see as many as you want. Sea lions, a baboon, parrots, and ponies are among the animals performing in the intimate outdoor theater. Students explain about the animals and take questions from the audience. Children get a chance to touch some of the animals, including a large snake. Between the shows you can visit the animals in their compound.

● Reagan Presidential Library and Museum

40 Presidential Drive, Simi Valley. From Highway 101, take the 23 Freeway north to Olsen Road and go north two miles (Olsen Road becomes Madera Road). Turn left on Presidential Drive. From I-5 or the 405 Freeway, take the 118 Freeway west and exit at Madera Road. Go south three miles and turn right on Presidential Road. Daily, 10 A.M.–5 P.M. Adults, $4; seniors, $2; under 16, free. **Ages 6 and up.**

A full-scale replica of the Oval Office and a recreated State Dinner are highlights of the Ronald Reagan Presidential Library and Museum. Other exhibits include a cruise missile once deployed in Europe, a piece of the Berlin Wall, gifts of state, and photographs and memorabilia from President Reagan's term in office. In addition to the permanent exhibits, the library hosts changing exhibits such as recent ones on the Civil War and the 1960s. Every year, the holiday season brings a Christmas tree extravaganza with trees decorated in the traditions of thirty nations. The Spanish Mission–style library is built around a courtyard and set on a hilltop that gives a view of the surrounding countryside.

● Ojai Valley Museum and Historical Society

109 South Montgomery, Ojai. A sign in the center of town on Ojai Avenue points the way. (805) 646-2290. Wednesday–Monday, 1–4 P.M. Adults, $1; children, free. **Ages 6 and up.**

Located in the former Ventura County Fire Station, the Ojai Museum displays Chumash Indian artifacts, early pioneer items, and stuffed animals and birds native to the Ojai Valley. The **Civic Center Park** on Ojai Avenue in the heart of town is a nice, shady spot for a picnic.

● Santa Paula Union Oil Museum

1001 East Main Street, Santa Paula. Santa Paula is located 53 miles east of Santa Barbara via Highway 150. From the 126 Freeway, exit at Tenth Street and go north two blocks. (805) 933-0076. Thursday–Sunday, 10 A.M.–4 P.M. Free. **Ages 6 and up.**

The Santa Paula Union Oil Museum traces the history of the search for crude oil in California and the subsequent development of the industry. On display are oil-drilling machinery and old tools, including an early wooden drilling rig. Other exhibits explain how oil pools are located and how the drillers reach them. There are many historical photographs, and Friday through Sunday you can take a guided tour of the turn-of-the-century business offices located upstairs. One room in the museum houses changing exhibits, which sometimes include hands-on activities for kids.

● Fillmore Historical Museum Park

350 Main Street, Fillmore. Fillmore is located on Highway 126 east of Santa Paula. (805) 524-0948. Phone for hours and prices. **Ages 6 and up.**

In a wonderful turnabout, Fillmore's 1887 Southern Pacific railroad depot, which had been moved away from the tracks to house the historical museum, has been moved back to the tracks. The depot, now the center of a new historic park, is back at work serving rail passengers. The park also includes a large rancho-era bunkhouse with exhibits relating to the history of the area, such as pioneer household items and tools, railroad and oil industry memorabilia, and Native American artifacts. Also on the grounds is a Victorian-era house furnished with period items. A large court connects the historic park with the railroad station.

● Fillmore & Western Railway Company

351 Santa Clara Avenue, Fillmore. From Los Angeles, take I-5 north to Highway 126, which leads to Fillmore. To reach Central Park Depot in Fillmore, turn north on Central Avenue and go one block. (805) 524-2546. Every Sunday, throughout the year. Phone for departure times. Adults, $14; children, $8; under 4, free. **All ages.**

You can board an old-time steam train or a full-sized 1940s-era passenger train at the Central Park Depot in the rural town of Fillmore for a one- to two-hour round-trip train excursion through picturesque eastern Ventura County. The outings are geared toward families, and snacks and beverages are sold on board. You don't need advance reservations; you buy your tickets in the caboose.

■ The Santa Ynez Valley, Lompoc, and Santa Maria

● Lake Cachuma Recreation Area

On Highway 154, twenty-five miles north of Santa Barbara. (805) 688-4658. Day use: daily, 6 A.M.–10 P.M.; $5 per vehicle. **All ages.**

Set in a valley of the Santa Ynez Mountains, this large man-made lake offers picnic and playground facilities, boating, and fishing in lovely surroundings. The freshwater lake is stocked with thousands of fish, including bass, catfish, bluegill and, from October to May, rainbow trout. Licenses, bait, tackle, and fish-cleaning stations are available at the marina. Boats, with or without motors, can be rented on a hourly, daily, weekly, or monthly basis.

A Nature Center features displays of local plants and wildlife and Native American artifacts. Other programs put on by the park's naturalists include year-round nature walks and wildlife cruises on the lake, summer fireside theaters, stargazing, and movies. Two swimming pools are open during the summer—because the lake serves as a reservoir, you can't swim, wade, or water-ski in it. Bike rentals are also available in the summer. Horseback riding is permitted, and there are both RV and tent campsites. Other facilities include a general store, gas station, snack bar, and grill.

● Solvang

Three miles east of Buellton and about forty miles northwest of Santa Barbara. You can either travel north on Highway 101 from Santa Barbara and east on Highway 246 at Buellton, or take the scenic route: Highway 154 from outside Santa Barbara, then west on Highway 246. Solvang Conference and Visitors Bureau phone: (805) 688-6144 or (800) 468-6765. Most shops and restaurants open daily. **All ages.**

Solvang is a blend of commercialism and cultural expression (leaning mightily toward commercialism). It was founded in 1911 by Danes who copied the architecture of their homeland. The businesses have an old-world appearance with thatched-style roofs, inlaid timbers on the outside walls, and stained-glass windows. Many of the roofs have the traditional stork perched on top; and, of course, there are windmills. The renowned bakeries are probably the highlight of the town. The shops generally feature imports from Europe. There are some toy, doll, and hobby shops that might interest children. A horse-drawn replica of a turn-of-the-century Copenhagen streetcar (called the Honen) gives tours of the town, starting at the Visitors Center on Copenhagen Drive near First Street.

Hans Christian Andersen Park (off Atterdag Road, three blocks north of Mission Drive from the center of town) is a relaxing place to have a picnic. The park has an old world–style entrance, beautiful trees, and a children's playground.

If you are traveling to Solvang on Highway 246 from the Buellton exit of Highway 101, keep your eye out for the ostrich farm on the south side of the highway. From Solvang, you also might want to head north toward Ballard on Alamo Pintado Road to visit the **Quicksilver Miniature Horse Ranch.** The ranch at 1555 Alamo Pintado Road (phone: 805-686-4002) is open to visitors from 10 A.M. to 3 P.M., daily.

● Mission Santa Ines

1760 Mission Drive, Solvang, a short distance east of the main business district. (805) 688-4815. Monday–Saturday, 9:30 A.M.–4:30 P.M.; Sunday, 1:30–4:30 P.M. Open until 7 P.M. during the summer. Adults, $3; under 16, free. **Ages 8 and up.**

Founded in 1804, Santa Ines is a well-restored mission with a red tile roof, a bell tower, an arched colonnade, and a beautiful church. Artifacts from the time the Santa Ynez Valley was first settled by the padres are on display. There is also a very pretty garden. Every August, the mission hosts a fiesta with food, rides, games for children, and music.

● Nojoqui Falls County Park

Seven miles southwest of Solvang on Alisal Road. Daily, 8 A.M. to dusk. Free.
All ages.

This park is named for its 164-foot-high waterfall, where, according to Chumash legend, a pair of star-crossed lovers from different tribes met their death. The beautiful falls are reached by an easy ten-minute hike. Depending on the rainfall and the season, the falls cascade or run gently over a moss-covered limestone cliff. Elsewhere on its 82.5-acre site, the park offers picnic and barbecue sites, softball diamonds, and children's playgrounds.

● Santa Ynez Valley Historical Museum

3596 Sagunto Street, Santa Ynez. Located about three miles east of Solvang. From Santa Barbara, take Highway 101 north, go east on Highway 246 through Solvang to Edison Avenue in Santa Ynez, and go north. Go to the next stop sign and turn right. The museum is on the corner. (805) 688-7889. Friday–Sunday, 1–4 P.M. Carriage house: Friday–Sunday, 1–4 P.M.; Tuesday–Thursday, 10 A.M.–4 P.M. Free. **Ages 6 and up.**

This small museum has exhibits on Chumash Indian culture and nineteenth-century pioneer life in the valley. A nearby carriage house displays wagons, buggies, stagecoaches, and carriages. Santa Ynez is a picturesque small town with high-front buildings that give it an Old West flavor.

● Pea Soup Andersen's Restaurant

Avenue of the Flags, Buellton. (805) 688-5581. Daily, 6:30 A.M.–10 P.M.
All ages.

Anton Andersen, an immigrant from Denmark, started selling pea soup here in 1924, and his restaurant is still serving travelers today. Breakfast, lunch, and dinner are offered, as well as their all-you-can-eat pea soup special. There are some coin-operated children's rides and a pretty garden outside.

● The Little Red Schoolhouse in Ballard

On Cottonwood Avenue, Ballard. Located about four miles north of Solvang. From Santa Barbara, take Highway 101 north, go east on Highway 246 through Solvang and north on Alamo Pintado Road. Go east on Baseline Avenue to Ballard. Turn north on Cottonwood Avenue to the school. Free. **All ages.**

In a setting that is absolutely genuine, children can experience the era of their great-grandparents when they visit the little red schoolhouse in the sleepy town of Ballard. The steepled, one-room schoolhouse was built in 1882 and has been in continuous use by schoolchildren since 1883. A sign at the schoolyard gate reads: "No dogs or livestock." The school is painted bright red with white trim. A rope swing usually hangs from a tree in front, a nice playground is in back, and there is also a big green lawn. Kindergarteners are still being taught in the schoolhouse, but the yard is open to visitors on weekends and in summer.

● Mattei's Tavern

On Highway 154, Los Olivos. Los Olivos is about six miles north of Solvang and about two miles north of Ballard. From Santa Barbara, take Highway 101 north past Buellton and turn right on Highway 154; or take Highway 154 directly from Highway 101 just north of Santa Barbara. (805) 688-4820. Dinner: Monday–Friday, 5:30–9 P.M.; Saturday and Sunday, 5–9 P.M. Lunch: Friday–Sunday, noon–3 P.M. **Ages 6 and up.**

Los Olivos was a stagecoach stop for the famous Butterfield Stage Lines. Mattei's Tavern, built in 1886, provided food and lodging for the tired and hungry passengers. The inn, now a state historic landmark, is still serving dinner to travelers. Of course, now the travelers arrive by car—but never mind, the tavern still retains some of its old atmosphere. It's in a lovely rural setting, and kids will enjoy looking around the old inn. Dinners are served in a number of attractive dining rooms furnished in the style of the late 1800s; the fare is predominately steak with bread and a soup and salad bar. Dinners range from about $14.95 to $25.95.

● Union Hotel/Los Alamos

Los Alamos. Fourteen miles north of Solvang and seventeen miles south of Santa Maria. Take the Los Alamos turnoff from Highway 101. Follow the signs to town. The hotel is on the main street; you can't miss it. (805) 344-2744. Hotel dining room open for dinner Wednesday–Sunday, 5–9 P.M., and lunch Saturday–Monday, 11:30 A.M.–3 P.M. **All ages.**

Kids can weigh themselves before and after dinner on a big butcher's scale in the lobby of the historic Union Hotel in Los Alamos. Built of wood in 1880, the original Union Hotel provided lodging for Wells Fargo stagecoach passengers. The hotel later burned down and was rebuilt of adobe bricks. When the present owner bought the old hotel in 1972, he restored it to look as it did originally, using wood from fifty- to one-hundred-year-old barns. The hotel is completely furnished in antiques, down to an old-fashioned telephone on the lobby desk. Parked outside the hotel is a 1918 fifteen-passenger White touring car. Next door is an out-of-use gas station with rusty pumps and gas prices frozen at 37.8 cents a gallon.

Dinners are served in the dining room, furnished with pieces from a Mississippi plantation, by friendly waitresses wearing old-fashioned dresses. You can order from the menu or select an all-you-can-eat family-style dinner. Lunch is served in the dining room or outside on the patio. Los Alamos is a quiet little country town of seven hundred people, and city kids may enjoy just strolling through it. Los Alamos also has a very nice **county park** (follow the signs) open daily from 8 A.M. to sunset. The park features a children's playground, lots of lovely grassy areas, wooden bridges, hiking trails, and picnic tables.

● La Purisima Mission State Historic Park

Northeast of Lompoc on Highway 246. Take Highway 1 from its junction with Highway 101 or take Highway 246 west from Buellton. The mission is about twelve miles from Buellton and about four miles from Lompoc. (805) 733-7781. Daily, 9 A.M.–5 P.M. $5 per car. **All ages.**

La Purisima is the most interesting of all the missions for children. Beautifully restored, it gives you the feeling you are actually visiting a mission in the early 1800s. The major restoration work was done in the 1930s by Civilian Conservation Corps workers. After careful research, they performed the restoration using the original tools and methods of the early 1800s. While only the church remains at most California missions, La Purisima has been restored almost in its entirety, enabling you to grasp more fully what mission life was like. The mission system was established as a way for the Spanish government to set up territorial outposts without great expense, and, as such, the missions had to be self-supporting. Each mission was a self-sufficient economic unit that, in addition to its religious functions, quartered soldiers, provided for visitors, raised livestock, grew crops, and produced tradeable commodities such as hides.

At La Purisima, you can see real cattle hides on the drying racks, reconstructions of the original tallow vats used for making soap and candles, the *cuartel*—used for housing soldiers—with its dirt floor and narrow cots, the candle maker's shop, the weaving room with its looms, the olive mill and press, the kitchens, the apartments of married soldiers, the carpenter's and potter's shops, as well as the church and chapel. Sheep, burros, horses, and goats are kept together in an old-style pen; and pigs are kept in another pen. You can even see the ruts of a segment of the old Camino Real—the original highway that connected the California missions. A museum near the visitors' entrance has displays on the mission and the Chumash Indians.

In addition to the fine restoration of the mission grounds, the sense of the mission's past is heightened by its location off the beaten track in a rural area surrounded by agriculture and grazing land. Plan to spend a couple of hours at this highly recommended family destination.

● Santa Maria Museum of Flight

3015 Airpark Drive, Santa Maria. Santa Maria is located about seventy-five miles north of Santa Barbara and thirty miles south of San Luis Obispo via Highway 101. From Highway 101, exit Betteravia Road; go west 2.3 miles and turn south on Skyway Drive. The museum is off Skyway Drive before you reach the airport. (805) 922-8758. Open April–November, Friday, Saturday, and Sunday, 9 A.M.–5 P.M.; rest of the year, Friday, Saturday, and Sunday, 10 A.M.–4 P.M. Adults, $2; seniors and students, $1; children, 50¢. **Ages 6 and up.**

A gull-wing Stinson V77 Reliant, a World War II SNJ, a MIG 21, and a Great Lakes biplane are among the aircraft displayed in this museum of aviation, housed in a pair of aircraft hangers adjacent to the Santa Maria Public Airport. One of the highlights is the once top-secret Norden bombsight and its accessories. Model planes, photographs, and other displays depict the history of aviation from its earliest days to the Stealth bomber.

● Waller County Park

Orcutt Expressway and Waller Lane, Santa Maria. From the Museum of Flight, take Skyway Drive southeast to Orcutt Expressway, turn north to park. Daily, 8 A.M. to sunset. Free. **All ages.**

This pretty 100-acre park makes a nice stop before or after a visit to the nearby Santa Maria Museum of Flight. The park features huge areas of green lawn, a lake with fountains, waterfalls, and ducks, a fitness course, several playgrounds, a number of picnic areas with barbecues, a softball field, basketball courts, and pony rides.

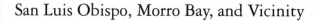

San Luis Obispo, Morro Bay, and Vicinity

● San Luis Obispo Path of History

San Luis Obispo Chamber of Commerce, 1039 Chorro Street (between Monterey and Higuera streets), downtown San Luis Obispo. (805) 781-2777. Monday, 9:30 A.M.–5 P.M.; Tuesday–Friday, 8 A.M.–5 P.M.; Saturday and Sunday, 10 A.M.–5 P.M. (Closed during lunch on weekends.) Free. **Ages 8 and up.**

Nestled in a beautiful rural valley, San Luis Obispo has preserved not only its small-town atmosphere, but also its history. Many of the city's original buildings remain, restored and adapted for modern use. The city has marked out a Path of History linking twenty historic sites in the downtown area. The path includes the mission, the history museum, and such intriguing places as the **Ah Louis Store** (800 Palm Street), founded in 1874 by a Cantonese entrepreneur to serve the Chinese community and still owned by his descendants. If your children are old enough and you have the energy, you can cover the two-mile tour in a leisurely two hours on foot. Otherwise, you can use the guide to select what you want to see.

If you get a chance—and something appropriate is playing—try to take in a movie at the historic **Fremont Theatre** (Monterey and Santa Rosa streets), listed on the Path of History. Built in 1941, the Fremont is an opulent and beautiful Art Deco movie theater. It has been not only restored to its 1940s glamor but updated with a wide screen, state-of-the-art sound, and new seats. For families accustomed to the multiplex, it is a real treat to learn—or remember—how movie theaters used to be.

Another way to see some of the historic downtown is by hopping on one of the open-sided old-fashioned trolleys on the **Old SLO Trolley Route.** The trolleys run daily from noon to 5 P.M. and on Thursday to 9:30 P.M. in an area framed by Nipomo, Marsh, Osos, and Palms streets. Catch the trolley on the right-hand side of the street. Rides are free.

● Bubble Gum Alley

Off Higuera Street between 733 and 737 Higuera Street. Between Garden and Broad streets, San Luis Obispo. **All ages.**

Although it has no historical or any other kind of significance, one place your children will definitely want to see in downtown San Luis Obispo is Bubble Gum Alley. As the name might suggest, this is an alley that has been brightly decorated with bubble gum. Grown-ups may wince, but kids love it.

● Farmers' Market

The 600 through 900 blocks of Higuera Street, downtown San Luis Obispo. (805) 781-2777 (San Luis Obispo Chamber of Commerce). Thursday, 6:30–9 P.M. (Set-up begins at 6 P.M.) Free. **All ages.**

Every Thursday evening year-round, Higuera Street in downtown San Luis Obispo is closed to traffic to become the scene of a lively farmers' market. Stalls of fresh produce line the street. There is an abundant variety of good-looking fruits and vegetables, and during the spring and summer fresh-cut flowers and herbs are added to the display. You can also buy chicken and juicy beef ribs barbecued on the spot. Street performances by jugglers, musicians, puppeteers, magicians, and other entertainers add to the merriment.

● Mission San Luis Obispo de Tolosa/Mission Plaza

782 Monterey Street, between Chorro and Broad streets, downtown San Luis Obispo. (805) 543-6850. Daily, 9 A.M.–4 P.M. Open until 5 P.M. during summer. Adults, $1 (suggested donation); children, free. **All ages.**

The fifth of the California missions was constructed in 1772 with adobe bricks made by the local Chumash Indians. The mission was restored in the 1930s and today serves as a parish church and museum, as well as the historic center of the city. In the museum, kids can see an acorn mortar used by the Chumash—along with other Chumash artifacts, a padre's bed, some antique dolls, and early California saddles, guns, saddles and tools, including a spinning wheel.

Historically a site for social gatherings—including bull and bear fights in the 1800s—the area between the mission and San Luis Creek has been redeveloped into a beautiful town square. With lush landscaping, brick paving, bridges, fountains, and creekside walkways, the Mission Plaza makes a lovely spot for resting or playing. The San Luis Obispo Art Center is located within the plaza, and many community activities take place in the Mission Plaza throughout the year.

Best of all for kids is **San Luis Creek,** once the mission's source of water. Today, kids can wade and skip rocks in the stream while the old folks sit on a bench in the shade.

● San Luis Obispo County Historical Museum

696 Monterey Street (opposite Mission Plaza, next to the mission), San Luis Obispo. (805) 543-0638. Wednesday–Sunday, 10 A.M.–4 P.M. Free, but donations appreciated. **Ages 6 and up.**

Housed in a 1904 red brick and sandstone Carnegie library (point out the face on the frieze above the front windows to your kids), this small, pleasant museum exhibits changing items from San Luis Obispo's past. Displays start with artifacts from the native Chumash and Salinans and move through the mission and rancho days to the recent past. Among the items in the museum collection you might see when you visit are an old-time U.S. mail carriage, a giant model of the RCA Victor dog, an RCA Victor Victrola, and the lens from the lighthouse at Port San

Luis. Behind the entrance desk is a room furnished in the style of an 1880s parlor, complete with models of women and children dressed in Victorian clothing. Although most of the exhibits are just for looking, kids will find a few that can be touched, such as a stereopticon with a number of photographs to examine—or, when we visited, an old Hoosier hutch containing such ancient artifacts as a rug beater and a spice grater.

● **San Luis Obispo Children's Museum**

1010 Nipomo Street (downtown), San Luis Obispo. Take Marsh Street exit from Highway 101. Follow Marsh Street north to Nipomo Street and turn left. The museum is on the corner of Nipomo and Monterey. (805) 544-5437. September to mid-June: Thursday and Friday, 1–5 P.M.; Saturday and Monday, 10 A.M.–5 P.M.; Sunday, noon–5 P.M. Mid-June to Labor Day, Monday–Saturday, 10 A.M.–5 P.M.; Sunday, noon–5 P.M. $3 per person ages two and up. Free first Wednesday of every month, 1–4 P.M. **Ages 1–11.**

Children have a museum designed just for them (and their parents) in historic downtown San Luis Obispo. In the bright museum galleries they can practice driving in a red truck with surfboards on top, race to the scene of a fire on the back of a fire truck, see themselves on television, zip down a dinosaur slide, and much more. Every available inch of space—or so it seems—is used creatively in this museum. Among the most fun exhibits are the ones above the main floor—a space capsule kids can enter and fly, an airplane cockpit from which they can soar into the clouds, and a Coast Guard cutter reached by climbing a ship's ladder. Toddlers have their own play area.

Outside in the museum yard is a train station play structure and a rainbow express train for climbing.

● **Cal Poly's Animal Farm**

School of Agriculture, California Polytechnic University, San Luis Obispo. From Highway 101, take the Grand Avenue off-ramp north and follow signs to campus. (805) 756-2419. The farm is open daily. Free. **All ages.**

Most of Cal Poly's beautiful 5,169-acre campus is devoted to agricultural studies. The campus includes some 3,400 acres of model farms, gardens, and livestock ranches where students get practical experience in their chosen fields. Visitors are welcome to tour most of the agricultural units. Kids will want to see the swine unit, which includes a nursery for baby pigs; the horses; the sheep unit; the dairy, where cows are milked every day at noon; and the cattle. The agriculture facilities are spread out, but you can get a map and pamphlet for a self-guided tour weekdays from the School of Agriculture (Agricultural Sciences Building, Room 210; the building is near the campus store). On weekends you can get directions from students on the campus or you can request that a map be sent to you ahead of time (although it is not hard to find your way to the animals on your own).

The horse and beef units and the feed mill are to the right of Via Carta up Campus Way. The swine units are to the left of Via Carta. The sheep unit can be reached from Highland Avenue, and the dairy, from Mount Bishop Road. Saturday is probably the best day to visit because everything is in operation and parking is easier than on the weekdays. (Although everything is not in operation on Sunday, you can still see the animals.)

● Apple Farm Restaurant and Mill House

2015 Monterey Street, San Luis Obispo. Take the Monterey Street exit from Highway 101. (805) 544-6100. Daily, 7 A.M.–9:30 P.M. **All ages.**

The Apple Farm is a country-style inn and family restaurant on San Luis Creek. The scenic grounds include an authentic water-driven grist-mill. Kids can watch the mill's system of pulleys and gears in action, then they can sample the homemade ice cream and apple cider produced by the system. The restaurant serves home-style American food, and is open for breakfast, lunch, and dinner. There is a children's menu, and you can order from the lunch menu at dinner if you like.

● Pismo Beach Butterfly Trees

About fifteen miles south of San Luis Obispo via Highway 101 to Highway 1. The Butterfly Trees are located just south of the North Beach Campground, just past the Grover Beach city limit sign on the ocean side. Park on the dirt shoulder and enter through the gate in the fence. For more information, contact the Pismo Beach Visitors Information Center, 581 Dolliver Street, Pismo Beach. (805) 773-4382. **All ages.**

Every winter thousands of migrating monarch butterflies make their home in this small grove of eucalyptus and Monterey pines. The orange and black butterflies begin arriving in late October or early November to escape the cold of more northerly regions and remain through February or March. The butterflies cluster so closely that their wings look like yellowish leaves on the tree. You can walk on a wooden-rail path in the eucalyptus grove that gets you up close to the trees while still protecting the butterflies, and there are benches in the grove.

Even if it is not butterfly season, the grove makes a nice stop. A trail leads from the grove across a stream and down to the beach.

● Atascadero Lake County Park

In Atascadero, about fifteen miles north of San Luis Obispo. Take Highway 101 north from San Luis Obispo and exit at Highway 41/Morro Bay. The park is located two miles west of Highway 101 on Highway 41. (805) 461-5000. Daily, 6 A.M.–10 P.M. Free. **All ages.**

A visit to this beautiful rural park is like returning to a slower, easier time. The lovely grounds are shaded with stately oaks, sycamores, and redwoods. There is fishing in the large lake, ducks to feed, and paddleboat rentals, plus the park has a nice playground with new equipment, picnic facilities, concession stands, and acres of shaded lawn. Best of all is the uncrowded, soothing atmosphere.

● Paddock Zoo

Located in Atascadero Lake County Park (see entry above). (805) 461-5080. Daily, 10 A.M.–4 P.M.; until 5 P.M. in summer. Adults, $2.50; ages 3–15, $1.50; under 3, free. **All ages.**

This small zoo was put together by ranger Chuck Paddock. It has more than one hundred different species of animals, including lions, bears, coyotes, monkeys, and a magnificent pair of jaguars. Some of the more exotic animals include rare golden-bellied mangabeys from Zaire, Arabian oryx, and Bengal tigers. There is a pleasant petting paddock, which includes a llama and turkeys along with the goats and sheep, and a lion-shaped drinking fountain for kids.

● Morro Bay State Park

Located a mile south of the town of Morro Bay on State Park Road. Take Bay Boulevard west from Highway 1 to the park; or, from town, take Main Street south to the park. (805) 772-2560 or (805) 772-7434. Open daily. Day use, $6. Campsite: weekdays, $17; weekends, $18; RV hookup, $23–24. For campsite reservations, phone DESTINET, 800-444-7275. **All ages.**

The nearly fifteen hundred seaside acres of Morro Bay State Park offer outstanding opportunities for picnicking, camping, hiking, bicycling, fishing, boating, and studying the wildlife of the central California coast. The park boasts one of the largest natural areas of marshland remaining along the coast, which serves as a haven for countless birds. In the spring, wildflowers are spread over the grass- and brush-covered hills. There are 135 family campsites, each with table, stove, and food locker, and the restrooms have hot showers. If you plan to stay overnight, you should reserve a campsite *at least* ten days in advance.

● Morro Bay Museum of Natural History

State Park Road, Morro Bay State Park. (805) 772-2694. Daily,
10 A.M.–5 P.M. Adults, $2; ages 6–12, $1; under 6, free. **All ages.**

Located on a rocky cliff overlooking Morro Bay, this nature museum
focuses on the birds and sea creatures of the area. There are exhibits on
tide pools, low-tide animals, local birds, abalone, and various fish, as well
as on the Chumash Indians. A discovery center for kids in a corner of the
museum has Chumash items such as musical instruments that children
can handle. Perhaps the nicest feature of this museum is that it overlooks
Morro Bay. Kids can use the telescope in the lobby or go out on the observation deck to match the specimens with the real thing.

● Morro Bay Aquarium

595 Embarcadero, Morro Bay. (805) 772-7647. Daily, 9 A.M.–5 P.M.;
until 6 P.M. in the summer. Adults $1; ages 5–11, 50¢; under 5, free.
All ages.

You walk through a door in the Morro Bay Gift Shop to find yourself
face to face with a group of barking seals and sea otters. Naturally, the
seals are adept at begging for handouts. Fortunately, the person who sells
tickets to the aquarium also sells fish food for the seals.

An inside area contains about twenty tanks with some three hundred
live marine occupants, including eels, octopi, abalone, crabs, lobsters, and
all sorts of fish. A display of preserved marine specimens includes a great
white shark. The inside of the aquarium is old, dark, and damp, and con-
sequently might frighten very young children. In this era of sleek amusement parks, however, there is something charming about this aquarium's
aging unpretentiousness.

● Tiger's Folly Harbor Cruises

1205 Embarcadero (behind the Harbor Hut Restaurant opposite the power
plant), Morro Bay. (805) 772-2255 (Harbor Hut Restaurant). Daily
during the summer. The rest of the year, open on weekends. Phone for the
schedule. **Ages 6 and up.**

You can take a one-hour narrated cruise of Morro Bay on the old-
fashioned paddle wheeler *Tigers Folly II* past Morro Rock, the Embarcadero, and the harbor entrance.

● Montana de Oro State Park

Located on the coast south of Morro Bay. From Highway 101 south of San
Luis Obispo, exit at the Los Osos off-ramp. Follow Los Osos Valley Road

through the town of Los Osos to Pecho Road. Follow Pecho Road to the park. (805) 528-0513. Open daily. Free. **All ages.**

Dramatic and unspoiled, Montana de Oro State Park is a vivid reminder of the natural beauty of this state. The park's seven thousand acres of rolling hills, rugged cliffs and capes, beaches, and small coves are breathtakingly lovely. In the spring, the area is covered with brilliant wildflowers whose mostly gold color gave the park its name: mountain of gold. Miles of hiking trails lead through hills that overlook the ocean, and camping is available in an undeveloped campsite. For kids, the park offers **Spooner Cove,** a quiet, beautiful beach covered with smooth, colored stones and protected by natural jetties. In addition to splashing in the ocean, kids can wade in a stream leading to it. They can also discover tide pools, climb rocks on the beach, and maybe even spot a sea otter feeding in the surf.

● Hearst Castle–San Simeon State Historical Monument

Off Highway 1 at San Simeon, forty-three miles north of San Luis Obispo. (805) 927-2000. Daily, except Thanksgiving and Christmas Day. Minimum tour hours are from 8:20 A.M. to 3 P.M., with tours departing every ten to sixty minutes, depending on the season (hours increase during summer and holiday periods). The ticket office is open daily, 8 A.M.–4 P.M. You can buy your tickets at the ticket office, but purchasing tickets in advance is strongly recommended. Phone (800) 444-4445 to charge tickets by phone or for a mail-in application. Adults, $14; ages 6–12, $8; under 6, free. No strollers are allowed. **Ages 8 and up.**

On a par with any castle that a powerful seventeenth-century monarch might have built is the residence that William Randolph Hearst created for himself. The vastly wealthy publisher began building his home —apparently he never referred to it as a castle—in 1919. The work was never completed, but by the time of his death in 1951, the estate contained more than a hundred rooms, including thirty-eight bedrooms, thirty-one bathrooms, fourteen sitting rooms, two libraries, a movie theater, and an indoor and an outdoor swimming pool. Hearst reportedly spent fifty million dollars collecting art treasures, many of them for showcasing in or as part of his estate.

In 1958, Hearst's descendants donated the mansion and 123 surrounding acres of terraces, gardens, and palatial guest houses to the state. Four separate two-hour daytime tours and one seasonal nighttime tour are available to the public. All the tours include a half-mile walk and climbing 150 to 300 stairs. Tour I is the least strenuous and is recommended as an overall first look. It includes the main floor of the castle, the gardens, pools, and a guest house. Tour II covers the upper floors of the castle, Hearst's private suite, the libraries, and the kitchen. Tour III includes a ten-room guest cottage, three floors of guest suites in the main house, the gardens, and the pools. Tour IV, available April through October, focuses on the grounds and gardens, including the wine cellar and pool dressing rooms. A more expensive evening tour, available in the spring and fall, includes docents in period costume appearing as guests and staff of the castle.

Given all the stair climbing and the no-touching, a visit to Hearst Castle is best made with older children.

Special Annual Events

All Ages

January

Tournament of Roses Parade

This New Year's parade has been a tradition for years. No matter how good your color TV set may be, you can't imagine how spectacular this event is until you see it in person. Hardy souls camp out the night before along the parade route to get a good vantage point. Grandstand seats usually go on sale in February and can be sold out by August. Check with the Tournament of Roses Association, Pasadena, CA 91184 (phone: 818-449-4100), early in the year to find out where to buy tickets. You can also see the floats the afternoon of the parade and the next day in Pasadena along Sierra Madre Boulevard between Paloma Street and Sierra Madre Villa Avenue.

Chinese New Year

Los Angeles's Chinatown celebrates Chinese New Year in January or early February. Highlights include the dragon parade and children's lantern procession. Phone or write the Chinese Chamber of Commerce, 977 North Broadway, Suite G/F, Los Angeles, CA 90012. Phone: (213) 617-0396.

February

Children's Camellia Float Parade

Kids design and propel their own floats in this annual parade in Los Angeles County, usually held on the last Saturday in February. Write or phone early to enter a float. Temple City Camellia Festival, c/o Temple City Chamber of Commerce, 5827 North Temple City Boulevard, Temple City, CA 91780. Phone: (818) 287-9150.

Festival of the Whales

The annual twelve-thousand-mile migration of the California grey whales is celebrated in this festival held in Dana Point. Events include a film festival, whale-watching cruises, and opportunities to meet famous scientists and adventurers. Dana Point is located between San Juan Capistrano and San Clemente. For more information, phone the Orange County Marine Institute, (714) 496-2274.

Laguna Beach Winterfest

This Orange County festival has folk dancing, an arts and crafts fair, surfing and sand castle contests, a pancake breakfast, a parade, and, often, art exhibits. Contact the Laguna Beach Chamber of Commerce, P.O. Box 396, Laguna Beach, CA 92652. Phone: (714) 494-1018, ext. 5.

National Date Festival and Riverside County Fair

Comical camel races, an amusement fair, and stands serving all sorts of date concoctions are some of the highlights of this ten-day festival in Riverside County. Contact the National Date Festival, 46-350 Arabia Street, Indio, CA 92201. Phone: (619) 863-8247.

Flying Leap Storytelling Festival

Storytellers from around the world gather in Solvang to spin their tales during this weekend festival. For more information, contact the Solvang Conference and Visitors Bureau, P.O. Box 70, Solvang, CA 93464. Phone: (805) 688-6144.

March

Blessing of the Animals

One of the loveliest events in Los Angeles occurs in front of the Plaza Church on Olvera Street on the Holy Saturday before Easter, when children bring their beribboned pets to be blessed by the priests. Even some of the animals from the zoo join the procession. Phone: El Pueblo Park, (213) 625-5045.

Ocean Beach Kite Festival

Both adults and children can participate in this San Diego County kite festival. The festival, which includes kite decorating and flying contests, is sponsored by the Ocean Beach Recreational Center and the Kiwanis. Phone: (619) 531-1527.

St. Patrick's Day Parade and Festival

The weekend before St. Patrick's Day is marked in old-town Ventura
with a hometown parade, Irish dancing, arts and crafts, and entertainment. For more information, contact the Ventura Visitors and Convention
Bureau, 89-C South California Street, Ventura, CA 93001. Phone: (805)
648-2075.

Fiesta de Las Golondrinas

The return of the swallows (*las golondrinas*) to Mission San Juan Capistrano
is celebrated in this festival in Orange County. There's a fiesta, a parade, a
dance pageant, art exhibits, and a pancake breakfast. For more information, phone Mission San Juan Capistrano, (714) 248-2049.

Hans Christian Andersen Fairy Tale Festival

Each spring in March or April, Solvang celebrates the fairy-tale writer
Hans Christian Andersen. Costumed storybook characters, musicians,
jugglers, and magicians add to the merriment of the street festival. For
more information, contact the Solvang Conference and Visitors Bureau,
P.O. Box 70, Solvang, CA 93464. Phone (805) 688-6144.

Calico Hullabaloo

The annual Hullabaloo at Calico Ghost Town near Barstow features
country and bluegrass music, gunfighter demonstrations, horseshoe
pitching, and more. This family event is held the weekend before Easter.
Call (619) 254-2122.

April

Renaissance Pleasure Faire

A whole Elizabethan village is set up in Glen Helen Regional Park in
San Bernardino every spring from late April through May. There are arts
and crafts booths, wonderful food, parades, dances, children's games, and
strolling musicians, jugglers, and other entertainers. Visitors come
dressed in their own period costumes. For more information, phone
(800) 52-FAIRE.

Ramona Pageant

Helen Hunt Jackson's early California love story, *Ramona,* is dramatized
three weekends every year in an outdoor amphitheater set in a canyon on

the slopes of Mount San Jacinto in Riverside County. The natural acoustics are excellent. It's a colorful production with a cast of more than 350; music, dancing, authentic Indian rituals, and even horses are presented on the stage. Early reservations for the play are a good idea. Ticket orders are accepted beginning January 1; phone (714) 658-3111 or (800) 645-4465.

Long Beach Grand Prix

This international auto race is held on the streets of Long Beach. Phone the Grand Prix Association, (310) 981-2600.

Orange Blossom Festival

Riverside celebrates its citrus fruit heritage in this two-day event featuring a turn-of-the-century-style parade complete with orange-decorated floats, flower-draped, horse-drawn carriages, elephants, clowns, and marching bands. There is gourmet food for the grown-ups. Children can enjoy elephant and camel rides, circus performers, a carnival, petting zoos, games, arts and crafts, and other activities. In the evening, there are fireworks in the sky above Mission Inn Avenue. Phone the Orange Blossom Festival office at (909) 715-3400 or (800) 382-8202.

La Fiesta de San Luis Obispo

The founding of San Luis Obispo in 1772 by Father Junipero Serra and the city's Spanish heritage are celebrated in this annual fiesta. Music, including strolling mariachi bands, food, colorful parades, an arts and crafts fair, live entertainment, a costume breakfast, and more are part of this four-day celebration centered around Mission Plaza. Contact the San Luis Obispo Chamber of Commerce, 1039 Chorro Street, San Luis Obispo, CA 93401. Phone: (805) 543-1323.

Santa Barbara County Fair and Expo

A traditional county fair comes to the Earl Warren Showgrounds for five days this month. Activities include a carnival, livestock exhibits, food booths, displays, and entertainment. Contact the showgrounds for more information. Phone: (805) 687-0766.

Del Mar National Horse Show

Held at the Del Mar Fairgrounds, this two-week event includes national championship riders. Phone: (619) 792-4288.

San Diego Earth Fair
This celebration of Earth Day, held in Balboa Park, features a children's activity area, exhibits, music, and dance. Contact San Diego Earth Day at (619) 496-6666.

May

Bishop's Mule Days
Mule-shoeing and mule-packing contests, mule races, a mule show, and a nonmotorized parade are some of the events of Bishop's Mule Days. There's a barbecue and a pancake breakfast, too. For details on this Inyo County event, write to the Bishop Chamber of Commerce, 690 North Main Street, Bishop, CA 93514; or phone (619) 873-8405.

Cinco de Mayo
One of Mexico's great holidays is celebrated in El Pueblo de Los Angeles Historic Monument with puppet shows, mariachi music, Spanish dancing, and food. Phone El Pueblo Park at (213) 625-5045 for information. In San Diego, a Cinco de Mayo celebration is held in Old Town State Historic Park. Phone: (619) 220-5422.

National Orange Show
Animated citrus exhibits, a Polynesian music and dance competition, a hobbies and crafts show, an Armed Forces parade, a championship rodeo, 4-H exhibits, a midway and carnival area, a youth band competition, model railroad displays, and a free marionette show are just *some* of the activities at the annual National Orange Show held on National Orange Showgrounds in San Bernardino in May. For more information, phone the National Orange Showgrounds, (909) 888-6788.

Strawberry Festival
Pie-eating contests, a parade, amusement rides, games, and the world's largest strawberry shortcake are all a part of this celebration, which is held in Garden Grove (Orange County) over the Memorial Day weekend. Telephone the Garden Grove Chamber of Commerce for more information. Phone: (714) 638-7950.

California Strawberry Festival
Another strawberry festival is held this month in Oxnard. Covering several square blocks surrounding Oxnard's Channel Islands Harbor, this

event features food, music, a strawberry shortcake–eating contest, a 10K run, and a Strawberryland for kids, featuring clowns, a petting zoo, crafts, and games. Phone Community Services of Oxnard Special Events, (805) 385-7578.

Children's Day Celebration in Little Tokyo

Boys and girls are celebrated in this two-day outdoor festival with its roots in Japan. Held on the first weekend in May in the plaza of Japanese American Cultural and Community Center in Little Tokyo, the event includes dances and performances, food, arts and crafts, games, and other activities for kids. Contact the Japanese American Cultural and Community Center, 244 South San Pedro Street, Los Angeles, CA 90012. Phone: (213) 628-2725.

June

Huck Finn Jubilee

Mojave Narrows Regional Park outside of Victorville is the site of this annual celebration of a bygone time held on Father's Day weekend. Events include river raft–building contests, nickel-in-the-haystack games, fence painting, clog dancing, bluegrass music, and more. For details, phone Mojave Narrows Regional Park at (619) 245-2226.

Cherry Festival

This festival in Beaumont (Riverside County) features a parade, fireworks, amusement rides, and a horse show. Kids can try their hand at picking cherries. Contact the Beaumont Chamber of Commerce, P.O. Box 637, Beaumont, CA 92223. Phone: (909) 845-9541.

Del Mar Fair

Held at the fairgrounds in Del Mar, this three-week-long county fair features carnival rides, concerts, exhibits, and an impressive performing horse show. Phone the Del Mar Fairgrounds, (619) 793-5555, for more information.

Whale Fiesta

Sand sculpture contests, arts, crafts, games, films, lectures, and much more are part of this annual celebration of the whale, sponsored by the Cabrillo Marine Museum and the American Cetacean Society. For details, phone the Cabrillo Marine Museum in San Pedro at (310) 548-7546.

Summer Solstice Celebration

The longest day of the year is celebrated in Santa Barbara with a color-ful parade down State Street and other activities. Phone the Santa Barbara Conference and Visitors Bureau at (805) 966-9222 for more information.

Lompoc Flower Festival

A parade of flower floats, tours of the flower fields, a carnival, and other festivities highlight this Lompoc celebration. Contact: Lompoc Valley Chamber of Commerce, 111 South I Street, Lompoc, CA 93436. Phone: (805) 736-4567.

Threshing Bee and Antique Engine Show

The Antique Gas and Steam Engine Museum in Vista, east of Oceanside in San Diego County, has a twice yearly show of its antique equipment. Held for two consecutive weekends in June and again in October, the show includes demonstrations of early American crafts and cooking, log sawing, and blacksmithing. There are hayrides, an antique tractor parade, old cars, and plenty of kids' activities.

Children's International Arts Festival

Puppet making, etching, weaving, and face painting are just a few of the hands-on activities featured in this children's arts festival held in Ventura. For more information, phone Ventura Parks and Recreation at (805) 658-4726.

July

Laguna Beach Living Art Pageant

Laguna Beach citizens are costumed and posed inside frames to recreate famous artworks during the nightly Pageant of the Masters in Orange County. During the day there is an outdoor display of arts and crafts. Write early for tickets: Festival of the Arts, 650 Laguna Canyon Road, Laguna Beach, CA 92651. Phone: (714) 494-1145.

Surf, Sand, and Sandcastle Days

Held in conjunction with the U.S. Open Sandcastle Competition, this event features a parade, fireworks, and, of course, sand castle building. The three-day event takes place in the City of Imperial Beach in July or August. For more information, phone the Sandcastle Committee, Box 476, Imperial Beach, CA 91933. Phone: (619) 424-6663.

July Fourth Street Fair in Ventura

The highlight of this street fair for kids is the "Push 'em–pull 'em" procession, where kids parade down the street in or on decorated strollers, wagons, bikes, skateboards, and all sorts of other nonmotorized conveyances. The event also features food, music, dancing, entertainment, and an arts and crafts fair. Contact the Ventura Visitors and Convention Bureau Information Center at (805) 648-2075.

Orange County Fiesta

Carnival rides, sports, cook-offs, musical entertainment, arts and crafts, and a fireworks show are just a few of the activities centered around this Fourth of July event held in Mile Square Park, Warner and Euclid streets, Fountain Valley. For more information, phone the Fountain Valley Chamber of Commerce at (714) 688-0542.

Santa Barbara National Horse Show

Held at the Earl Warren Showgrounds, this is one of the best horse shows in the nation. Phone: (805) 687-0766.

Orange County Fair

A rodeo, a horse fair, 4-H project displays, motorcycle races, an arts and crafts show, a laser light show, a carnival, and professional entertainers are a few of the main events in this ten-day fair held in Costa Mesa. For more information, phone the Orange County Fair at (714) 708-3247.

San Bernardino County Fair

Victorville is the site of this county fair held from July through early August. The event features a rodeo, a carnival, livestock and agricultural exhibits, and more. For details, contact the San Bernardino County Fairgrounds at (619) 951-2200.

Old Miner's Days in Big Bear

Long before the skiers started coming here, these San Bernardino County Mountains were inhabited by gold miners. This Old West–style celebration commemorates that time with parades, dances, contests, and a burro derby. Contact the Big Bear Lake Chamber of Commerce, P.O. Box 2860, Big Bear Lake, CA 92315. Phone: (909) 866-4607.

Santa Barbara County Fair

Santa Maria is the site of the old-fashioned, weeklong Santa Barbara County Fair. The fair includes 4-H exhibits, horse shows, animal judging,

homemade food, a carnival, music, and entertainment. For details, phone
the Santa Barbara County Fairgrounds at (805) 925-8824.

August

Santa Barbara's Old Spanish Days Fiesta

This five-day festival celebrates the heritage of Santa Barbara. The
highlight is the historical parade including brightly decorated, antique
horse-drawn carriages. Other events include Spanish, Mexican, and Aztec
performances, an arts and crafts show, food, a rodeo, and a children's
parade. For details, call the Santa Barbara Conference and Visitors Bureau
at (805) 966-9222.

Little Tokyo Nisei Festival

Karate, judo, and sword tournaments; a carnival; and a street parade are
among the attractions at this celebration in Los Angeles's Little Tokyo.
Contact the Japanese Chamber of Commerce of Southern California,
244 South San Pedro Street, Los Angeles, CA 90012. Phone: (213)
626-3067.

Antelope Valley Fair

Tractor races highlight this six-day fair held at Lancaster in Los Angeles
County. For more information, phone the Lancaster Chamber of Commerce at (805) 948-4518.

Old Mission Santa Ines Fiesta

Food, rides, games for kids, folklorico dancing, and mariachi music are
all part of a weekend fiesta to celebrate the valley's rich Spanish/Mexican
heritage. The fiesta is held early to mid-August on the grounds of Mission
Santa Ines in Solvang. Phone: (805) 688-4815.

Long Beach Sea Festival

Boat races, a swim meet, and a sand-sculpture contest are some of the
events of this monthlong Los Angeles County summer festival. Contact
Long Beach City Parks for more information. Phone: (310) 570-3100.

Ventura County Fair

A parade, rodeo, and carnival are some of the highlights of this county
fair, held on the Ventura Fairgrounds. Contact the Ventura Visitors and
Convention Bureau Information Center, 89 South California Street,
Ventura, CA 93001. Phone: (805) 648-2075.

Tehachapi Mountain Festival

A professional rodeo, Western parade, 10K run, music, games, and food
are all a part of this old-fashioned family festival held the third weekend
in August in Tehachapi in Kern County. For more information, contact
the Tehachapi Chamber of Commerce, P.O. Box 402, Tehachapi, CA
93581. Phone: (805) 822-4180.

America's Finest City Week

San Diego celebrates itself in this annual event. Activities include a
half-marathon run, fireworks, Special Olympics, a Bay Day for children,
and more. Phone the San Diego Visitors and Convention Bureau at (619)
236-1212.

Mission Rancho Days

Mission San Juan Capistrano celebrates Orange County's rancho era in this
festival. Food, entertainment, lawmen, desperados, and, of course, Western
exhibits are all part of this popular August event. Contact Mission San
Juan Capistrano for more information. Phone: (714) 248-2048.

September

Los Angeles County Fair

One of the largest fairs in the nation, the Los Angeles County Fair in
Pomona lasts most of the month of September. Featured are rides, food,
livestock, arts and crafts, horse shows, and you name it. Phone: (909)
623-3111.

Eastern Sierra Tri-County Fair and Bishop Wild West Rodeo

This event over Labor Day weekend includes a county fair, rodeos, and
Old-West–style family entertainment. For more information, phone the
Tri-County Fairgrounds in Bishop at (619) 873-3588.

California Beach Party

Live surfer music, beach volleyball, canine Frisbee-catching contests,
windsurfing, 5K and 10K runs, arts and crafts, seafood, and a children's
entertainment area highlight this celebration of California beach culture
held along the Beachfront Promenade between Ventura Pier and Surfer's
Point in Ventura. For more information, contact the City of Ventura
Special Events Office, Box 99, Ventura, CA 93002. Phone: (805)
654-7830.

Newport Seafest

A variety of sea-related festivities, including a sand castle–building contest, boat races, entertainment, and sports events are featured during this two-weekend celebration in September in Newport Beach. For more information, contact the Newport Harbor Area Chamber of Commerce, 1470 Jamboree Road, Newport Beach, CA 92660. Phone: (714) 729-4400.

Kern County Fair

A junior livestock auction, games, and rides are featured at the fair. Telephone the Bakersfield Chamber of Commerce for details at (805) 327-4421.

California American Indian Days Celebration

American Indian singers and dancers and tribal arts and crafts are showcased at this two-day event held at the Museum of Man in San Diego's Balboa Park. For details, phone the Museum of Man at (619) 239-2001.

Cabrillo Festival

This festival celebrates the discovery of the West Coast with a reenactment of Juan Cabrillo's landing at Point Loma. For details, call the San Diego Convention and Visitors Bureau at (619) 236-1212.

Solvang Danish Days Festival

Denmark's Independence Day is celebrated with Danish music, costumed singing and dancing, and special pancakes cooked outdoors and served along the main street. For more information, contact the Solvang Conference and Visitors Bureau, P.O. Box 70, Solvang, CA 93464. Phone: (805) 688-6144.

Valyermo Fall Festival

The monks of St. Andrew's Priory host an annual fall festival featuring arts and crafts, food (including locally grown fruit), games, a children's farm, music, and dancing on the priory's 750-acre ranch. The event is always held on the last two-day weekend in September. Exit Longview Road off Highway 138 in Valyermo (near Palmdale), Antelope Valley. Phone: (805) 944-2178.

October

Calico Days

A greased-pig contest and mock gunfight are two of the events held during Calico Days at Calico Ghost Town (San Bernardino County), P.O. Box 638, Yermo, CA 92398. Phone: (619) 254-2122.

Pismo Beach Clam Festival

All sorts of activities are held during this weekend-long event in San Luis Obispo County, including clam-digging contests, sand castle–building contests, and arts and crafts exhibitions. Telephone or write the Pismo Beach Chamber of Commerce, 581 Dolliver Street, Pismo Beach, CA 93449. Phone: (805) 773-4382.

Morro Bay Harbor Festival

A live chess game with costumed performers as the pieces, a kid's cove with signs warning of pirates and other adventures, and a family-fun lagoon with boat rides are just a few of the highlights of this festival in Morro Bay. There are also boat tours, Hawaiian-shirt contests, fishing, a marine-life touch tank, seafood dishes, and much more on the first two-day weekend in October. For more information, write or phone the Morro Bay Harbor Festival, Box 1869, Morro Bay, CA 93443. Phone: (805) 772-1155.

Goleta Lemon Festival

The historic Stow House in Goleta is the site of this one-day event in Santa Barbara County. There is lemonade to drink, lemon pies to eat, as well as arts and crafts, and entertainment and activities for kids. Phone the Goleta Chamber of Commerce for details, (805) 967-4618.

Pumpkin Patch and Harvest Festival

Every October, the Ayers family opens its farm in Santa Paula to the public. Kids can pick their own Halloween pumpkins. Wagons, drawn by teams of Clydesdale horses, provide hayrides on weekends. The Faulkner Farm and Ayers Pumpkin Patch is located at the corner of Briggs and Telegraph roads in Santa Paula. Phone: (805) 525-9293.

November

Hollywood's Santa Claus Lane Parade of the Stars

Santa Claus is joined by television and movie stars in this parade along Hollywood Boulevard on the Sunday after Thanksgiving. Call the Hollywood Chamber of Commerce at (213) 469-8311.

Mother Goose Parade

Mother Goose characters are portrayed on colorful floats during this parade in El Cajon designed entirely for children. For details, contact the Mother Goose Association, Box 1155, El Cajon, CA 92022. Phone: (619) 444-8712.

December

Long Beach Christmas Water Parades
Boats decorated with Christmas lights make their way through the Naples canals in Long Beach while a choir sings from barges during this Los Angeles County Christmas pageant. Other lighted boat parades take place in Shoreline Village and the Port of Los Angeles. Contact the Long Beach Convention and Visitors Council, One World Trade Center, Suite 300, Long Beach, CA 90831, for details. Phone: (310) 436-3645.

Lights on the Water
Boats strung with Christmas lights parade through San Diego's Mission Bay. The parade ends with the lighting of Sea World's Sky Tower Christmas tree. In a separate water parade, lighted boats tour San Diego Bay from the Embarcadero to Shelter Island. Contact the San Diego Convention and Visitors Bureau, 1st Avenue and F Street, 11 Horton Plaza, San Diego, CA 92101. Phone: (619) 232-1212.

Newport Harbor Christmas Boat Parade
Still another boat parade takes place in Newport Harbor with more than two hundred decorated, illuminated boats. For a viewing schedule, write or phone the Newport Harbor Chamber of Commerce, 1470 Jamboree Road, Newport Beach, CA 92660. Phone: (714) 729-4400.

Christmas on the Prado
On the first three Sundays in December, Spreckels Outdoor Organ Pavilion in Balboa Park is the location for a fifty-foot lighted Christmas tree, Nativity scenes, and special programs. Phone: (619) 239-0512.

Las Posadas
A traditional Mexican Christmas festival is held for nine days on Olvera Street in Los Angeles. Each night at 8 P.M. there is a candlelight procession through the street, reenacting the journey of Mary and Joseph into Bethlehem. After the procession each night, children break an enormous candy-filled piñata. Phone: (213) 625-5045. Las Posadas celebrations are also held in Old Town State Historic Park in San Diego (phone: 619-220-5422) and at Mission San Luis Rey in Oceanside (phone: 619-757-3651).

Index by Age Group

All Ages

Alphabetical Index